The Mass Consumption Society

Other Books by George Katona

The Powerful Consumer
McGraw-Hill Book Company, 1960.

Psychological Analysis of Economic Behavior
McGraw-Hill Book Company, 1951.

Organizing and Memorizing
Columbia University Press, 1940.

The
Mass Consumption
Society

GEORGE KATONA

Survey Research Center, The University of Michigan

 McGRAW-HILL BOOK COMPANY

New York
San Francisco
Toronto
London

II

THE MASS CONSUMPTION SOCIETY

Preface

Much of today's economic research is organized research in which a group of people participate. This is particularly true of surveys and research on economic behavior. Many of the findings presented in this book are the result of investigations carried out over a time span of fifteen years at the Survey Research Center, a division of the Institute for Social Research of The University of Michigan. I, as Director of the Economic Behavior Program of the Center, have drawn on the work of my colleagues and have been greatly stimulated by daily contact with them. As a member of both the Department of Economics and the Department of Psychology of The University of Michigan, I have profited from exchanging ideas with social scientists across the boundaries of the established disciplines.

Only a few of the many persons who participated in the research studies and who gave me an opportunity to discuss my ideas with them can be named here. The book could not have been written without close collaboration with Eva Mueller, James N. Morgan, and John B. Lansing, who have shared with me for more than ten years the excitement of theorizing and fact-finding in the new field of psychological economics. Rensis Likert, Director of the Institute for Social Research, and Angus Campbell, Director of the Survey Research Center, as well as Leslie Kish, Director of sampling, and Charles F. Cannell, Director of interviewing, at the Center contributed greatly to creating a psychological climate conducive to new kinds of studies and to the development of the research methods used. Sincere thanks are also due to numerous associates and assistants, to the interviewing staff of the Center, and to the thousands of respondents all over the country who participated in the surveys. The list of foundations, business corporations, and government agencies which financed the studies through grants or contracts is too numerous to mention.

I am greatly indebted to Sylvia M. Kafka, whose editorial skills helped to make the book more readable. Sincere thanks are also due to Nancy McAllister for efficient secretarial assistance.

Search for knowledge and its utilization are closely related in the behavioral and social sciences. Therefore this book is not addressed exclusively to students of economics, sociology, psychology, or marketing, but to a broader audience as well.

George Katona

Contents

Part Five: SAVING

Part Six: SPENDING

Part Seven: TOWARD NEW ECONOMIC INSIGHTS

PART ONE

The New Setting

1

Mass Consumption Society and Affluence

The past few decades have seen the rise, here in America, of a new and unique phenomenon in human history, the mass consumption society. It is unique by virtue of three major features:

Affluence. Not a few individuals, nor a thin upper class, but the majority of families now have discretionary purchasing power and constantly replace and enlarge their stock of consumer goods.

Consumer power. Cyclical fluctuations, inflation or deflation, and the rate of growth of the economy—all now depend to a large extent on the consumer.

Importance of consumer psychology. In our economy, consumer demand is no longer a function of money alone. Discretionary demand, which has assumed a decisive economic role, is influenced and sometimes even determined by consumers' willingness to buy. In turn, the willingness to buy is a reflection of consumer motives, attitudes, and expectations.

All three of these characteristics emerged only in recent decades. All three now prevail in the United States, and increasingly in Western Europe as well. Together, as this book will show, they require us to reexamine and indeed to revise several important tenets of traditional economic thought—propositions of theory as well as rules of policy.

Accordingly, the aim of this book is to describe and analyze the nature of the mass consumption society and to explore the new requirements it imposes on economic thought and economic policy.

3

As a corollary aim, it proposes to describe the new discipline of psychological or behavioral economics and to explain its value, its present uses, and its future potential.

It is this new discipline that has enabled us to acquire the information necessary for understanding the economy as it functions in the United States today. This book is not a "think piece." Ideas and even speculations will be presented, since they serve as hypotheses that are the first steps of research. But the discussion of research findings that support, clarify, or modify the original ideas represents the core of the book.

The distribution of purchasing power among the American masses and their economic behavior represent one set of relevant new developments. The attitudes and expectations, as well as hopes and fears, of millions of individuals constitute, however, the principal subjects of research. Although the era of mass consumption results from the sum total of the behavior of many people, this behavior stems from the way individuals think and feel.

What emerges, then, is a somewhat unorthodox view of what has been happening in post-World War II America. Where others have portrayed American consumers as irrational and grossly materialistic, we found them to be less than ideal "rational men," to be sure, and yet to be sensible and not easily swayed when it matters and to be spurred on by success to higher levels of aspiration. Our so-called wealth has not blunted incentives; rather, concrete and attainable rewards were found to motivate millions of people to work hard to improve their lives still further. Higher living standards in turn appear to set the stage for, rather than to impede, cultural aspirations. The picture that emerges from a study of consumer motives, attitudes, and expectations is not a dismal one. There is much cause to be grateful for the fact that ours is a consumer-oriented society.

What name to give to the present-day economy, and to the society based on it, was a question not easy to answer. Best known, of course, is Galbraith's expression of the affluent society. This designation seemed inappropriate on two counts. First and foremost, affluence represents but one aspect of the new economic picture, and secondly, America is affluent only in relative terms, that is, only as compared with the past or with other nations. In choosing the term mass consumption society, the author used a designation that had likewise been used by others before him.

W. W. Rostow, in distinguishing five stages of economic growth, has called the last stage, the one which now prevails in the United States, Canada, Australia, the Western European countries, and Japan, "the age of high mass consumption."[1] Again, Barbara Ward has written: "The mass consumption economies of the Atlantic world represent a wholly new phenomenon in human history. In them, not simply individuals, or groups, or classes but society as a whole is rich and expects to become richer."[2]

Neither Rostow nor Barbara Ward used the expression mass consumption in exactly the same sense in which it is used in this book. The main interest of both authors lay in historical and international developments rather than in changes in the psychology of the masses. Yet nothing conveys what is new in America better than the term mass consumption society.

Of the three major characteristics of this new society—affluence, consumer power, and importance of consumer psychology—only the first may be said, in a certain limited sense, to represent a carry-over of something that was known in the past. Yet even in this respect, the present situation in the United States differs greatly from the past. Throughout the course of human history, poverty has been the rule, riches the exception. Societies in the past were called affluent when their ruling classes lived in abundance and luxury. Even in the rich countries of the past, the great majority of people struggled for mere subsistence. Today in this country minimum standards of nutrition, housing, and clothing are assured, not for all, but for the majority. Beyond these minimum needs, such former luxuries as homeownership, durable goods, travel, recreation, and entertainment are no longer restricted to a few. The broad masses participate in enjoying all these things and generate most of the demand for them.

What is known all over the world as the American standard of living does not consist of luxurious living by the wealthy. Prosperity by a thin upper class would be neither new nor envied by millions abroad. What is new is the common man's sharing in the

[1] See W. W. Rostow, *Stages of Economic Growth*, Columbia University Press, New York, and Cambridge University Press, London, 1960.

[2] Barbara Ward, *India and the West*, W. W. Norton & Company, Inc., New York, 1961, p. 247. I took advantage of Barbara Ward's insight into the significance of mass consumption in our times and borrowed from the quotation above for the first sentence of this book.

ways of living that in the past were reserved for the few. The common man's ability to use some of his money for what he would like to have rather than for what he must have represents the revolutionary change.

We are rich compared with our grandparents and compared with most other peoples of the world. In fact, however, we are still a middle-class society, enjoying middle-class comforts. Affluence as we use the term has the new meaning of more for the many rather than much for the few. The drudgery of seeking subsistence has been supplanted for millions of people, not by abundance and indulgence, but rather by a new concept of what are necessities and needs. The new ability to satisfy wants, which has become the rule among broad groups of the American people, makes life easier but does not necessarily result in soft living and waste.

The present-day distribution of consumer possessions and especially of consumer demand in the United States and a few other countries constitutes one of the new facts of our times. A second set of new facts is closely linked with it. The outlook of consumers also has changed greatly. New perspectives have opened up, and confident and optimistic expectations prevail among the majority of the people. Many people know and many others feel dimly that they have made progress, and they strive for further progress. This is not assured, but new hopes have arisen, and many people are confident that still higher material standards will be achieved.

Possibly the American people are least conscious of the new perspectives, since in the United States they have become commonplace. In Western Europe the change has been more sudden, and mass consumption economies are not yet fully realized. But people have begun to feel in Western European countries as well that forces beyond their control no longer set rigid limits to the average person's standard of living. They are beginning to understand that limits set by the availability of fertile land, natural resources, and the weather can be overcome by human ingenuity.

The ideal of progress, of the "possibility of material change leading to a better world, not hereafter, but here and now," as Barbara Ward has recently expressed it,[3] is still more revolutionary in underdeveloped countries. "The revolution of rising expectations," to use Adlai Stevenson's phrase, drives people to action. This is also true

[3] *The Rich Nations and the Poor Nations,* W. W. Norton & Company, Inc., New York, 1962, p. 15.

in America, where individuals exert great efforts to improve their own and their children's material standards. If successful, the impact goes far beyond the material. If frustrated, tragic consequences may ensue. Progress in avoiding starvation or malnutrition and in controlling the elements has been achieved at the price of restlessness and of the danger of mental breakdown for individuals and destructive war for nations.

When we argue that a great many people's subsistence needs are now assured, we do not imply that people feel secure or free from worry. Insecurity remains widespread, though its causes have changed. Concern with the so-called higher order of wants may be as great as concern with subsistence. The age-old threat of insufficient supply of goods has disappeared thanks to mass production and automation, but consumers cannot feel assured that they will be able to satisfy their ever growing wants. More goods for more people has not solved the problems of mankind; it has changed them. An era of satisfaction has not yet been achieved, and incentives for exercising great effort still abound. When the primary needs are gratified, human beings turn to other tasks. How well society will accomplish them depends on the degree of understanding of the problems confronting it. We are far from fully grasping the problems of a mass consumption society. But we can and must take a few steps in this direction.

Part One of the book contains an analysis of the three major characteristics of the mass consumption society. It will be shown that affluence has emerged from recent great changes in the distribution of income in the United States and that consumer power has resulted from the fact that consumers now make sizable expenditures which may legitimately be called investments. An analysis of the third feature—the important economic role played by consumer attitudes and expectations—calls for an acquaintance with the origins and purposes of psychological studies of economic processes. Part One ends with a description of the sample interview survey, which represents the major methodological tool of psychological economics through which most of the data used in this book were collected.

It is often easier to explain what something is by explaining first what it is not. This procedure, used in Part Two, seems particularly appropriate in the present instance, since we have but to recall descriptions of today's economy which have been provided by some outstanding social critics and which differ greatly from the picture that emerged from the studies reported in this book.

One aspect of psychological economic research, doubtless the one for which it is best known, concerns short-range economic fluctuations. In Part Three we shall show how consumer motives, attitudes, and expectations influence the business cycle and how the ability to measure changes in consumer sentiment contributes both to the prediction and to the understanding of cyclical fluctuations.

But consumers' influence on the economy far transcends the role they play in shaping short-term changes. In Part Four the long-range effects of the influence of consumers will be considered. From an analysis of consumer attitudes toward the future and toward some major public issues, we shall derive certain general principles of social cognition that may serve as guidelines to an understanding of consumers' reactions.

In Parts Five and Six we shall report on what our studies revealed about consumer behavior in areas of personal finance, including various forms of saving, of incurring debt, and of making major discretionary expenditures. In all these areas it will be shown how greatly consumers' motives and attitudes influence their behavior. It will also become apparent that, despite the great value placed on saving by the American people, no mass saving society has as yet emerged comparable in any way with the mass consumption society.

In the final part of the book an attempt will be made to summarize the major insights gained, as well as to draw consequences for economic policy and for the behavioral sciences.

2

Discretionary Income

How has the miracle of consumption come about? It derives from the interaction of a variety of forces. Changes in the composition of the population, in education, as well as in customs, attitudes, and aspirations, have all contributed to the emergence of discretionary purchasing power among the American masses. But the *sine qua non* of mass consumption economy has been a substantial increase in the average family's income together with a great change in the distribution of income. We shall devote much of this book to a study of the new psychological forces brought into being by the "income revolution." We must first, however, take note of the great change that has taken place in the distribution of purchasing power among the American people.

FOUR INCOME GROUPS

In 1961 two out of every five American family units belonged to the "discretionary-income group," and they controlled more than one-half of all personal income. This group is defined as having earned more than $6,000 and less than $15,000 before taxes. These limits are rather arbitrary.[1] Probably some families with less than $6,000 income had somewhat more than they needed for absolute necessities and should have been considered as possessors of dis-

[1] The argument presented in this book would remain valid if a somewhat different definition had been chosen.

9

cretionary income. Undoubtedly many families with more than
$6,000 income would deny that they had more than they had to
have for minimum necessities. Yet as a rough approximation we
may take those limits and argue that the income revolution consisted of the emergence of a large group of families with incomes
between $6,000 and $15,000. These families constitute the backbone
of the mass consumption economy. It is the sharp increase in their
number and in the share of the total income controlled by them
which set the stage for the new era.⟩

Four groups are presented in Chart 1. We give them names
which may not be fully appropriate but which will serve to make
them easily recognizable. Those with incomes higher than the "dis-

CHART I

Distribution of Spending Units and Family Units
and of Their Income by Income Groups in 1961

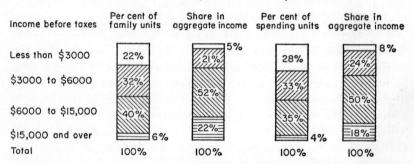

SOURCES: For spending units, 1962 Survey of Consumer Finances, conducted
by the Survey Research Center, The University of Michigan. For family units,
same source adjusted according to methods used by U.S. Department of Commerce in order to make survey totals identical with data obtained in national
income accounting (see *Survey of Current Business*, April, 1962).

A spending unit is defined as all related persons living in the same dwelling
who pool their incomes. A family units consists of all related persons living
in the same dwelling. There are more spending units than family units because
some sons, daughters, or other relatives do not pool their incomes with their
parents, even though they live together. Some spending units as well as some
family units consist of single persons.

The adjustments by the Commerce Department are made because survey
data exclude the institutional population, disregard income in kind and imputed
income, and understate total income slightly. The adjusted data represent
the distribution in 1961 of approximately 400 billion dollars income among
56 million family units.

cretionary-income group" we call the "wealthy," and among those with lesser income we distinguish the "poor" from the "lower-middle-income group."

There have been some rich people in most societies at all times, usually representing 1 or 2 per cent of the total population. If we had set the lower limit of the wealthy families at an annual income of $25,000 rather than $15,000, in 1961 there would have been less than 2 per cent wealthy and more than 44 per cent upper-middle-income families. The importance of the top-income groups has not increased and has probably declined slightly during the last few decades. In 1947, 5 per cent of the population received 20 per cent of the aggregate income, and in 1961, 6 per cent received 22 per cent. According to the best available estimates, 25 per cent of the total income in 1929 went to 5 per cent of the people.

The poor are those at the bottom of the income distribution, (while the lower-middle-income groups may be defined as those (not poor) whose share in aggregate income is less than would accrue to them if income were equally distributed.)

Recent studies by the Survey Research Center have given an answer to the question, Who are the poor? Morgan and his associates[2] compared incomes received in 1959 with the minimum budgetary requirements necessary to house, feed, and clothe the people who shared the family income. They found that 20 per cent, or about 10½ million family units, had less income in that year than would have been required for decent living. This estimate, then, is not much different from our simple tabulation which shows that 22 per cent of American families in 1961 had an income of less than $3,000. The great majority of the poor, as defined by Morgan, are described by at least one (often several) of the following statements:

They are old (over sixty-five years of age).

They are disabled.

They are nonwhite.

They are single with children at home (most often widows).

They are farmers or businessmen (having sharply fluctuating incomes, their income in a given year may not have been typical).

Not all the old, the nonwhite, or the widows are poor, but most of the poor fall into one or the other of these categories. The first

[2] J. N. Morgan, M. H. David, W. J. Cohen, H. E. Brazer, *Income and Welfare in the United States,* McGraw-Hill Book Company, New York, 1962.

three are most important in creating poverty. Most commonly, poor people are unable to earn enough because of age, physical handicaps, or discrimination. Families headed by women are likewise discriminated against in their ability to earn a living, especially if they have small children to care for.

Lack of skills and lack of education characterize many of the poor. In modern society specialized skills are a necessary requirement for advancement. Workers without such skills have a low level of earnings and are subject to frequently recurring periods of unemployment.

Our second broad classification—the lower-middle-income group which had $3,000 to $6,000 income in 1961—includes one large segment of the population, the young people. In a society such as existed in the United States as recently as thirty to fifty years ago, in which farmers and unskilled workers predominated, the earning power of young family heads was not much lower than that of middle-aged family heads. One of the radical ways in which today's American society differs from that earlier one is that skilled workers and white collar workers, and generally the better-educated people, represent the great majority rather than a small minority. We shall present data in Chapter 12 on the age brackets at which different population groups obtain their top income and shall discuss the impact of prevailing expectations of steadily rising income. At this point, it suffices to state that among the families with less than $6,000 annual income, there is a sizable group of younger people who have every reason to expect their income to rise substantially in the future.

Since the two lower-income groups (less than $3,000 and $3,000 to $6,000) are made up largely of people who might be expected not to play a leading role in the national economy for reasons other than income (age, disability, etc.) and others who may be expected at some time to join the ranks of the $6,000 to $15,000 group, it follows that some adjustment of the set of percentages in Chart 1 would give a truer picture of the important role played by the discretionary-income group. Rather than exclude several specific segments, such as all farmers or all nonwhite families, we used the simplest possible method of clarifying the actual present-day situation. We excluded the young and the old and considered only those heads of spending units who are between thirty-five and fifty-four years old, that is, at or close to the peak of their earning power. The findings are presented in Chart 2 and can best be seen by comparing the right side of Chart 2 with the right side of Chart 1. (In 1961 one-half of American spending units in their main earning period belonged to the upper-middle-income group which uses part of its income for discretionary purposes.)

CHART 2

Distribution of Spending Units with Head 35-54 Years of Age and of Their Income by Income Groups in 1951 and 1961

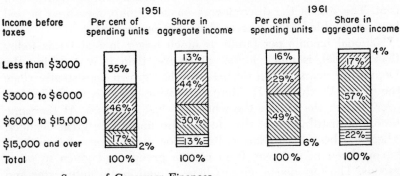

Income before taxes	1951 Per cent of spending units	1951 Share in aggregate income	1961 Per cent of spending units	1961 Share in aggregate income
Less than $3000	35%	13%	16%	7% / 4%
$3000 to $6000	46%	44%	29%	57%
$6000 to $15,000		30%	49%	
$15,000 and over	17% / 2%	13%	6%	22%
Total	100%	100%	100%	100%

SOURCE: Survey of Consumer Finances.

GROWTH OF DISCRETIONARY INCOME

Comparable data on the distribution of income in the United States of many years ago are not available. The first reliable surveys to provide such information were made only after World War II, and inflation sharply impairs the comparability even of data collected ten years ago. Nonetheless, certain major conclusions about the growth of the upper-middle-, or discretionary-, income group since 1929 emerge clearly from available figures and estimates.

(First of all, it is known that in the past thirty-odd years growth has taken place (1) in the total population, (2) in the national income in constant dollars, and (3) in the number of families in the upper-middle-income group. The crucial facts to be kept in mind are that, in relative terms, (2) has increased at a greater rate than (1), and (3) at a greater rate than (2); that is, the increase in real national income has been greater than the increase in population, and the growth of the discretionary-income group ran far ahead even of that.

Thus, from 1929 to 1961 the number of family units increased by approximately 55 per cent. National income, in constant dollars, advanced by almost 160 per cent. But the number of families in the $6,000 to $15,000 group, even when the limits of the group are adjusted for price increases, rose by 400 per cent; that is, there were five times as many such families in 1961 as in 1929.[3]

Even since World War II the growth in these three areas, both in absolute and in relative terms, has been remarkable. From 1947 to 1961 the number of family units increased by 28 per cent. National income, in constant dollars, advanced by more than 60 per cent. The size of the discretionary-income group, measured in real income, doubled (i.e., increased by 100 per cent).

National income per family is much larger in real terms today than in 1929, is much larger, of course, than it was during the Depression years of the thirties, and has grown consistently since the end of World War II. More purchasing power is available than ever before: the size of the whole pie has increased. At the same time, the distribution of the pie has also undergone great changes. There has been hardly any redistribution in the sense of something having been taken away from certain groups and given to other groups. The top-income groups have gained in absolute terms and had more income in 1961 than ever before. But their relative share in the much bigger pie has not grown and may even have declined slightly. The same is true of the lower half of the income distribution: the less well-to-do have improved their position in absolute terms but not their share of the total income. The largest part of the increase in the total accrued to the upper-middle-income group. This group was fairly insignificant before World War II. It is estimated that in 1929 only about 12 per cent of all families had an income which in purchasing power would correspond today to an income of $6,000 to $15,000. The group grew to 25 per cent by the end of World War II and, as shown in Chart 1, to 40 per cent by 1961. In 1961, then, among all family units there were approximately 22 million (40 per cent of 56 million units) with an income of $6,000 to $15,000, and they controlled over 200 billion dollars of income out of a total of 400 billion dollars.

While developments before and during World War II made the greatest changes in income distribution, the trend has continued during the postwar years. The very nature of a mass consumption

[3] Adjustment for price increases has been made on the basis of the cost-of-living index. The use of different methods would not affect the main argument.

economy tends to strengthen the discretionary-income group. A few comparisons between the income position of spending units with thirty-five- to fifty-four-year-old heads in 1951 and in 1961 will make this clear. In 1951, 65 per cent of units in their top-earning period had incomes over $3,000 (see Chart 2); in 1961, 67 per cent had incomes over $5,000. These figures indicate great progress, since the consumer-price index advanced only 15 per cent in those same years. In 1951, 29 per cent had incomes over $5,000; in 1961, 55 per cent had incomes over $6,000. Those who could have been called members of the upper-middle-income group in 1951, namely those thirty-five to fifty-four years of age who had an income between $5,000 and $10,000, represented only 25 per cent of all units and controlled 36 per cent of the total national income. In comparison, in 1961 the $6,000 to $15,000 group represented 49 per cent of the units and controlled 57 per cent of the total income.[4]

Similar findings have been obtained with a somewhat different procedure by Arno H. Johnson.[5] He calculates basic living costs per capita and deducts the sum total of these costs from aggregate personal income. (Taxes and amounts saved are likewise deducted.) The resulting amount he calls "discretionary spending power." This amount has risen since World War II to a much greater extent than either income or prices. Before 1940 American consumers as a whole had insignificant amounts at their disposal beyond what was calculated to be needed for basic living costs. During the forties the overage—that portion which permits the exercise of consumer discretion—advanced from 40 to 100 billion dollars; after having exceeded 100 billion dollars in 1950, it surpassed 200 billion dollars in 1959. The increase in discretionary spending power has been phenomenal.

---

[4] These great changes are rarely noticed because economists and social reformers pay most attention to (1) the extent of poverty and (2) the rate of income concentration. It is true and shameful that, in spite of growing affluence, little progress has been made in abolishing poverty. Concentration of income is usually measured by calculating the share of total income which is received by the top 10 or 20 per cent of all income receivers. These measures show that income was much less concentrated toward the end of World War II than in 1929 but that there was no substantial change from 1947 to 1961. But these calculations combine the income share of the truly rich with that of many in the discretionary-income group and are not relevant for our purposes.

[5] Arno H. Johnson, *Advertising Age*, May 14, 1962.

3

Consumer Investment

The first major feature of mass consumption economies, affluence, has developed gradually. Only after World War II was a stage reached when as many as one-fourth or one-third of American families had discretionary spending power. But the middle class emerged much earlier, and with its emergence purchasing power broadened considerably. While the living standards of the masses changed little from the dawn of history until the nineteenth century, new trends set in with the advent of the industrial revolution. Science and technology started to exert an impact on human life more than one hundred years ago, although the impact was much larger toward the end than in the middle of the nineteenth century and much larger again in the middle of the twentieth century.

The impact of mass consumption has come upon us more suddenly. In the first two decades of this century the influence of consumers on the business cycle was limited, and consumer psychology had no fundamental effect on economic events. To be sure, there were antecedents for the recent changes in these respects as well. Technology must be recognized as having made it possible for consumers to exercise their power. When consumers spend their money on perishable goods and on some services, such as rent, which are fairly short-range, they are not in a position to withhold their purchasing power or to bunch their expenditures. The invention and production of automobiles and many other consumer durable goods during the last sixty years, and their widespread acceptance by consumers, opened the way for the consumer to exert an influence on the economy.

A few decades ago business investment was, with much justification, considered to be the only dynamic private factor in the economy. In many minds it has remained so. It is our purpose in this chapter to indicate how the role of consumers has changed so that the private sector of the economy today depends upon three forms of investment: business investment in plant and machinery, consumer investment in housing and durable goods, and investment in human capital (primarily education, skills, and health).

THE CHANGED ROLE OF THE CONSUMER SECTOR

Theories that were true in the nineteenth century but are no longer true today still exercise a great influence on economic thinking. Language habits persist. The belief that consumers consume, that is, use up and destroy, what agriculture and industry produce serves to elevate business investment to the dominant position in economic policy and to relegate the consumer to a minor place. True, lip service has always been paid to the consumer. He was called king in the nineteenth century, and the statement that the end of production is consumption is as old as economics itself. But traditional economic analysis did not assume that consumer wants and consumer demands represented major forces in the economy. On the contrary, the consumer was considered incapable of generating income or of determining its allocation. It was postulated that consumers on the whole received their incomes from business and government and spent it at a fairly steady rate.

Of the three sectors of the economy—business, government, and consumer—only the first two were recognized as exerting an autonomous influence on economic developments: The business sector was thought to be able to do so by raising or lowering the volume of business investment and the government sector by incurring deficits or withdrawing funds from the other sectors in excess of what it paid out. But the consumer sector, by spending what it received from the other two sectors at a fairly stable rate, was viewed as an unimportant transmitter of income.

Prior to fairly recent major changes in the economy, this may well have been a correct description of economic processes. In feudal societies a few landlords, and in early industrial societies a few entrepreneurs, alone represented the forces bringing about change. The government's role in shaping economic processes has increased in most countries of the world during the last one hundred years. At the same time, consumers remained close to the subsistence level except for a few whose principal influence on the economy was in their role of entrepreneur.

One major change which has invalidated traditional economic views, namely, the change in the level and distribution of income, has already been discussed. Added to it in the United States have been changes in the financial reserves of consumers and in the availability of consumer credit. Higher incomes, more extensive assets, and greater use of credit have given the consumer latitude of action, which he has been in a position to exercise because of the technological changes that had previously occurred.

Liquid-asset holdings by consumers were unimportant in total amount before World War II and were restricted to a small minority. Bank deposits and government bonds were probably held by less than 10 per cent of all American families in 1939 but by the great majority of families in 1946. The total amount increased approximately threefold in those few years. Even today the great majority of consumers own only negligible amounts of assets that can readily be converted into cash, but as we shall see later, these assets add to a general feeling of security and help people exercise greater discretion in using their income and in borrowing.

Availability of mortgage credit represents a nineteenth-century development, and yet it was only after World War II that the majority of Americans became homeowners through its use. Early in this century approximately 40 per cent of 20 million family units lived in one-family houses which they owned; in 1946, close to 50 per cent of 38 million families and in 1962, 60 per cent of 53 million families lived in private households.[1] In the last sixteen years the number of homeowning families has increased by 12 million. Installment credit rose substantially during the first three decades of this century, but its almost universal acceptance is likewise a post-World War II development. Statistics on the use of credit, especially by younger families in the middle-income group who have children, as well as data about the growing popularity of consumer credit will

[1] Families and individuals living in institutions or military reservations are not included in these figures, because they are excluded from the surveys conducted by the Survey Research Center.

be presented later. It suffices to state here that at any time during the late fifties and early sixties, close to one-half of all American families owed installment debt, and many more made use of it in the course of a few years' time.

The possibility of making purchases on credit adds greatly to consumers' discretion of action. It enables them to buy durable goods before they assemble sufficient funds. Postponement of purchases is likewise facilitated, because people know that credit will be available later. The use of this discretion in timing purchases is one major new factor that makes the expenditure flow diverge from the income flow. Consumers are in a position to spend more or less than the income they receive in any given period of time.

Discretionary expenditures show much greater fluctuations than nondiscretionary expenditures. Sharp fluctuations of certain consumer expenditures have been widely noted, even though some of our traditional accounting conventions tend to conceal them. The most widely publicized data on the subdivisions of the gross national product are compiled by the U.S. Department of Commerce and contain information on three major sectors: (1) government receipts and expenditures, (2) business investments and their sources, and (3) total consumer income and expenditures. In order to avoid double counting, not all that business spends or takes in appears in the tables summarizing the data on national product. Business outlays for plant and machinery and for inventory accumulations, which are included, fluctuate much more than business outlays for wages and raw materials, which are not. When consumer outlays are tabulated, no similar comparable differentiation is made. Consumer expenditures reported include amounts spent for food and necessities which do not fluctuate greatly. Since these constitute the major proportion of all expenditures, they overshadow the sharply fluctuating discretionary expenditures to such an extent that consumers' incomes and their total expenditures always correlate highly. Viewed in this manner, the consumer sector appears relatively stable and therefore predictable and unimportant in a study of business cycles.[2] Even though data on the sharp ups and downs

[2] Sometimes, in popular writings, the importance of the consumer sector in shaping business cycles is acknowledged in the light of an argument that sounds plausible but is not correct. For instance, the Secretary of Commerce said in a speech made in 1963: "Consumer expenditures for goods and services account for about two-thirds of our GNP and, thus, to a great extent determine

of consumer expenditures for new durable goods are published—data on most other widely fluctuating discretionary consumer expenditures, including expenditures on used cars and travel, are not readily available from government sources—many competent economists continue to call business investment "the most mercurial" of expenditures. This is true only when certain business expenditures, namely investments, are contrasted with total consumer expenditures.

It may be worthwhile to reshuffle the Department of Commerce data in a manner not found in official publications. The heading "Construction Expenditures" included in "Gross Private Domestic Investments" is divided into "Residential construction" and "Other" (mainly business construction). The latter we shall add to "Producers' durable equipment" to obtain a new item called "Business construction and equipment," representing business investment in buildings and machinery. In this way the figures in Table 1 contrast the enduring expenditures of consumers with those of business firms.

Table I. Recent Changes in Widely Fluctuating Money Outlays
(*In Billions of Dollars*)

Annual outlays	1950	1955	1958	1960	1961	1962
Business construction and equipment	29.0	39.3	40.5	47.3	46.1	50.1
Consumer durable goods	30.4	39.6	37.6	44.8	43.7	47.5
Residential construction	14.1	18.7	18.0	21.1	21.0	23.3

The statistical data presented are not exactly what we need. The Commerce Department's compilations of expenditures on consumer durables are somewhat overstated for our purposes, for they include, in addition to the purchase of new automobiles and major household appliances, expenditures on many small nondiscretionary items as well (for instance, tires). Turning to residential construction,

---

what happens to GNP and our rate of growth." If two-thirds of a total is stable or rises at a steady rate while the other third fluctuates greatly, the two-thirds does not determine the ups and downs of the total. Furthermore, if two-thirds grows steadily at a 2 per cent annual rate while one-third rises by 5 per cent in one year and declines by 3 per cent the next, then the variable factor should be given major attention by those who are concerned with the rate of growth.

the purchase of newly built owner-occupied houses may be attributed to the consumer. The construction of apartment houses, however, which is included under residential construction, may be viewed as business activity, even though the apartments are rented by consumers. On the other hand, a very important item of tangible investment expenditures made by consumers is not fully reflected in the statistics, namely, expenditures for additions to and modernization or repair of homes, estimated at approximately 10 billion dollars a year.

Whatever the shortcomings of the statistical data, it is apparent that consumers' investment expenditures on durable goods and housing are at least as large as business investment expenditures. We find further that both have fluctuated greatly and that there is an upward bias in the figures due to inflation. Nevertheless, 1958 and 1961 appear as bad years, to a great extent because of declines in the investment expenditures of both consumers and businessmen.

The current market value of owner-occupied one-family houses is estimated at 400 billion dollars. The value of automobiles and other durable goods owned by consumers may be set at close to 200 billion dollars after depreciation. By comparison, business investment in plant and machinery has been valued at approximately 400 billion dollars.

The most relevant statistics concern the rate of change in these values. William Butler, of the Chase Manhattan Bank of New York, assembled data on the rate of increase in the stock of consumer durable goods.[3] The net value of the stock of consumer durables per household in constant dollars:

Rose by 3½ per cent per year from 1920 to 1930

Declined slightly from 1931 to 1945 (during the Great Depression and World War II)

Increased at the rate of 6 per cent per year from 1946 to 1956

Increased by only 1 per cent per year from 1957 to 1962

The rate of growth of the economy is strongly affected by the rate of change in consumer investment. During the five years prior to 1962, the rate of growth of the American economy was much slower than during the preceding ten years. Dissatisfaction with

[3] See the article by William F. Butler, "Consumer Durables: Stocks and Expenditures," in *Consumer Behavior in 1961*, Foundation for Research on Human Behavior, Ann Arbor, pp. 13–22; and *Business in Brief*, bimonthly report of the Chase Manhattan Bank, May–June, 1961.

this rate of growth has been voiced both in comparing it with growth in other countries and in noting that recessions have recurred at relatively short intervals and that sizable unemployment has persisted. In the early sixties management and labor, Republicans and Democrats, all agreed about the sluggishness of the American economy, even though they disagreed about possible remedies. Behind the disagreement about future economic policy lie fundamentally different views about what has gone wrong in the past.

At this point it may suffice to refer to Table 1. It indicates that there was a somewhat less pronounced retardation in the rate of growth of business investment during the period 1955 to 1962 than of consumer investment. But it is not argued here that business investment represents a less significant factor than consumer investment. The argument is that business investment is not the sole important factor. Investment is not carried out by business alone. There are three forms of private investment: business investment in plant and machinery, consumer investment through tangible expenditures, and investment in human capital.[4]

THREE FORMS OF INVESTMENT

Private capital or wealth consists of (1) the productive facilities of the nation, including, in addition to natural resources and factories, such business assets as trading, banking, and insurance facilities without which production would not be possible; (2) the housing of the people, supplemented by their durable wealth in home appliances, and automobiles; (3) the health, education, and skills of the people.[5] Rich countries differ from poor countries, and the wealth of the present American economy differs from that of the economy of earlier years, not in the first factor alone but in the second and third as well.

What consumers spend on buying and improving their homes and on automobiles or appliances adds to the enduring wealth of a nation. What to some extent consumers, and to a larger extent governments, spend on education and health represents another

---

[4] The term *investment* as most commonly used includes what is called here business investment, residential construction, and change in inventories. The last of these is not a permanent addition to wealth.

[5] In addition to private capital there is, of course, government capital, consisting of office buildings, schools, hospitals, highways, recreational facilities, etc.

most significant addition to national resources. The sum total of skills and education of the people, as well as their health, represents economic assets even though the significance of these assets goes far beyond economics.

Expenditures in all three areas are future-oriented and enduring, although just as business machinery wears out or becomes outdated in a fairly short period of time, so do the appliances and automobiles owned by consumers. Expenditures in all three areas add to productivity. To increase productivity we need skillful, well-educated, and healthy people—and therefore investment in human capital. We need well-equipped factories and businesses—and therefore business investment. We also need a population that is well-housed, within easy commuting distance from home to place of work, and in possession of laborsaving devices—and therefore consumer investment. Increase in productivity depends not only on people's skills and on business tools, but also on the material standards of the people. (In addition, of course, material goods in the possession of consumers produce satisfaction directly.)

All this appears obvious and not controversial. Yet attribution of investment activities to consumers is contradicted by most economists and, what is worse, is disregarded by most policy makers. The reasons for the prevailing doctrine can be found in cultural lag. It was true in the nineteenth century, and in fact even in the twentieth century before the advent of mass consumption economies, that enduring wealth was created mainly by business and government. Old truths linger on and, as time goes by, seem to require less and less factual support. The exclusion of consumers from capital formation may best be understood by following the arguments put forth recently by a leading economic statistician, Simon Kuznets. He undertook the task of measuring capital formation over the past one hundred years and began by defining it.[6]

"Capital is a productive factor," Kuznets writes. "It is intended for use in producing goods or income" (p. 16) and is thus distinguished from consumption, which is the disposal of goods. Production is defined as making goods for units other than the producing ones. The term *producing income* is introduced in order to include the contributions of commerce, banking, transportation, and the like, in capital formation. Thereby the way is opened for arbitrary dis-

[6] Simon Kuznets, *Capital in the American Economy*, National Bureau of Economic Research, Princeton University Press, Princeton, N.J., 1961.

tinctions. Kuznets includes in capital formation all construction in addition to expenditures for producers' durables (as well as net change in inventories and in foreign claims). Not only the construction of office buildings and apartment houses, but also that of one-family houses, by households, is included in capital formation, because "Housing involves decisions akin to business behavior," and all dwellings are called capital goods. Why capital formation should not be extended further is not discussed. Many large appliances are purchased together with new one-family houses, and the decisions involved in buying automobiles are similar to those involved in buying houses. Some automobiles owned by individuals, rather than business firms, are also used to produce income.

A somewhat different definition likewise fails to settle the question. "Capital formation represents the saved part of current production" says Kuznets (p. 9). In defining personal saving, the acquisition of houses as well as durable goods should be included (net of depreciation, to be sure), in addition to the accumulation of financial assets. Since consumer durables do not wear out in the year in which the expenditures are made but are used, on the average, as long as business machinery, they, too, represent a saved part of production and should be considered capital.

The traditional concepts of capital and capital formation are not logically consistent. What was derived from nineteenth-century conditions should be reconsidered in the light of mid-twentieth-century developments. The parallel between capital formation by business and by consumers may be illustrated by studying the opposite process, namely, the destruction of capital (often called capital consumption). Kuznets correctly states that "consumption of producers' durable goods" is due primarily to economic obsolescence rather than to physical wear and tear. Obsolescence occurs because of technological progress and changes in taste or desirability. Factories remote from raw materials are abandoned even when in good condition; machinery loses value when more efficient machinery is invented; office buildings in fair condition are replaced by new buildings having more desirable features. Similarly, one-family houses in decaying neighborhoods are not kept up and lose value; automobiles and appliances are scrapped when newer ones are desired. Obsolescence and insufficient upkeep destroy capital—business as well as consumer capital. Consumption of food and even the wear and tear of clothing represent different forms of dynamic processes. Truly the consumer is the only one who consumes, but he does something else as well.

Toward the end of the last and the beginning of the present century, business investment was the major dynamic factor in the private economy. Its mercurial character, making for boom or bust, provides much of the explanation for the widespread demand at that time for government regulation and control. When private economic activities seem unable to provide economic stability, and seem unable to avoid sharp ups and downs, including deep depressions, the government is called upon to step in or even to take over.

Since World War II we have been confronted with two new factors. The first is the emergence of the mass consumption economy in which consumers are one of the factors determining cyclical fluctuations and the rate of economic growth. The second is the change in the character of the business cycle. Before World War II the United States, as well as other highly industrialized countries, experienced prolonged prosperous periods followed by long-lasting deep depressions. Since World War II good times have been interrupted by short and rather mild recessions. This change in the nature of cyclical fluctuations is usually attributed to the changed role of government. Today's economy is characterized by high rates of taxation, by government expenditures that represent a large share of national product, and by a variety of social-security provisions. Some of the government's expenditures increase when bad times set in, and the withdrawal of funds from the economy through taxation declines at the same time. Contrariwise, in good times payments of unemployment insurance decrease, and tax receipts go up. Thus, automatic stabilizers help keep the economy on an even keel.

Without neglecting the importance of fiscal policy on business cycles, it will be shown in later chapters that these two new factors —the greatly increased role of consumers and the change in the character of business cycles—are closely related. In analyzing features of the consumers' mode of thinking, we shall discover strong countercyclical tendencies that serve to forestall excessive behavior upward as well as downward. We shall show consumer influence on the economy to be a stabilizing force, because most of the time most consumers behave in a conservative and sensible manner rather than go overboard. The spread of opinions and attitudes will be proved to operate differently among the unorganized masses of consumers from among the close-knit groups of business leaders. Business cycles are still with us. But government action to forestall inflation or depression assumes a different character when the question is not one of controlling or influencing a few businessmen but rather of stimulating millions of consumers.

What has been shown up to now is that consumers have discretion of action. How they exercise their discretion has not yet been discussed. Consumers do not spend their income at a steady rate, and therefore the amount of their income is not the sole factor that determines economic developments. What factors, other than the money available to them, influence consumers' behavior?

4

Psychological Economics

It will startle no one to hear that changes in such psychological factors as confidence or pessimism play a role in stimulating or retarding economic processes. Such statements were frequently made in the past—even as long ago as the second half of the nineteenth century—and remained without influence on the study of economics. True, they usually referred to the psychology of the entrepreneur rather than the psychology of the consumer, but this does not constitute the major difference between their significance then and now. Past statements indicating that psychological factors influenced economic trends did not really represent economic psychology because of two fundamental shortcomings. First, they remained at the level of assertions and did not stimulate attempts at measurement. In the absence of measurements of the influence of changes in attitudes and expectations, the thesis could be neither supported nor contradicted and could not contribute to a scientific discipline. We shall devote the next chapter to the subject of measurement and shall discuss here a problem that must precede it. In order to proceed with measurements, tools and methods are needed, but first of all what is to be measured must be specified. Past assertions about the influence of psychological factors were vague and imprecise. They were stopgap statements, prompted by occasional failure to explain economic processes without recourse to psychology, and had no theoretical basis. Such notions as "small causes may have huge effects because of the psychology of the people" are compatible with any theory of the business cycle[1] and do not qualify as a theory of psychological economics.

WILLINGNESS TO BUY

The basic principle of psychological economics was formulated by the author some fifteen years ago as follows: Discretionary demand is a function of both ability to buy and willingness to buy. The principle applies to business firms as well as consumers. Yet it has been elaborated in the past and will be developed in this book primarily regarding consumer behavior. The principle says nothing about nondiscretionary demand. It suggests that the role of willingness to buy is contingent upon the presence of some discretion to the decision maker. Discretion is not an all or none phenomenon; to some extent consumers have a latitude of choice even when buying necessities. Yet willingness to buy influences behavior to the greatest extent when the purchases are discretionary.[2]

Income, previously accumulated financial assets, and access to credit constitute ability to buy and, thereby, the conditions without which inclinations to buy cannot be transformed into demand. Willingness to buy is represented by psychological predispositions or motivational vectors in the individual who makes the purchase. Motives, attitudes, expectations, felt needs, and wants are some of the factors that enter into it. But such description does not suffice. Willingness to buy or rather, as we shall show later, changes in willingness to buy must be measured.

As we have said, consumer discretion prevails first of all in the timing of purchases. Even when a specific need is felt and money is available, the would-be buyer may be unwilling to proceed and may decide to postpone his purchase. Alternatively, the felt need for a certain expenditure may be slight, but the purchaser may act. In the first case adverse attitudes, and in the second case favorable

[1] This is how Gottfried Haberler summarized the influence of psychological factors on the business cycle in his *Prosperity and Recession,* League of Nations, Geneva, 1937.

[2] Consumer discretion has been analyzed in Chap. 2 of George Katona's *The Powerful Consumer* (Ref. 2). (Books and articles frequently cited are numbered in the Bibliography, p. 335). The distinction between genuine decision making and habitual behavior is crucial in determining what expenditures are discretionary. This distinction was introduced in Ref. 1.

attitudes, are assumed to be the determining factor. When many people have similar attitudes at the same time, aggregate demand is influenced.

It has been said that consumers' discretion in timing their purchases is of little economic import, since it exerts a short-range influence only. Postponement of purchases creates a slack that is made good a little while later; buying in advance and in excess of immediate needs makes a bulge, compensated for later by lesser purchases on the part of saturated buyers. This argument is not valid, because fluctuations in consumer demand at a given time may determine cyclical trends which, in turn, affect long-range developments. The postponement of some purchases may develop into a full-fledged recession; it may have an adverse effect on incomes, followed by widespread abstinence from buying, rather than by a period of larger purchases. Contrariwise, increased buying inclinations may lead to a general upswing in which new wants arise, rather than saturation. In short, changes in the timing of purchases may, under certain circumstances, lead to fundamental changes. The long-range impact of changes in willingness to buy depends on what later changes occur both in the ability and in the willingness to buy.

Consumer discretion extends far beyond discretion in the timing of expenditures. A basic proposition of yesterday's economics—that consumer expenditures are a function of income—must be amended in two ways. The first way we have just described, namely, that some expenditures are a function of motives, attitudes, and expectations as well as of income, assets, and debts. The second correction consists of a reversal of the basic proposition: To some extent at least, consumer incomes are a function of consumer expenditures or consumer wants. The economic model according to which two sectors—business and government—fully determine the income of the third sector—the consumer—by hiring and firing workers and setting wages, salaries, interest, and dividend rates must be abandoned. Consumers can and often do exert an influence on the level of their income. Rather than sitting back as passive agents or mere recipients, they sometimes actively seek more income and at other times refrain from doing so.

Conspicuous instances of striving for higher income occur when heads of families take second jobs and wives return to work after their children have reached school age. These will be analyzed later, together with the impact of education on income. Education represents the major means of augmenting lifetime income, even though longer years of schooling mean that income is foregone at a certain stage of the life cycle.

The analysis of consumer discretion in this area must be connected with a search for the causes of striving for larger income. Greater effort and exertion, we shall find, is typically a function of desiring a better standard of living and wanting more consumer goods. In our society, success is demonstrated by a better home, better car, more travel and recreation, larger expenditures on social life, and so on. All this requires greater income. Money is desired, not for its own sake, but for the sake of what it buys.

Consumer discretion is limited. Even people's striving and wishing have their limits; most commonly, desires are reality-bound and exceed levels of accomplishment slightly, rather than greatly. In addition, the environment severely limits what consumers can accomplish. Still, consumers' margin of action is sufficient to influence economic processes.

PSYCHOLOGY AND ECONOMICS

Why is psychological economics needed? One way to answer this question is to picture a science of economics that does not make use of psychology at all. For many decades in economic analysis the actors—businessmen and consumers alike—were pushed off the stage, and economics was restricted to studies of the *results* of their behavior without regard to factors shaping that behavior. Even though this program has not always been adhered to rigorously, it is worthwhile to contemplate what form economic studies take in which the decision makers and their psychology are ruled out of bounds. We begin by giving the most radical example.

In practical matters, as they concern the producers and distributors of goods, the studies are restricted to an analysis of sales and their trend over time. It is of no consequence to the seller who buys his products or why. Only data to which the dollar sign is attached matter. What and how much is sold, and at what price, in a given period in comparison to previous periods—such data serve to measure the impersonal market forces.

Or, proceeding to an analysis of economic developments of the country as a whole, trend lines are constructed of total retail sales or business investments and projected into the future. Interrelationships among these data are explored; changes in GNP and its components are studied and related to changes in other aggregates. The image of exact natural science looms large in these studies. What is given—the facts or data, be they plants and stones or sales and investments—represents the object of investigation. Supply and demand are considered as given. Inferences are drawn about the origin of changes from the relationships between present and past data. The possibility of a direct study of the decision-making process, or what is in the minds of businessmen who supply the goods and consumers who demand them, is not considered.

The picture just presented is extreme. In one respect economic analysts have introduced people into their studies, albeit not the people's psychology. In addition to the questions of what and how much, the question of who has also been raised. Marketing has resorted to nose counts and studied the question of who the buyers of a given product are—the old or the young, the rich or the poor, the urban or the rural people. Business investments have been classified according to the kinds of firms making the investments (manufacturers, utilities, retailers, etc.). The first widely accepted uses of survey research in economics concerned the distribution of national income and the collection of demographic data. However, to know the size of national income and the extent to which it was composed of wages, salaries, interest, dividends, etc., was not considered enough, and the question of how it was distributed by size was raised. How many families were there with, say, more than $10,000 or less than $2,000 income a year? Similarly, many analysts were not satisfied with knowing that national income had increased by, say, 10 per cent over the preceding year; they wanted to know how many families and what kinds of families had large or small increases, or unchanged or declining incomes. When macroeconomic statistical analysis was thus strengthened by microeconomic data, the introduction of demographic data—the determination, for instance, of the age distribution of high-income people or of those with income increases—was a step easily taken.

How about the crucial question of why? It was not raised directly, but it was often answered, in a manner called satisfactory and efficient, by studying the answers to the question of who. It was found, for instance, that there was a high correlation between bank deposits and income or between flying on commercial airplanes and income. It was then thought probable that high income was the cause for the larger bank deposits or the more frequent flights.

The manifold economic data which became available permitted detailed and exact analysis. Relationships between different economic components, expressed in equations in which the parameters were supplied by past experience, could be subjected to tests over time. Numerous equations could be constructed about economic processes occurring at the same time, and their mutual fit could be studied. Variables with time lags could be introduced to investigate, for instance, the relation between sales or profits in an earlier period to investments in a later period. Econometric studies of interrelationships among results of behavior represent enduring achievements of modern economics. But they alone do not suffice. There are several paths leading to the same mountain peak. By ruling out the exploration of one of those paths, we lose information and may even arrive at misinformation.

This point becomes clear when we consider that traditional economic analysts, although they did not study the psychology of decision makers, did not dispense with psychology. They drew conclusions about motives, attitudes, and expectations, partly from available nonpsychological data and partly from what has often been called common sense.

There are hardly any propositions of economic theory which do not imply something about the psychology of the businessman or consumer. Psychological statements have been made on an a priori basis by economists ever since there was a field of economics. Consider, for instance, the study of the saving process. Statistical data have shown that high-income people save a larger proportion of their income than low-income people. With this as the starting point, economists have concluded that motives to save become more powerful when people are well provided with necessities. But further observations have also shown a lack of correspondence between fluctuations of income and amounts saved, thus indicating that income could not be the sole determinant of saving. Some economists turned to interest rates to explain changes in rates of saving. If higher interest rates are assumed to induce people to save more, again a psychological process is postulated: People are seen to be striving for future earnings in preference to gratifying their present needs. Or, to mention a problem to which special attention will be given in this book, it has been postulated that amounts saved are negatively correlated with wealth: The larger the financial assets, the smaller the incentive to add to them. This represents a psychological proposition that has been deduced either from alleged common sense or from principles of marginalism.

These examples may suffice to indicate that there is great need for answers to questions of why in economics, over and above the answers supplied by correlations of economic processes with other economic or demographic variables. Psychological economics is not satisfied with commonsense answers or with homemade psychology and seeks information through empirical studies. By supplying empirically validated generalizations about factors shaping economic behavior, psychological studies add to our understanding of economic processes. Principles and generalizations derived through traditional economic methods may then usefully be supplemented by studies of motives, attitudes, and expectations, presumably without detracting from the value of older teachings.

The statement that we expect to gain a better understanding of economic processes and improve our ability to predict by introducing psychological studies in economics may have a different meaning as well. It may imply that information about people's motives and expectations may not only add to previous knowledge but also change it.

The influence of psychological factors on economic decisions may be viewed in either of two ways. One may think that financial-economic factors dominate economic processes, while changes in motives and expectations color, exaggerate, or diminish their importance. Then market conditions would exert the only significant and enduring impact, and the study of psychological factors would merely supplement traditional economic studies. Alternatively, it is conceivable that economic motives and expectations change, at least at certain times, autonomously, that is, independently of and differently from changes in incomes, prices, interest rates, and the like. Then the impact of psychological factors might fundamentally alter the economic decisions of consumers and businessmen. In the latter case psychological economics might lead to new insights into economic processes. Prior to World War II, occasional advocates of contact between economics and psychology leaned toward the first point of view. During the late 1940s, the first empirical studies of consumer attitudes stemmed from theoretical notions not far removed from such modest expectations. Yet the studies carried out during the last decade have demonstrated this first moderate thesis to be inadequate. Economic activity can sometimes be explained only in terms of the second proposition. Some basic psychological facts may help to explain why.

INTERVENING VARIABLES

Stimuli elicit responses on the part of the organism. Only in certain lower-order responses do we find a one-to-one correspondence between the stimulus and the response. The major form of stimulus for economic behavior is information. Information on changes in the environment is filtered through a variety of intervening variables. These consist, in addition to innate capabilities and personality traits and sociocultural norms acquired in early childhood, of the sum total of the individual's past experience. The information transmitted which impinges on the individual is not identical with the information received. Our perceptions are a function of intervening variables, and our responses depend both on perceptions and on intervening variables.

Past experience, molding our habits, motives, and attitudes, constitutes the most relevant intervening variable. Expectations are a subclass of attitudes that point to the future, since our time perspective extends both backward and forward in a highly selective manner. There is no place for a sharp distinction between attitudes toward the past and the future or between cognitive and affective processes. Attitudes always have affective connotations. Whether a thing is considered good or bad, whether we approve or disapprove of it, is often the most salient aspect of an attitude.[3]

Because of differences in intervening variables, two individuals' responses to identical stimuli need not be the same. The same individual's response to identical stimuli at two points of time likewise need not be the same. The second proposition expresses the basic psychological fact of learning. Human beings are capable of learning.

Yet the diversity of psychological factors influencing responses

---

[3] For a detailed discussion of the principles of psychology used in our studies of economic behavior, see Ref. 1. The term *intervening variables* is widely used to denote those factors or constructs that are not directly observable by recording stimuli and responses and that are postulated to explain behavior.

does not represent our major theme. Even though a multitude of factors account for human actions, it is possible to study the antecedents of action and to discern their major features and regularities. Human beings belong to groups, and group members tend to be influenced by similar motives and attitudes. In addition to learning by individuals, there is social learning. Group belonging causes the acquisition of similar motives and attitudes among many people. At any given time, changes in motivational patterns and in attitudes tend to be similar among group members.

An illustration of how these principles of psychology apply to economic behavior may be in order. Let us consider perceptions of, and reactions to, rising prices. Assume that the stimulus consists of the news that automobile prices have been increased by 10 per cent. People who hear the news will react according to their motives, attitudes, and expectations. Some may have been highly motivated to buy a car, while for others buying a car was out of the question. Some of the former may view the price increase as unjustified profiteering and decide not to buy a car. Others may see the price increase as part of a long-lasting inflationary process; they expect further price increases to follow and decide to buy a car in short order before prices go up still further. Similarly, some people who had not thought of buying a car may view the news as the signal for a new wave of inflation; other people may consider it as a unique event, restricted to the automobile industry; others again may be indifferent to the news.

Does it follow that the psychological analysis is worthless because it discloses, at best, a variety of possible reactions? Nothing could be further from the truth. First, it is possible to determine the prevailing motivational and attitudinal factors and thereby to predict the most probable reactions of different population groups or even of the majority of the people. Secondly, it is possible to study the origin of changes in motives, attitudes, and expectations and thereby to understand the probable reactions and improve the predictions.

At times such psychological studies may fail to add much to economic knowledge. In the extreme case, in which consumers spend all their income in period 1, and incomes remain unchanged but prices rise (and neither financial reserves nor credit is available) in a subsequent period 2, it can be deduced that demand will be smaller in period 2 than in period 1. But such an extreme case in which psychological studies can be dispensed with is hardly ever realized. In a second, more realistic case—when incomes and prices increase in period 2, and some part of income is saved in both periods—there exists a potential impact of psychological factors. Even then market forces may determine the reaction of most consumers. Psychological economics is nonetheless useful in this case. It can indicate why motives and attitudes did not change (for instance, why people did not become concerned with inflation). Finally, the clearest case of a need for psychological studies occurs when autonomous changes of psychological factors are the major determinants of mass action. In such a case, consumers may step up demand beyond the rate of increase in income or, alternatively, reduce demand with no unequivocal economic reason. It is the task of psychological economics to find out how attitudes changed and what kinds of motives and attitudes shaped the response.

In what way psychological factors influence or even determine consumers' response to information about changes in the environment—this is the task of psychological economics to be studied in this book. At this point we are concerned with the postulates of psychological economics and may summarize them as follows:

1. Market forces—incomes, prices, assets, and the like—and psychological factors—motives, attitudes, past experiences, and expectations—jointly determine economic behavior.

2. Both market forces and psychological factors are measurable. It is possible to discern the extent of change in both and to study the factors responsible for the change.

3. Economic knowledge must be derived from the study of both kinds of forces, even though under certain conditions the one and under other conditions the other may predominate. In principle, both purely economic causation and purely psychological causation must be ruled out because it is not changes in incomes, prices, orders, and the like, but the perception of these changes which influence decisions by businessmen and consumers. The consumer is not a puppet governed by the impersonal market, though his discretion is not unlimited.

4. With increasing discretionary income and affluence, the role of the psychological factors is growing. In a mass consumption society, psychological economics is far more important than in any other economic system; psychological studies of economic behavior do not just supplement traditional economics but form a part of its basic operations.

5. Motives, attitudes, and expectations do not change capriciously; the origin of their changes can and must be studied. Even before these studies approach the stage of solving problems, rudimentary data on prevailing motivational patterns and on the dynamics of change in economic attitudes may serve to improve our understanding of economic processes.

In closing we turn our attention to the research methods used in psychological economics. Human behavior is complex, multimotivated, and subject to learning as well as to the influence of inertia. The question is: How, under such circumstances, is it possible to conduct research which will serve to provide understanding and improve prediction? We shall outline here the program of such research as it has been conducted by the Survey Research Center.

The first step in such a program is to eliminate from consideration those factors which do not cause changes in aggregate behavior. These include ephemeral moods which change rapidly and personal idiosyncrasies which average out. Frequently they include also those factors which change very slowly. Sociocultural norms, for example, or the age distribution and the family composition of the population, are relevant for the analysis of changes over fairly long periods but not for the study of cyclical fluctuations.

Second, we focus on three types of variables: (1) those that indicate changes in ability to buy (income, assets, debts, as well as prices); (2) those that represent perception and understanding of new information transmitted—be it on business-cycle trends, politics, or any other relevant subject; and (3) those attitudes and motives that point to changes in willingness to buy.

Third, regarding changes in willingness to buy, we must make use of several indicators and search for uniformity of change in direction. The attitudes of different population groups may be tapped by questions in different areas; changes in some people's willingness to buy may be influenced primarily by personal financial attitudes and other people's by their general economic outlook. Substantial changes in attitudinal measures are recognized as deserving more attention than small changes.

In Chapter 9 we shall describe the results of extensive empirical studies on diverse attitudinal measures and their relation to discretionary expenditures. We shall also show that an additive index constructed from six attitudinal measures has performed rather well. Linear models are economical, and a simple unweighted index of a selected subset of variables can be used as a benchmark measure. But in human behavior a variety of interactions play a role, and therefore the detailed examination of each variable must supplement the use of an index.

These considerations lead to the fourth and last point in the program of studies: In addition to data on changes in ability to buy and willingness to buy, the reasons for those changes must likewise be considered. Evidence of learning by broad groups of consumers, indicated by patterns of reactions different from those observed on previous occasions, is of particular interest.

Information on such intervening variables as motives and attitudes is obtained from individuals. It is the individual who feels, thinks, and decides to make or not to make discretionary expenditures. Yet, for purposes of economic analysis, changes in the attitudes of individuals matter only if they are uniform among broad groups of consumers and thus indicate changes in aggregate demand that will influence the markets. The aggregation of individual data of a psychological nature represents a major problem of measurement.

5

Measurement

Scientific progress depends upon measurements that serve to support or to refute theories and hypotheses. During the past twenty-odd years, change in consumer sentiment has become measurable. It has become possible, first, to find out whether consumer attitudes and expectations are more or less confident and optimistic at a given time than at an earlier time and, second, to demonstrate the relationship between such changes in consumer sentiment and subsequent demand for durable goods.

It is not unusual in the history of science that improvements in methods coincide with developments which create the need for them. Fifty or even thirty years ago, there was neither the urgent need nor the necessary tools for the study of consumer psychology. Before the emergence of the mass consumption economy there was little reason to measure the economic attitudes and expectations of millions of people and no techniques were available to make such measurements. It was only in the thirties of this century that the mathematical, sociological, and psychological foundations of a new method, the *sample interview survey,* were developed. This method has become the basic tool for measurements in consumer psychology.

Economic statistics has made enormous progress in the present century. Following conceptual developments about the relationships among the different sectors of the economy—business, consumer, and government—means were found to measure the respective contribution of each sector, the interaction among the sectors, and the total output of the economy (GNP). All these are aggregate, or macroeconomic, measures. National income, total retail sales, business capital outlays, and the like, relate to the performance of the entire economy or its major parts, as do indexes of production, prices, and employment. The usefulness of these global measures long blinded economists to the need for breaking down the aggregates. But aggregates, and what amounts to the same, that is, averages (means), do not provide all the information needed and may even be misleading. Aggregate statistics, usually derived from records rather than surveys, inform us, for instance, that the average American family owns common stock valued at close to $2,500. (This is the total value of stock owned by individuals divided by the number of families.) Hearing this, few would suspect that about 80 per cent of the families own no stock whatsoever, and about 3 per cent own stock worth more than $25,000. Clearly there is need for microeconomic data on the distribution of incomes, assets, debts, and purchases. Data on many of these distributions were obtained by the survey method in the 1940s. Prior to that time it was not even known how national income was distributed by size or what share of national income accrued to families with high or low incomes.

Economic-financial surveys collect data on the incomes, assets, and purchases of individuals in a representative sample. Our concern is not with the individual, however, but with the economy or the markets. The sample interview survey represents the bridge between collecting data about individuals and drawing conclusions for aggregates. Sampling theory and practice enable us to draw small samples, say of 1,000 to 3,000 families, which are representative of the more than 50 million families in the United States. It is a simple matter to divide the sample into easily identifiable subgroups of the population—income groups, age groups, and residents of central cities, suburbs, and rural areas, etc.—and present data for such subgroups as well as for the entire population. It is fairly simple to add up data to which the dollar sign is attached, such as incomes, assets, and expenditures, and to build up national totals or group totals from survey data on individuals. Thus economic-financial surveys, even though they obtain their data from individuals, supply information relevant for the entire economy.[1]

[1] Sample surveys provide information on the order of magnitude of values rather than exact information. Survey data are subject to errors which do not exist when the data are obtained from all members of the universe. These sampling errors are, however, measurable, provided scientific sampling methods

Data on economic attitudes and expectations can hardly be collected except through surveys of relatively small size. This is the consequence of difficulties involved in uniformly applying indirect methods to probe for elusive motives. Respondents' answers to attitudinal questions depend to a large extent on the questions asked as well as on the personality of the respondents. Differences in the way the questions are formulated and differences among individuals in their manner of responding affect the answers. Interpersonal comparisons are difficult, if possible at all, because the same feeling may be expressed by one person in words that sound quite optimistic

---

are used, and therefore it is possible to present the findings together with their confidence limits. For instance, the finding in Chart 1 of Chap. 2 that 35 per cent of spending units had incomes between $6,000 and $15,000 in 1961 should have read, if expressed precisely, 35 per cent ±2 per cent, indicating that there is 95 per cent probability (two standard errors) that the "true value" would not be lower than 33 or higher than 37 per cent. The larger the sample, the smaller the sampling error, but the reduction in error is very slight beyond a few thousand cases. Newspaper editors as well as their readers often find it difficult to understand that a sample of, say, 2,000 cases may correctly represent a universe of 50 million families, and they prefer to rely on a sample of, say, 20,000 cases. Yet it is rare that greater precision is needed than can be obtained with a sample of a few thousand cases, and no organization except the U.S. Bureau of the Census uses much larger samples. The major reason why the Census Bureau spends the taxpayers' money for larger samples is, not that it is intent on reducing the sampling errors still further, but that it desires to break down its samples into small subgroups. For instance, it wishes to present employment and unemployment data not only for the nation as a whole but also for each state separately. In small samples important subgroups contain only a few hundred cases, and those data are subject to very large sampling errors.

The frequent public discussion of sample size overlooks the fact that reporting errors represent a much bigger problem for survey research than sampling errors. Misunderstanding by respondents or interviewers and incorrect recall, modesty, exaggeration, or even deliberately false answers given by respondents (the latter more often on assets than on attitudes!) constitute the greatest challenge to survey research. One of the most important means of minimizing reporting errors is careful selection and training of the interviewing staff. Obviously this is easier with the small staff needed for a survey of 2,000 cases than with the large staff needed for a survey of 20,000 cases or the enormous staff needed for the decennial population census. The census is not subject to sampling errors, but it is checked and corrected through sample surveys conducted by the Census Bureau.

The bibliography at the end of this book contains a special section listing some important publications from the vast literature on sampling methods and survey methods in general. Additional information on the surveys conducted by the Survey Research Center is also given there.

and by another person in words that sound quite pessimistic. Optimistic or pessimistic attitudes, in contrast to amounts spent, are not
additive, and it is not possible at any time to express people's
optimism in a single value.

Fortunately, absolute measures are not needed. Relative measures
representing quantification of the extent of change suffice. For most
economic analysis it is enough to know whether there has been a
change and, if so, to know its direction and magnitude. We may
therefore proceed by drawing representative samples of consumers
at three- or six-month intervals. Different samples are drawn each
time, but each sample is representative of all consumers. We ask
the same set of questions each time of each individual and select
the questions so that together they yield information on the
respondent's psychological predispositions for his economic behavior.
We tabulate the answers by using crude groupings and thus obtain
distributions indicating, for instance, that at a given time 60 per cent
of all consumers expect good times during the next year, 20 per
cent are undecided or have no opinion, and 20 per cent expect bad
times. Such findings in themselves are of little value. But three and
six and twelve months later we ask the same set of questions and
use the same methods of scaling the answers. By comparing the
admittedly inexact measures obtained at different points of time,
we obtain fairly reliable measures of change. This conclusion
emerges if we assume, and there is much justification for the
assumption, that within each of the representative samples interviewed at different times similar individual differences occur. Also,
response errors due to misunderstanding of the questions or the
answers and even intentionally false replies, as well as errors due
to the methods of categorizing the answers, tend to be constant in
each of the successive representative samples.

Data on trends over time of distributions of answers represent
one of the two major contributions of survey research and will be
reported extensively in this book. Changes in measures of consumer
attitudes from one period to the next can be expressed in the form
of index values, and the same is true of aggregate economic data,
for instance, of changes in the dollar amount of sales of durables.
Then it is possible to calculate the correlation between the two sets
of data.

The second major function served by survey measurements is to
reveal relations among variables and thereby to contribute to our

understanding of why the changes occurred. From survey data functional relations between financial variables are studied (for instance, between income and asset holdings), as well as between financial and demographic variables (for instance, between income and age). Measurements of the relation of psychological variables to either demographic or financial variables are of particular importance for economic psychology. We may, for instance, determine the proportion of optimists among upper-income people, and by making comparisons with past distributions determine whether an increase in the proportion of optimists among all consumers was or was not due to changes in the attitudes of upper-income people. Further, we may find that optimism and confidence are associated with a certain form of behavior, e.g., greater purchases of durables, and may trace this relation over time. We may also study the relation between different attitudes, say, between the expectation of income increases and the expectation of price increases, and derive conclusions from the findings about consumer thinking at a given time. That only approximate measures are available for either of the expectations does not make it impossible to generalize about the relation that prevails between them. These examples serve to indicate that information on functional relations may shed light both on the origin and the effect of changes in motives and expectations.

A change in the distribution of attitudes from one period to the next is most reliably measured by using different representative samples in each survey. A person, once interviewed, may give subsequent thought to the problems raised in the interview and might therefore not be representative were the same questions asked of him at a later time. For purposes of studying certain functional relations, however, it is often valuable to adopt the panel method of interviewing, that is, to interview the same respondents on repeated occasions. This is useful, for instance, in identifying the factors that contribute to changes in attitudes, and it is necessary for comparing the purchases of groups of people who, at an earlier time, had been characterized either as optimists or as pessimists.

Psychological tests frequently require the use of open questions to which respondents answer freely in their own words. The Survey Research Center tends to avoid questions that can be answered by yes or no or by any other single word. Many questions begin in a rather simple and direct way, such as, "Do you think that a year from now you will be better off financially, worse off, or just about the same as now?" Yet questions of this type are always supplemented by asking, "Why do you think so?" in order to induce the respondent to explain his answer in detail.

In surveys the question of why can be asked directly. For instance, after finding out that a respondent has purchased common stock, one may ask, "Why did you buy common stock at that time?" Or the question of why can be determined in an indirect manner through the use of a variety of questions about opinions and expectations (for instance, about price and income expectations). Finally, answers to the question of why may be sought through applying such psychological techniques as picture-, story-, or sentence-completion tests. During the last few years the direct question of why has been disparaged by practitioners of motivation research. It is correct to argue that such questions are often useless, because people are not clearly aware of their motives; or that the questions are sometimes even dangerous, because they may yield biased answers. Yet under certain circumstances the direct question may yield valuable insights and has occasionally been used in our studies.

Periodic surveys then, in addition to recording changes in consumer sentiment, may serve to answer such questions as the following: How did it happen that at a given time many people became optimistic or pessimistic? What developments in personal finances or in the economy in general have been salient to masses of consumers? What, if any, noneconomic news has influenced people's economic attitudes? Are there differences in how new information is apprehended by different groups of the population? These and similar objectives govern the formulation of survey questions. Surveys carried out with representative samples yield quantitative data the interpretation of which leads to conclusions that either support or contradict the assumptions guiding the studies.

From this description of the methods used, we may outline the philosophy of science which underlies the study of economic psychology. The initial step is theoretical, consisting of vague and imprecise notions about the influence of certain factors on behavior. Testable hypotheses are then derived which guide empirical research. Empirical tests never prove a hypothesis and hardly ever refute it; they help to improve and refine the hypothesis. There is an unending procession from hypothesis to empirical test, then to improved hypothesis and further test, and so on. New data indicate the shortcomings as well as the values of earlier generalizations and suggest improvements. Theory construction, that is, the integration of a variety of hypotheses into a broad and logically consistent framework, may take place at any stage of the process; there are early, there are middle, and there are late theories. A theory of economic behavior, and of social behavior in general, represents the ultimate goal; empirically validated generalizations, the proximate goal. Theorizing as well as empirical research are required for both goals.

This book contains data obtained through quantitative research, tentative generalizations derived from the data, and low-level theorizing on the mass consumption society. An attempt has been made to give meaning to a great amount of information accumulated about the mid-twentieth-century American economy. It is not possible to produce conclusive evidence for every statement made. The reader is presented with well-established findings, as well as implications from combinations of findings about which some assurance of truth exists, and occasionally also generalizations from scanty data. The book is based on the belief that, particularly in the social sciences, some restructuring of theory is in order before a solid basis can be provided for every aspect of the new structure.

A strategy of science is implied in this procedure. If we were to wait until we were sure before accepting new ideas, it seems likely that progress would be slow indeed. In the attempt to fill the need for a reasonably workable theory of consumer behavior, it may be necessary to forge some links without proof. Such proofs require time and funds, and devoted scientists are urged to select the weak links and to test them.

PART TWO

Social Critics

PART TWO

Social Critics

6

The Penalty of Affluence

Rarely are new developments, whether social or economic, greeted with rejoicing. With every change, however desirable it may be, there are always those who bemoan the "good old days." Traditionally, prophets of doom find a wide audience in times of prosperity. Thus with the widespread distribution of discretionary purchasing power in the United States, affluence was first recognized, not by those who welcomed it as a unique accomplishment of our times and our country, but by social critics who deplored it. In popular books, Galbraith's *Affluent Society* becomes an overabundant society; the wealth of consumer goods is equated, not with the high American standard of living, but with gadgetry and waste.

Unjustified though their criticisms may be, our affluent society has every reason to be grateful to its critics. However slight the writers' influence on consumer habits and practices, it should be beneficial. Fortunately, those thinkers and writers who attack our society do not have it in their power to destroy its affluence. They may, on the other hand, serve the useful purpose of pointing up its possible dangers. It is true that there could be too much of a good thing, and changes might sometimes take undesirable directions. There is virtue, therefore, in our being constantly reminded that the lives of our grandparents, burdened as they were with a neverending struggle for mere subsistence, had many values worthy of being retained.

I am greatly indebted to the social critics.[1] Their writings eliminate the necessity of erecting a "straw man" or employing the common technique of setting forth imaginary conditions in order to demonstrate more clearly the opposite point of view. In the literature of recent years, it is contended that our economic structure is largely based on artificially contrived demand, that private wealth is associated with public poverty, that consumer debt presents grave dangers, that dependence on the behavior of the masses increases the instability of the economy. If such contentions were not persuasively made and believed, it would be necessary to invent them, since the mass consumption economy cannot be understood without a discussion of precisely these issues. Since these are not mere straw men but rather notions being given serious credence, it becomes important to bring empirical evidence to bear upon them; this, then, will be the major task undertaken. First, however, let us consider the general or philosophic aspects of the attacks being made against the concept of affluence.

The first argument we have to consider is that our present-day society constitutes a betrayal of the American Revolution. Arnold J. Toynbee calls the Revolution glorious because "It staked out human rights and staked them out for all men." After thus setting forth this magnificent achievement of the United States in the history of mankind, Toynbee continues:

> Though I am a foreigner, I can tell you what was *not* one of the aims of the American Revolution. It was not its aim to provide the people of the Thirteen Colonies with the maximum amount of consumer goods per head. . . . It [affluence] has side-tracked America from the main line of her own revolution. (*Op. cit.*, p. 150.)

There is little question that the great men of 1776 were concerned with other matters than consumer goods. But must we believe that the ideals they staked out were intended to be rigid and fixed for all time? Is it not possible that succeeding generations best preserved their great heritage by broadening the scope of the Founding Fathers' aspirations to conform to changing conditions? The new

[1] John K. Galbraith, *The Affluent Society*, Houghton Mifflin Company, Boston, 1958; Arnold J. Toynbee, *America and the World Revolution*, Oxford University Press, London, 1962; Vance Packard, *The Hidden Persuaders* and *The Waste Makers*, both published by David McKay Company, Inc., New York, 1957 and 1960.

conditions created by the Revolution inevitably necessitated actions which, in turn, resulted in new goals. Shall every new step be considered a deviation from the path of our forefathers—or rather progress along the same path but farther than could have been dreamed of in the eighteenth century?

Human rights and political freedom, constitutional guarantees and independence—these were the goals of the first struggle. Then came the struggle for social justice. Finally—and the word *finally* reflects our own myopia since there is no end to the fight—came the struggle for economic democracy. In our early history it was conceivable that equal justice for all might have been provided even if productive facilities were controlled by a few rich people who alone reaped profits and lived abundantly. For the millions of immigrants of the second half of the nineteenth century, freedom from persecution and oppression was its own reward, justifying even the drudgery and poverty of life in the mines and mills of America. Wages remained low and working hours long while a few captains of railroad and industry amassed huge fortunes and the Newport set lived in luxury surpassing that of Europe's aristocracy. But the American frontier provided livelihood to many, and the success of a few second-generation immigrants sufficed to create the dream of unlimited economic opportunities in a classless society.

The American dream was dreamed long before it was realized. Until World War II the middle-class bourgeoisie improved their standard of living to a similar extent in Europe and in America. Yet the new middle class shared only some of the amenities available to the rich; money for discretionary expenditures beyond the necessities of life remained in the hands of the few. More important still, the middle class itself was small; the broad masses of the population were still struggling to satisfy subsistence needs.

Although some of its aspects appeared earlier, it was only after World War II that the first great mass consumption society came into existence in the United States. In this instance, the advent of a new kind of society preceded the concept of it even as an ideal. The majority of Americans were freely making discretionary purchases before they realized that they were living in a new era.

The change may have been understood abroad before it was understood at home. What was an unsung fact in the United States was a revolutionary idea in Europe, namely, that economic equality might be approximated by raising the living standards of the masses rather than by appropriating the wealth of the rich. Europeans soon recognized that the high American standard of living differed radically from the way of life of their own upper classes. The latter—which American millionaires of an earlier era had taken over from their European counterparts—was a life of country estates and many servants, lavish parties, and jewelry and art collections. The former, by contrast, was seen as the standard of the average people, which permitted them to concern themselves no longer with averting hunger but with the amenities of life—cars and washing machines, vacations and savings accounts. For European consumers the vision was of a new American revolution, but one which was a continuation of, not a deviation from, the revolution of 1776.

The great change in ideals cannot be better described than in the words of Toynbee himself. Unbelievably, the following passage contains no reference to America. And Toynbee's discussion of America's having abandoned its old leadership contains no reference to the following:

> For the first time since the dawn of civilization about five thousand years ago, the masses have now become alive to the possibility that their traditional way of life might be changed for the better and that this change might be brought about by their own action. This awakening of hope and purpose in the hearts and minds of the hitherto depressed three-quarters of the World's population will, I feel certain, stand out in retrospect as the epoch-making event of our age. (*Op. cit.*, p. 40.)

Just as surely as America pointed the way to human rights for all in 1776 did she show the way to material well-being for all in the mid-twentieth century.

Toynbee argues that there is a "penalty of affluence." Affluence cuts people off from the common lot; it insulates the rich minority from the poor majority. There is truth in this observation: The rich are surely not loved. Those who have what others desire or envy are seldom popular. Then, too, there have been some Americans abroad who have stirred up a dislike of Americans in general. It does not follow, however, that Americans would win more popularity contests or would make more headway among allies and neutrals if they were poor. Toynbee seriously advises America to give up its affluence. We should stop spending, says he, on "unwanted consumer goods" (we shall return to this phrase in a few moments) and rather devote that money to "meeting the basic and pressing needs of the majority of our fellow human beings." The intention may be good, but the advice is bad, not only because it is not feasible, but first of all because it is based on fallacious economic principles. A redistribution of existing resources is not the solution to worldwide needs. Taking away from the rich minority to give to the poor majority has never provided the long-term help needed. One of the merits of the mass consumption society has been to teach the new economic lesson that the solution to mass poverty is not cutting the pie into different-size slices, but rather exerting every effort to increasing the size of the pie.

Toynbee's advice serves us ill on the ideological level as well. By raising the living standards of the American masses and demonstrating to the world at large that it is possible for the great majority of the people to live decently, the United States has once again presented new goals and aspirations for all the world. Rather than having betrayed the ideals of her early history, she has once more demonstrated a dedication to the faith that mankind has it within its own power to better its way of life.

Toynbee maintains that America by renouncing its affluence would not really make any sacrifice, since that affluence is, in any event, doomed to perish. Says he, "An economy that depends for its survival on an artificial stimulation of material wants seems unlikely to survive for very long." (Speech by A. J. Toynbee, quoted in *Time* magazine, September 22, 1961.) He is not alone in believing that our economy is saturated and that it can only flourish for a short time because of the artificial creation of demand for goods not really needed or wanted. This is the second major argument condemning mass consumption economies. On closer inspection it, too, will turn out to be mistaken.

7

Artificially Created Wants

In contrast to the argument that America has betrayed its own ideals, the proposition that its affluence is based on artificially created wants is not original with Toynbee and has a respectable ancestry among economists. Nevertheless, we shall begin by quoting Toynbee because he has provided the simplest formulation of the position.

Demand for consumer goods, according to Toynbee, stems (1) from our needs, (2) from our wants, and (3) from "bogus wants" which make for "unwanted demand in excess of genuine wants." Needs for necessities of life are primary, but genuine wants are also acceptable. These are "the wants that we become aware of spontaneously, without having to be told by Madison Avenue that we want something that we would never have thought of wanting if we had been left in peace to find out our wants for ourselves" (*op. cit.*, p. 145). The third category, the unwanted goods, are of course easy to give up: "We have merely to stop listening to Madison Avenue."

An analysis of this point of view must first consider the allegation that we become aware of certain wants "spontaneously." We shall do no more than remind the reader of the age-old discussion about innate versus acquired behavior. Even our innate or inherited capabilities, needs, and personality traits are modified by experience. Economic behavior is learned behavior in the sense that it develops and changes with experience. Learning is intercommunication. In addition to the learner, there always must be stimuli from the environment: a teacher, a book, an event, a newspaper, or even an advertisement. It makes no sense whatsoever to distinguish between wants, desires, or behavior that we have acquired spontaneously and not spontaneously. If the distinction were made, we would find that the ways in which we satisfy our basic needs are the least spontaneous. Habits of eating and drinking, toilet training, and the like, are impressed upon us in early childhood. Sociocultural norms which fashion our behavior and our wants are likewise conditioned in our early childhood, rather than selected spontaneously later.

Toward the end of the last century, nobody "wanted" an automobile. Whether the invention of the horseless buggy was due to accident, play, tinkering, or rational thinking on the part of people endowed with mechanical abilities is immaterial for our purposes. Surely, the invention did not originate with the consumer and was not made with an eye to prevailing consumer wants. Even when the first cars appeared on the road and for many years thereafter, their use for mass transportation was envisaged neither by producers nor by consumers. But today even small children in America feel the need for a car to take them and their parents shopping, visiting, and later to school. Between the early days of the automobile and the present situation there was a long period of social learning. The learning process was, of course, not spontaneous: first of all, it could not have taken place without the original invention; second, it was a function of numerous stimuli—personal experience, education, and reading, as well as propaganda and advertising. Thus it may be said that wants for automobiles were induced, or to use Galbraith's term, "contrived." But are not most of our wants contrived in this sense? And are not most of our contrived wants, in a certain sense, original with the buyer? It can hardly be said that such want-creation is artificial.

Similarly, cigarette smoking and even the craving for cigarettes on the part of many people are dependent on numerous changes in our environment and their impact on the smoker. Another example about which empirical evidence is available is air conditioning. Shortly after World War II air conditioning was used in many movie theaters and office buildings, and people became familiar with it. At the same time many people in large American cities were probably suffering from the heat and humidity of summer. Thus one could assume that there existed what might be called a spontaneous need or want. Nevertheless, wants or desires for room air conditioners were found to be practically nonexistent in 1946–1947. In surveys with representative samples of consumers, when people in all walks of life were asked about the things around the house they would *like* to have—assuming that money played no role and that technology provided whatever one wanted—practically nobody mentioned home air conditioners. Even though attempts were made to stimulate imagination and fancy, the consumer did not point the way to the producer. Before a new product reaches the market, before the consumer is told by the producer what is available, wants do not take a form specific enough to serve as a guideline for industry. Shall it then be said that room air conditioners did not fill a real need or want when finally they were produced and sold by advertising? On the other hand, it does not follow that any new product developed by industry will be a wanted product. It is well known that many widely advertised new consumer goods fail to find a market because they are not in line with consumer predispositions.

Now we are ready to turn to Galbraith's more sophisticated argument about the creation of wants. His basic premise is: "When man has satisfied his physical needs, the psychologically grounded desires take over" (*op. cit.*, p. 143). The latter are said to be of "a lower order of urgency" in the sense, for example, that a car would be given up before food would be given up. But it is essential to remember that psychological wants can be as insistent as physical needs and, more importantly, that there is no such thing as reaching a point of satiation with "higher-order wants" (which, with much justification, the wants of a lower order of urgency are commonly called).

Galbraith, like most economists, does recognize the incorrectness of any notion that there are rigid limits to human needs and wants.[1] He recognizes that the wants of an individual do not become less urgent as more of them are satisfied. He nonetheless holds on to the notion of saturation of the economy with consumer goods. We shall see later that there is indeed a real problem of saturation, not in the sense of absolute limits to possessions, but in the sense of temporary feelings of having enough goods. This problem is

[1] Toynbee, on the other hand, maintains that there is a narrow limit "to the quantity of goods that can be effectively possessed" and even believes that most present-day American consumers have already exceeded that limit.

relevant, however, to an understanding, not of economic development, but only of business cycles and must be studied from the
point of view of the psychological principle of varying levels of
aspiration.

For the moment, it suffices to say that in spite of his different
starting point, Galbraith propagates the same view which has been
described as Toynbee's (which in fact Toynbee borrowed from
Galbraith). "If the individual's wants are to be urgent, they must
originate with himself. They cannot be urgent if they must be contrived for him," writes Galbraith (*op. cit.*, p. 152). In view of what
has already been said about Toynbee's theory of spontaneous wants,
nothing needs to be added about Galbraith's original wants. But
Galbraith proceeds to further arguments, linking want-creation with
debt-creation and envisaging an urgent and immediate danger in the
growth of consumer credit. As popular followers of Galbraith have
written, "We are buying goods we do not need with money we
do not have" and "The average American is three months away
from bankruptcy."

Consumer credit has become one of the prime controversial issues
of our time. Many of my studies have been directed to an analysis
of consumer attitudes toward credit and of the impact of the
increase in consumer borrowing on the economy. This problem
requires detailed treatment which, however, may be postponed (see
Chapter 22), because the increase in consumer borrowing is related
only to the dispersion rather than the creation of wants. Suffice it
to say now that (1) consumer credit is something liked by consumers rather than something they are coerced into using; (2)
there is no question of bankruptcy for many consumers; most
consumers carefully budget their borrowing, and default rates on
consumer credit are as small as, if not smaller than, on business
credit; and (3) consumer borrowing has added little to the instability of our economy, though it has contributed much to its
growth by facilitating the gratification of wants.

Galbraith's discussion of want-creation leads him to the following
major conclusion: "One cannot defend production as satisfying
wants if that production creates the wants." According to him,
modern advertising and salesmanship have given the American
economy a new direction, which he deplores. Private opulence
represents a maldistribution of national resources because it is associated with "public poverty." Clearly, if it were true that it was

because America has devoted too large a share of her resources to consumer goods that we have too many slums and not enough schools or hospitals and if this allocation of resources were due to advertising, we should most heartily join with Galbraith in attacking both the composition of the goods currently being produced and the agents responsible for it. The next chapter will be devoted to the relation between private opulence and public poverty. Let us study here, briefly, the role assigned to advertising in creating consumer wants and thus determining the allocation of resources.

There is nobody who attributes greater power to Madison Avenue than its critics. Serious spokesmen of the advertising industry do argue that advertising has contributed to an increase in consumer demand and a change in its composition, but they would rarely if ever dare to credit themselves with being as successful as Galbraith, Toynbee, and Packard claim they are. Let us first review the assertion that advertising "brings into being wants that previously did not exist" (Galbraith, *op. cit.*, p. 155).

THE INFLUENCE OF ADVERTISING

The original function of advertising, and the one in which it is most successful, is to transmit information. The consumer is provided the means of finding out what products are available on the marketplace. As we have argued, most new products are not created because consumers have expressed a desire for them. The consumer must, therefore, be informed of their existence and of the purposes they serve, as well as of their prices.

So far we are not on controversial grounds. Providing information is not what is usually meant by influencing the consumer. The problem becomes more complicated when we consider persuasion, unreasoned appeals, and the changing of people's tastes, opinions, and beliefs as possible functions of advertising. No doubt, there is advertising that attempts to persuade prospective buyers, and the constant repetition of brand names and the virtues of specific brands often takes the form of unreasoned appeals. The rule relating to the success of such endeavors is simple: The influence of advertising, just as of any other mass medium, decreases in proportion to the importance the consumer attaches to a matter. This follows from the presence of genuine decision making in important matters but can be illustrated even without reference to the psychological principles involved.[2]

Surveys have revealed that most Americans hold that the various leading and widely advertised brands of gasoline do not differ from one another in any significant way; this is true even of those who regularly buy one particular brand. Matters connected with the gas station and the people operating it, e.g., convenient location, good service, and personality of the serviceman, are primarily responsible for establishing a habit of purchasing at one station and, therefore, one kind of gasoline. Under such circumstances, advertising is important for the seller. The brand name must constantly be kept in the public eye, just because it does not matter to the public whether it buys one brand or the other. Similar situations prevail, for some people though not necessarily for all, regarding brands of toothpaste, orange juice, and many other products. We let ourselves be reminded and even persuaded because the decision is not of great importance.

Since beliefs and attitudes usually concern important matters, changing behavior is often easier than changing attitudes. But there are certain major forms of behavior that are based on our beliefs and attitudes. In an important situation, the American consumer is sensible and critical rather than foolish and gullible.

If modern psychology has proved anything, it is that changing other human beings, and especially changing them without personal contact, is a very difficult task. Frequently, husband and wife learn to share each other's tastes and opinions. This may be due to purposive selection (people with similar tastes and opinions marry), as well as to a slow process of change resulting from close contact over many years. Personal interaction and intercommunication also occur at places of work: employees learn to share the attitudes of their colleagues, and sometimes even of their superiors.

Groups to which we belong—trade associations, labor unions, professional societies, etc.—exert an influence on us, because we specifically seek the group's influence in joining it, or because group

[2] For a brilliant analysis of the vast literature on what has been called the "mass society," see R. A. Bauer and A. H. Bauer, "America, Mass Society and Mass Media," in *Journal of Social Issues*, vol. 16, no. 3, 1960. The authors cite evidence that the alleged omnipotence of mass media is a myth and conclude that "mass media of communications exercise a distinctive advantage in *inverse* proportion to the importance of the issues involved" (p. 24). They also suggest that a change of attitudes is more difficult to achieve than a change of behavior.

belonging makes for a selection of the communications that reach us. Democrats, for example, tend to listen to Democratic campaign speeches; and Republicans, to Republican campaign speeches. In addition, over a long period of time group belonging may result in genuine social learning, that is, in the acquisition of new beliefs, attitudes, and wants that prevail in the group.

To conclude the discussion of the extent to which people's behavior and even personality may be changed, we may recall the contention that psychoanalysts do sometimes succeed in exerting a certain influence. When they do, let us credit their influence to an intercommunication between therapist and patient which lasts over an extended period of time and is sought by the patient.

Such examples make it clear that changing the masses of consumers, through advertising, concerning matters that are important cannot happen frequently. Social influence which is effective rarely comes from the outside or from above. We are influenced by the group to which we belong, that is, by a horizontal rather than a vertical process.[3]

Is this conclusion contradicted by the occasional quick success of some widely advertised products or the changes in fashion and consumer tastes that have occasionally been observed? The great increase, for example, in the sales of Revlon cosmetics following the nationwide attention paid to the "$64,000 Question" television program is hardly evidence of induced changes in consumer tastes when they matter. The increase in the sale of cosmetics in general at the same time, or the preference for large cars equipped with fins and lots of chrome in 1955, may perhaps be cited in support of the contention that changes in consumer tastes result from persuasion and that they may be made to conform to changes in production. But let us not forget the existence of contrary evidence. In 1957, for instance, the American people turned away from large cars with fins, even though they were the only American cars available and were widely advertised. In 1958 automobile advertising was as extensive as in the preceding years, but auto sales dropped sharply. Not all advertising campaigns are successful, and not all widely advertised products penetrate the market.

We should know much more than we do about the dynamics of change in consumer tastes. Some of these changes no doubt occur

[3] See E. Katz and P. F. Lazarsfeld, *Personal Influence,* The Free Press of Glencoe, New York, 1955.

without purposive action by producers, while others are induced by them. Under what conditions are the "persuaders" successful? Quite simply, when they swim with the current. Market research, intended to find out what consumers want and why they want it, is important; if and when advertising conforms with trends in consumer wants, it exerts some influence. We shall come back to this point in Chapter 26.

As has been said, all learning requires interaction between the teacher, or other stimuli, and the learner. The persuader, whether open or hidden, is successful insofar as the persuaded cooperates. There is, of course, interaction between the consumer and the seller or advertiser. But it is equally correct to say that the advertiser manipulates the consumer as that the consumer manipulates the advertiser. The good advertiser is a middleman between producer and consumer; he senses consumer reactions and helps fashion the product accordingly; at the same time he interprets the consumer and tries to make nationwide trends from small beginnings.

The consumer was never sovereign in the sense of being wholly autonomous, and he is not sovereign today. However, the assertion that his sovereignty has diminished during the last twenty or fifty years is most questionable. But even if it had, the consumer is still neither a puppet nor a pawn. For a while some consumers may be stimulated into buying something that is useless or wasteful, but they do eventually learn better. A study of empirical evidence will show that most consumers, though they are not ideal "rational men," are circumspect and sensible.

Consumer demand is not fixed in quantity. Consumption can be and has been stimulated by salesmanship, marketing, and advertising. But the extent of such influence is far too small to justify the broad statements that are made about advertising's creating our wants. Production and advertising, when in line with prevailing sociopsychological tendencies, do contribute to the actualization of certain wants but are not the creators of the manifold wants that stimulate our mass consumption society.

8

Private Opulence and Public Poverty

This is the most serious argument against the mass consumption society: The consumer exercises his influence in a socially undesirable manner. It is Galbraith's accomplishment to have presented the argument to the American public in a most convincing way. We do not have enough schools and spend far too little on education; we do not have enough hospitals and spend far too little on the health of our people; there are too many slums which breed delinquency and crime; scarcity prevails in the entire domain of public expenditures, such as highways, parks, and recreation facilities. Such realities represent Fact No. 1. Fact No. 2 is the affluence in the private sector of the economy, the extent to which we are endowed with consumer goods. Galbraith argues that there is a causal connection between the two facts: It is because of Fact No. 2 that we are suffering from Fact No. 1. To reestablish the social balance, he would have us change the allocation of our resources. He would have us cut down on consumer expenditures in order to increase public investments.

Again the argument goes far beyond economics and concerns human values. The social critics deplore our preoccupation with material goods, our gadget-mindedness, and our wastefulness on the ground that they detract from the true goals of man, which are spiritual. In the phrase of Toynbee: "The true end of Man is *not* to possess the maximum amount of consumers goods" (*op. cit.*, p. 144).

The philosophic and historical basis of the argument is complex, and its roots are not always consistent. To some extent the argument stems from the longing for the proverbial "good old days," which are recalled as having been peaceful and quiet, while modern life is thought to be anxiety-ridden. Puritan notions about the dangers of self-indulgence also play a role. It has been said, in every era, that wealth blunts incentives and makes people soft. Historically the decline of civilizations is commonly thought to be associated with the acquisition of material goods.

Such condemnation of American society is, of course, not connected with present-day affluence. American society has been called money-minded and acquisitive for more than one hundred years. That America was wasting its natural resources was argued, with some justification, in the nineteenth century. Conspicuous consumption and luxurious living by the rich were widely criticized toward the beginning of this century. When it is deplored today that we buy gadgets rather than books, or spend more on liquor and cosmetics than on health or education, we must recall that contrasting cultural aspirations with material interests is an old tradition. The *nouveaux riches* have always been ridiculed for allegedly neglecting the arts and culture. That the arts flourish best when not hindered by the burden of wealth is an old romantic notion. I recall, for instance, how as a child in Europe I admired the painting of a romantic German artist. The picture showed a young hungry-looking man in a torn shirt, sitting in a leaking attic in front of a wooden plank, writing on a torn sheet of paper. The caption under the picture read, *The Great Poet*. With increasing affluence, the notion that artistic performance is incompatible with prosperity has gained in popularity.

The praise of frugality and austerity and the condemnation of extravagance and self-indulgence are part of our religious, philosophic, and artistic tradition. They also conform to general economic beliefs. Thus, if business investment represents the only source of enduring wealth, as economists have assumed, and if resources are scarce, which is a basic postulate of economics, future-oriented activities can be carried out only at the expense of present need gratification. Consumption must give way if we are to build for the future. Should the present generation consume at a great rate, the next generation would be deprived of its due. An economy in which a large share of national resources goes into business investment is then an economy in which consumer expenditures use up relatively little of the gross national product. Workers who toil hard and efficiently at low wages are considered to be building for the future of the country. Contrariwise, large-scale consumption expenditures are believed to result in a slow rate of growth of productive facilities.

This argument obviously disregards the possibility that some consumer expenditures represent enduring investments. It also presupposes fixed resources. It is true, of course, that if resources were fixed, the balance could be redressed only by changing each sector's share in the pie, that is, redistributing the existing wealth; an increase in the size of the pie would be ruled out.

The readers of Galbraith's *Affluent Society* will have noticed that we have departed in one respect from his argument. Galbraith believes that production is no longer of major concern to our society. He argues for an increased share of resources to be channeled to the government rather than to the business sector. But in one crucial respect, in the assessment of the consumers' role in the economy, Galbraith goes along with those who call for austerity for the sake of industrial expansion.

In a certain sense the belief that the public sector of our economy has been neglected is quite surprising. In the years of affluence since World War II, the share of the gross national product spent by the government has been higher than ever before in peacetime. Yet the largest part of government expenditures has been used for national defense, not for health, education, slum clearance, and the like. Let us not forget this unparalleled peacetime rise of defense expenditures as proof that consumers, in their role of taxpayers, acquiesce in being deprived of a large share of their earnings and in letting the government use that share. The argument that public poverty is due to huge defense expenditures would be more justified than the argument that it is due to private affluence. Were it not for the necessity of fighting the cold war, America could have and doubtless would have spent much more on such things as education and health than she actually did.

The greatly increased cost of welfare expenditures is likewise borne by the affluent consumer. Old-age insurance, unemployment insurance, aid to farmers and many other groups not participating fully in prosperity, represent collective arrangements, all of which support the argument that the mass consumption economy has not developed without a social conscience. Increased government expenditures, both for defense and for social welfare, have been financed through progressive taxation that has greatly reduced the private spending of the middle- and upper-income groups. The condemnation of affluence would stand on better grounds if, during the last few decades, the distribution of income had become less egalitarian. Nevertheless, we cannot but agree with Galbraith that we are faced with what we have called Fact No. 1. The share of national income devoted to government services, other than defense, is low. There are indeed too few well-equipped schools and hospitals and too many slums in the United States, and an increase in outlays for these and related purposes is of prime importance. The area of disagreement concerns the question of how to remedy the situation. A redistribution of our present national resources is neither the only way nor even a desirable way of achieving the goal.

In fact, such redistribution would have little chance of being successful. Any attempt to cut down on consumer spending for the sake of increasing public expenditures might easily plunge the economy into stagnation or recession. Even maintaining current levels of consumer living standards would not suffice to do the job. It is precisely the wanting and striving for improvement in private living standards that forms the solid basis of American prosperity. Only if the so-called private opulence increases still further can we hope to overcome public poverty. The question is not one or the other; it is both or none.

The reason for our not having enough schools, hospitals, and parks is not that we have too many consumer goods nor that the government must spend large amounts on national defense. The major reason is that the rate of growth of our economy has been too slow.

The most important single factor that spurs the growth of an economy is the amount of work that is done and the efficiency with which it is done. The crucial question, therefore, concerns people's motivation to work hard and efficiently. Recent research (more of it will be presented in later chapters of this book) has given an answer to the question of what motivates people to work hard. People are willing to exert great effort if the effort helps them to achieve their own concrete goals, namely, a better life for themselves and their children.

True, Americans also recognize the necessity of working for the achievement of national goals. We grumble about high income taxes but understand that national defense is necessary and expensive. Most of us also believe in paying for old-age and unemployment insurance, as well as for schools and hospitals. But, as we said before, there is a psychological difference between money we must spend and money we like to spend. The desire for more and better things is one of the most powerful incentives to induce people to work hard and to stimulate production, efficiency, and economic growth.

Ours is a middle-class society with middle-class comforts. Only in comparison with former times and other countries are we rich. Most of us in the middle classes are far from being saturated with goods. During the last decade of growing affluence, our desires for new goods and new services have steadily grown. Survey studies show that in the early 1960s the American people desired a variety of goods that were hardly known to them ten years earlier. Owners of fairly new homes wanted larger homes or homes in better neighborhoods, summer houses, second cars, new appliances, and boats. Shortly after the end of World War II, middle-class people, in replying to a question about things they would like to have or would like to spend money on, mentioned only a few basic desires— a house, an automobile, and a few major appliances. Over the fifteen-year period, 1947 to 1962, the list grew steadily longer. Many of the newly mentioned desires were in the field of services rather than goods. Vacation trips and other travel, recreation, hobbies, and leisure-time activities in general gained in importance with growing affluence. So, too, did the cultural desires of those same people.

Americans buy gadgets instead of books—so it has been argued in envious Europe for many decades. Today Americans buy both gadgets and books. They have laborsaving devices which give them more free time to read books and attend lectures, go to concerts and theatrical performances, and visit museums. Sales of nonfiction paperback books showed a proportionately larger gain than the sales of most other products in the late 1950s and early 1960s, and the shares of book publishing companies have been considered growth stocks on the New York Stock Exchange. The more consumer goods people have, the more they spend on books, lectures, and concerts, as well as on schools and hospitals.

We are still far from a genuine mass culture. It is still a minority of families that spend more than a tiny portion of their income on educational and cultural needs. But the direction in which the society is moving is clear. The well-to-do, who are in possession of many amenities of life, are the first to recognize the value of education and health and are now willing to spend on these values. The idea of austerity, of sacrificing for the things that are really worthwhile, appeals perhaps to a few exceptional people. Most people attend to spiritual needs only after material wants have been taken care of, which is the case for a steadily increasing number of people in a mass consumption society.

We have said that people are willing to exert great effort to satisfy their own concrete goals and to be able to spend on what they themselves want to spend. This is individualism and private initiative at its best, but it does not operate in opposition to collectivist ideas and goals. It has often been emphasized, and rightfully so, that the American people are social; they belong to groups, are dependent on groups, and are influenced by groups. Concern with neighborhood and community leads them to approve of public expenditures. Economists distinguish sharply between the private and the public sectors of the economy. In fact, the solution of the great problems raised by Galbraith is to abolish the distinction. The government need not be considered as "they"; it can become "we." People should find it satisfying to spend on hospitals, schools, and slum clearance rather than feel compelled to do so. Psychologically, our clothes and eyeglasses become parts of our body. Family and friendship groups, even the community and the nation, can and often do become parts of our extended ego. This is true, however, only if more immediate wants are satisfied, if we already have the consumer goods we feel necessary for our basic comfort.

A society which strives for material wants that are artificially stimulated cannot survive, says Toynbee. Having disagreed with the derogatory meaning attached to material satisfactions and with the notion of artificial stimuli, we may turn now to the problem of survival. Survival in the nuclear age is not an economic problem. What are our hopes for peace? Does a mass consumption society detract from peace, or may it contribute to it?

Just as the ideal of human rights and freedom spread from America to the rest of the world, so is the ideal of higher living standards and consumer comforts now penetrating into Europe, Asia, and Africa. Even communist countries are not immune to the sweet poison emanating from America. There are increasing indica-

tions that the desire for consumer goods and consumer comforts
has gained in importance among the Russian people. The greater
this concern, the greater the hope for peace. It is the have-nots
who think they have little to lose in case of war. Unscrupulous
leaders can easily create war frenzy if the people are poor. But
fighting for national or ideological glory appeals less to those who
have a decent standard of living and who can look forward to a
better life for themselves and their children. Decent material standards for all the peoples of the world and a justifiable expectation
of their improvement represents, therefore, our best hope for peace.

PART THREE

Business Cycles

9

Predicting Short-range Fluctuations

The new discipline of psychological economics has often been identified with the study of the business cycle. Although that was not its starting point—studies of inflation and of motives for the purchase of war bonds came earlier—both theoretical and practical considerations soon dictated a concentrated effort to study the short-range fluctuations of the American economy. Preliminary theoretical notions about the importance of the consumer sector and of the motives, attitudes, and expectations of consumers called for a study of the influence of psychological factors on subsequent discretionary consumer demand.

The first large-scale consumer surveys were carried out toward the end of World War II, when the threat of a postwar recession represented the major problem of the day. While the absence of a recession, in spite of the termination of war production and the demobilization of millions in the armed forces, was not predicted on the basis of the first studies, optimistic attitudes and strong demand for durable goods by consumers were indicated in advance. By 1948–1949 methods of conducting surveys and analyzing data were developed to such an extent that it was possible to make definite predictions. Studies of attitudes and expectations at that time indicated continued strength of consumer demand, and this indication subsequently proved correct, in contrast to the forecasts then being made by traditional methods of an imminent general recession. During the Korean War, short-range economic fluctuations again loomed large and offered unique opportunities for psychological studies of business-cycle trends.

Yet the research carried out at that time by the Survey Research Center was not restricted to short-range effects of psychological factors. The analysis of fluctuations in consumer demand was related to the study of enduring changes in consumer behavior. I published papers shortly after the war on expectations of inflation, on the impact of income increases, and on dissaving and consumer borrowing. Nevertheless, the reassessment of factors relevant to the business cycle constituted a central part of the development of psychological economics. These were the studies that helped to make the psychological approach known and thereby to obtain the financial means necessary to conduct nationwide consumer surveys. These studies will continue to occupy an important part of psychological economics, even though this discipline extends far beyond them. Therefore, in this and the next chapter we shall examine the following questions: Why is psychological economics important for business-cycle studies? What are its methods, its accomplishments, and its shortcomings in analyzing short-run fluctuations?

SELECTING AND MEASURING CYCLICAL ATTITUDES

The first task was to measure changes in willingness to buy and therefore in those psychological predispositions that are subject to fairly frequent variations. In present-day usage, the term *psychology* is commonly associated with personality studies and Freudian principles. The starting point of economic psychology, however, had to be different. Neither the Oedipus complex nor differences in childhood upbringing, because of either stern or permissive parents, could be expected to contribute to an explanation of changes in sentiment, say, from times of prosperity in 1928 to times of depression in 1930. On the other hand, the psychology of learning, especially studies of habit formation and problem solving, did supply clues to an understanding of the origins and changes of economic expectations. Similarly, sociopsychological findings about the effects of group belonging on the selection and understanding of information provided a key for the study of the spread of uniform attitudes.

But such general notions did not suffice. It was necessary to specify the economic attitudes that served as intervening variables in codetermining discretionary purchases. Studies over several years were required before it was possible to come up with some service-able answers. We shall relate here briefly some major aspects of the search for the psychological predispositions associated with cyclical fluctuations.

The concept of intervening variables was first applied to eco-nomics in connection with the study of reactions to changes in income. Relating major consumer expenditures to one year's income appeared unjustified because of the known variability of income. Taking into account, in addition to current income, the income of the previous year or of several previous years, likewise appeared insufficient because of the possibility of radical differences in the subjective meaning of an increase or a decrease in income. An in-come increase may be subjectively unsatisfactory if it is considered temporary, i.e., if it is expected to be followed by a decrease, or if it amounts to less than what is expected, or what seems justified, or what members of a reference group have been getting. Contrari-wise, an income decline might appear quite satisfactory under certain conditions.[1] Willingness to buy was assumed to be influenced not by the income change alone but by the subjective meaning of the change. Therefore it appeared necessary to find out, through a representative sample, how the people felt about their personal financial progress and what changes they expected in personal finances, both in the short and in the long run.

While attitudes toward personal finances were the first candidates for inclusion in a study of consumer sentiment, other attitudes had to be considered as well. It was found that for many blue-collar workers, direct questions about income expectations did not produce relevant information. Most workers understood the questions in terms of wage rates which, in their opinion, either rose gradually or remained unchanged but could not conceivably decline. Infor-mation about the number of hours to be worked and therefore about prospective changes in total income was not available to most workers, and they often had not even vague expectations on these matters. Thus, lengthy questioning about personal financial prospects frequently failed to indicate people's feelings of security and degree of confidence. A somewhat similar situation was found to prevail regarding the income expectations of many white-collar workers in steady positions, such as government employees and

[1] See my article, "Effect of Income Changes" in *Review of Economics and Statistics*, vol. 31, 1949; and Ref. 1.

teachers. To some extent even employees of large corporations were found to be unable to envisage the possibility of financial setbacks and differentiated only between faster and slower advancement. Thus many of these people, too, proved rather insensitive to questions about income expectations.

Restricting the study of consumer sentiment to personal financial attitudes appeared unjustified on other grounds as well. Since people live in groups rather than in isolation, not only what happens to themselves but also what happens to their relatives, friends, and neighbors, and even to their community and country, influences their attitudes. Finally, for methodological reasons, clues to affective as well as cognitive changes had to be sought in several different ways rather than in one way only. Asking questions about other people's prospects or the prospects of the economy was expected to produce insights additional to those obtained from respondent-oriented questions.

These considerations led to survey questions concerning people's information about, attitudes toward, and expectations of business-cycle developments. What people know about recent changes in economic trends, and the news they have heard and can recall, obviously represent highly variable items of perception and cognition. Expectations about what will happen in the economy may be thought of as clues to feelings of confidence and security or their absence.

Survey questions about these matters have frequently been misunderstood by critics. The question "whether the next five years would be years of unemployment and depression, or of prosperous times, or what" was once ridiculed by such comments as that the Survey Research Center "asks Southern sharecroppers and unskilled laborers to make five-year business-cycle forecasts!" Indeed, all members of a representative sample are asked this question—business leaders and economists, as well as laborers. Many people say at first that they don't know or "Who am I to say?" but most of them can then be induced to express an opinion. At certain times a large and at other times a small proportion of the people reply in an optimistic manner. It is the changes in the distribution of optimistic or pessimistic replies from one time to the next that are sought as clues to changes in economic trends. The question is not intended to induce people to make a forecast; it represents an indirect way of probing whether at the time of the interview people feel more or less confident about the economy. Intervening variables that shape people's responses must often be studied in such an indirect way.

How could the notions of individual survey respondents about the prospects of the economy be best determined? Translation of the objectives into survey questions was not an easy matter. Attempts to make precise measurements by inquiring about the extent of economic improvement or deterioration respondents expected would have been doomed to failure, since answers to such questions would have fallen outside the range of most people's way of thinking. The findings obtained with samples interviewed at different points of time could be compared in two respects. First, the degree of uncertainty could be measured. The proportion of a representative sample of all consumers, and also of such major segments of consumers as age and income groups, that could not be prompted to express an opinion of the direction in which the economy was moving proved to be an important indicator in itself. Uncertainty is not just a neutral factor of indifference or absence of information. In most instances being uncertain about what will come represents an unfavorable factor that dampens initiative. Thus an increase in the proportion of uncertain people proved an adverse indicator.

Disregarding uncertain respondents, the relation of those who expected improvement to those who expected deterioration in business conditions could be ascertained. Changes in the ratio of the two answers provided the second useful measure.

The wording of the questions about economic trends also caused problems. Answers to the question whether business and the economy would be better or worse, say, a year from now than it is currently proved difficult to interpret, since they depended on opinions about the current situation. The highest frequency of the answer "Things will be better a year from now" was obtained during recessions. The most fruitful question, chosen after much experimentation, simply asks whether, speaking of business as a whole, the next year would be good or bad. If the question is asked once, the answers are of no value. Many people do not like to complain, and there may prevail an underlying optimistic bias in our society. But the extent of the difference in the number of people answering "good" or "bad" has undergone substantial and often rapid shifts from one time to another. These changes are taken as indications of greater or lesser optimism and confidence and are studied regarding both short-range and longer-range economic trends.

A third and final area of relevant economic attitudes concerns

the market situation. In this respect again information on external
conditions may or may not be available to consumers and may or
may not alter attitudes. Yet satisfaction or dissatisfaction with prices
and market conditions and the assortment of goods offered can be
studied to discover favorable or unfavorable changes. Studies carried out over several years revealed that a simply worded question
served the purpose of revealing changes in people's sentiment. "Is
this, in your opinion, a good time to buy or a bad time to buy
(cars, appliances, houses, etc.)"—any of several large potential
purchases were mentioned—has been asked to indicate consumers'
underlying attitudes rather than to obtain their rational judgments.
A follow-up question, "Why do you think so?" helped in understanding the answers. Reactions to recent past and expected price
trends greatly influenced the answers to this question. On the other
hand, the question "Do you expect prices of things you buy (or of
cars, houses, etc.) to go up, go down, or remain stable during the
next year?" proved to be too factual to reveal economic attitudes. It
took extensive studies before a simple way was found of including
a question on prices in the set of attitudinal measures. Immediately
following the question on price expectations, respondents were
asked, "Would you say this is to the good or bad?" The question
is not precise and permits a variety of interpretation. Price increases
may be thought to be good or bad for the economy or for the
respondent himself. But such differences could be neglected, because only changes in the distribution of replies over time were of
interest. A greater frequency of the answer "good" served as an
indication of increased optimism or confidence; and a lesser frequency, of increased pessimism or mistrust.[2]

THE PREDICTIVE VALUE OF THE INDEX OF CONSUMER SENTIMENT

By 1954, after extensive empirical studies which included much
experimentation involving the above considerations, the Survey Research Center had constructed an Index of Consumer Sentiment.
The Index is available from 1952 to date—at first half-yearly and
later at quarterly intervals. It consists of six questions: two each on

[2] The question on price expectations is nevertheless the least satisfactory of
the indicators of consumer sentiment. The relevance of attitudes toward inflation
will be discussed in Chap. 14.

personal finances, the general economic outlook, and market conditions. Since many additional questions were introduced in later years, for the period after 1957 it would have been possible to construct the Index from twelve or even more questions, rather than from six questions. Experimentation with such variations showed, however, that such changes would not have consistently improved the results. Similarly, attempts to attach weights to the questions did not prove fruitful.

As soon as a sizable number of observations was available, econometric calculations were made in order to test the performance and the predictive value of the Index. The latest of these has been presented by Eva Mueller in an article in the *Journal of the Ameri-*

CHART 3

Actual and Estimated Durable Goods Expenditures (1953—1963)
(Data adjusted for changes in prices and in population)

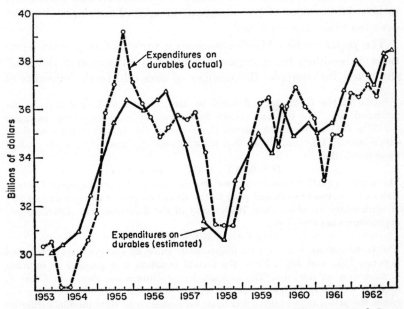

NOTE: Expenditures on durable goods (actual): U.S. Department of Commerce. Durable goods expenditures (estimated) based on personal income during the 6 months prior to durable goods sales (Y_{-1}) and Survey Research Center Index of Consumer Sentiment (S) plotted at the time of the survey. The equation used was $D = 0.18 Y_{-1} + 0.40S - 48$.

can Statistical Association (Ref. 4). She presents a strong test. Rather than comparing fluctuations of the Index with data on consumer purchases taken from the same surveys and thus eliminating variations in sampling, she submits the Index to comparison with data compiled by the Commerce Department. This Department publishes quarterly data on aggregate expenditures on consumer durable goods, and the data are seasonally adjusted and can be deflated for increases in prices and population. The available data are far from ideal. They exclude many of the major discretionary purchases by consumers (for instance, travel expenses) and include many small items, such as tires and chinaware, which are commonly purchased because of wear and tear and are thus not really discretionary. A substantial part of the fluctuations in the Commerce Department series is nevertheless explained by the Index of Consumer Sentiment. When the Index and consumer incomes in the preceding period are both taken into account to test the basic hypothesis that demand is a function of both ability and willingness to buy, 76 per cent of the variations in sales of consumer durables over ten years are explained.[3]

The paper by Eva Mueller presents a variety of regression equations. In addition to aggregate expenditures on consumer durables, she takes, for example, the number of cars sold or the amounts of

---

[3] Two of the equations calculated by Eva Mueller in Ref. 4 may be reproduced here. The first one relates fluctuations in expenditures on consumer durables (D) to disposable personal income in the half year prior to those expenditures (Y_{-1}) and shows that prior income explains only 29 per cent of those fluctuations.

$$D = 0.13 \, Y_{-1} + 3.7 \qquad r^2 = .29$$

The second equation uses both prior income and the Survey Research Center's Index of Consumer Sentiment prior to the six-month period of expenditures (S) as explanatory variable. Then 76 per cent of the fluctuations in durable-goods expenditures are explained.

$$D = 0.18 \, Y_{-1} + 0.40S - 48 \qquad r^2 = .76$$

The equations are based on 22 observations since 22 surveys were conducted between 1952 and 1961. From the second equation it is possible to estimate expenditures on durables. The estimated expenditures are shown in Chart 3, together with actual expenditures. It can be seen that the correspondence between the actual expenditures and those estimated six to eight months earlier on the basis of prior attitudes and prior income is quite close but not perfect.

The Index values are reproduced in the series of books *Surveys of Consumer Finances* (Refs. 5 to 8), published by the Survey Research Center. The Index was originally published in the book *Consumer Expectations,* by George Katona and Eva Mueller (Survey Research Center, Ann Arbor, Mich., 1956).

installment debt incurred as the variables to be explained. In all these cases the Index proves its explanatory value.

One of the crucial problems of predictions is that of *lead time*. If one variable predicts an upward or downward movement of another variable, the question of how much time separates the changes in the two variables must be asked. The longer the lead, the more powerful is the predictor. Experience with the Survey Research Center's Index of Consumer Sentiment indicates that it leads expenditures on consumer durables by six to eight or nine months. Such a lead time was used in the equations as well as in Chart 3. The surveys are usually conducted in February, May, August, and November, and changes in attitudes are compared with sales of durables during the two calendar quarters that follow the quarter in which the attitudes are measured. For instance, attitude measurement in May is taken as indicative of sales of durables between July 1 and December 31.

In the regression equations consideration is given to the predictive value of each observation made over a period of ten years. Obviously, there are times when the prevailing trends continue and prediction is a fairly simple matter. On the other hand, there are also crucial times, namely, turning points in the cycle about which advance information is more difficult to obtain. It would, of course, be of particular value to be able to predict the approach of these sharp changes in the economy. In addition, the theoretical notion to the effect that attitudes may at times change independently of income and other economic trends also called for a separate analysis of turning points. At this time, it may suffice to point to Table 2, which shows the changes in the Index prior to three turning points experienced during the last decade.

It can be seen from the table that the Index values obtained in June, 1954, were much higher than those of a few months earlier; by October, 1954, a further rise had taken place. Consumer durable sales were fairly stable during the entire year 1954; the sharp increase took place in the first quarter of 1955 and signaled several years of prosperous times. Similarly in June, 1957, and again in May, 1960, consumer sentiment showed a sizable deterioration much in advance of the recessions that culminated in the first quarters of 1958 and 1961. The worsening of sentiment continued during the second half of 1957 but not during the second half of 1960. This difference may be thought to be related to the severity of the

Table 2. Movements of Consumer Attitudes and of Expenditures on Durable Goods in Three Crucial Periods

SRC index of attitudes and inclinations to buy		Expenditures on durable goods (U.S. Dept. of Commerce)	
Time of survey	Fall, 1956 = 100	Quarter	In billions of current dollars*
Jan.–Feb., 1954	88.5	1954: I	31.2
June, 1954	95.6	II	32.2
Oct., 1954	102.4	III	32.3
		IV	33.9
		1955: I	38.2
Nov.–Dec., 1956	102.4	1957: I	40.3
June, 1957	95.1	II	40.3
Nov.–Dec., 1957	86.7	III	40.9
		IV	39.7
		1958: I	36.9
Jan.–Feb., 1960	99.3	1960: I	44.2
May, 1960	91.7	II	44.5
Jan.–Feb., 1961	91.8	III	42.7
		IV	43.2
		1961: I	39.2

* Seasonally adjusted annual rates.

respective recessions. The stability of the Index during the second half of 1960 permitted the prediction that the expected recession would be short and mild.

Thus at some of the most crucial times during the past decade the Index of Consumer Sentiment gave correct indications of future economic changes. (In the next chapter we shall place these forecasts in their proper frame by discussing the reasons found for the improvement or deterioration of consumer sentiment at different times.) Considering each survey finding separately, however, instances of incorrect indications have likewise been found. A perusal of Chart 3 shows, for instance, that the extent of the upswing in durable sales in 1955 was not predicted by the available survey data. After the fact we may assume that certain factors not considered by us, such as the extension of installment maturities or self-generating features of the automobile boom of 1955, explain the difference. In 1961, on the other hand, the decline in the sales of durables was larger than would have been called for by the deterioration of sentiment possibly because of cumulative features of the downturn; during that recession for one quarter, sales of durables were very small.

Obviously, major extraneous events that took place after the survey measurements were made and that had not been anticipated should destroy the predictive value of the Index of Consumer Sentiment. Such events—the outbreak of war or new legislation or regulations—are, however, quite rare. Yet in a certain sense new events counteracting the fulfillment of predictions should be the rule rather than the exception. Suppose that, sometime in the future, survey indications of a forthcoming depression or boom induce government and business to take measures that are successful in forestalling the depression or boom. The failure to correctly predict prospective trends must then be called a success of the forecast rather than its failure.

IMPROVEMENTS AND VARIATIONS IN ATTITUDE MEASUREMENT

What has been said thus far pictures the contribution of psychological economics to forecasting as purely mechanical. Once the measurements are made—the survey questions fixed, the samples drawn, the interviews collected and transformed into numerical values through an operation called coding—the computer can and does take over. It calculates the Index values and thereby makes the prediction. The result may inspire either belief or disbelief. Whichever it may be, the Index itself supplies no reasons for either a greater or a lesser degree of confidence in the forecast.

Improvements in the predictive value of the Index may no doubt be sought through better measurements, better questions, for instance, or through a selective use of the data. The computer supplies Index values not only for the entire sample, representing all consumers, but also for its parts. It might be assumed that certain groups of consumers would prove better predictors. This might be true on two grounds. First, purchases of durable goods are not evenly distributed; upper-income people and younger and middle-age people purchase more durables than lower-income and older people. Secondly, some people may be considered better informed about economic affairs. Therefore the opinions and attitudes of well-educated people might be given greater weight. Since education is associated with income, one might single out high-income people and use their attitudes alone as predictors.

Studies along these lines did not prove fruitful. To be sure, there were periods when it was found, after the fact, that the attitude changes of upper-income people would have provided better predictions than those of all the people, but there were other periods as well in which the opposite conclusion emerged. A somewhat more sophisticated notion, namely, that upturns are indicated by the attitudes of upper-income people and downturns by the attitudes of lower-income people (the latter suffer more in recessions and therefore should be more sensitive), was also considered, sometimes with success, sometimes without. Possibly, future studies will bring progress along these lines. For the moment the Survey Research Center persists in using data for the entire population and may point to the following argument in favor of this position: Although the crucial factor is the discretionary income groups' willingness to buy, the limits of these groups are not rigidly fixed; therefore restricting the studies of attitudes to a fixed definition of discretionary consumers is not preferable to including other groups which also occasionally make discretionary purchases. Even more powerful is the argument that substantial changes in sentiment have usually been uniform among various groups of the American people. When the Index of Sentiment, computed for different population groups, indicates similar changes for each of the groups, confidence in the findings is enhanced. When, as has happened occasionally, the overall change is due to certain selected groups only, there appears to be reason for more cautious interpretation.

In calculating the Index the same kinds of data are treated in the same way each time. Selective use of the data would be possible, for instance, by giving certain attitudinal indicators a greater weight at certain times and a lesser weight at other times. With this remark we have gone beyond the discussion of mechanical forecasts.

Before turning to an analysis of further, possibly more important, uses of attitude measurement, it must be stated that the function which has been attributed to the Index of Consumer Sentiment has also been fulfilled to some extent by another type of consumer study. In fact, the Survey Research Center and its predecessor organization[4] began their studies of consumer behavior during World War II by asking direct questions about *buying intentions* and extended these questions only later to studies of what have been dubbed by some scholars as "other attitudes." In recent years surveys of buying intentions have also been conducted by various other organizations, including the U.S. Bureau of the Census.

The theory behind forecasting through a measurement of buying intentions is simple. The purchase of a house, a car, or a major appliance has antecedents. Although some consumer purchases are made with hardly any advance planning, either in a routine manner or on impulse, most large discretionary purchases are preceded by deliberation, discussion, and even shopping around.[5] If the planning process is sufficiently extensive and has a lead time of several months, measures of buying plans may represent the best prediction of subsequent purchases. Buying plans may be viewed as the resolution of diverse motives, attitudes, and expectations. By measuring buying plans the analyst transfers the resolution of conflicting forces where they belong, namely, to the consumer, rather than undertaking himself the task of constructing an index of attitudes and then predicting the result in terms of purchases.

Even if the basic assumption—there is a lengthy planning period regarding a substantial portion of major purchases—were not valid,

---

[4] The Division of Program Surveys in the U.S. Department of Agriculture.
[5] See G. Katona and E. Mueller, *Consumer Behavior I*, edited by L. H. Clark, New York University Press, New York, 1954; and Ref. 1.

expressed buying intentions could nonetheless be used for forecasting provided the unplanned purchases were randomly distributed. There is reason however to doubt that this is so. The planners
with definite intentions may at certain times be influenced by
considerations different from those which motivate the uncertain
or marginal buyers. The predictive value of expressed buying intentions is by far the greatest for the period immediately following
the survey in which the intentions are ascertained. Then, clearly,
unplanned purchases occur least frequently. But predictions for a
very short period, say, for the following three months, are the least
important of all forecasts. A variety of other data are available about
the immediate future, and therefore the measuring of buying intentions must be judged according to its success in predicting purchase
trends over the following six, nine, or twelve months.

Measurement of consumers' buying intentions has proved successful at various times but not consistently. Combinations making use
both of buying plans and of the Index of Consumer Sentiment have
often performed better than buying plans alone. Concerning the
ten-year period 1952–1962, calculations by Eva Mueller indicate
that the Index of Sentiment far outperformed buying intentions
(see Ref. 4). Data on buying intentions are of special value when
demand for one or another commodity develops in a manner that
differs from the trend in general consumer demand. Thus the data
on intentions to buy cars in 1961 to 1963 provided information
additional to that derived from the data on consumer sentiment.[6]

Even in the matter of predicting whether the individual will
indeed make the purchase he has expressed the intention of making,
the record is only fair. According to repeated studies,[7] on the
average 60 per cent of those who had said that they expected to
buy a car during the following twelve months did buy a car. On
the other hand, only 20 per cent of those who had said they would
not buy a car bought one. From the point of view of explaining

---

[6] Intentions to buy new cars rose sharply by May, 1961, that is, earlier than
the Index of Consumer Sentiment, and remained very high during the following two years. In the summer and fall of 1962 a new peak was registered,
indicating in advance the success of the 1963 car models (see Chap. 23).

[7] G. Katona and collaborators, "Fifteen Years of Experience with Measurement of Consumer Expectations," *1962 Proceedings of Business and Economic
Statistics Section,* American Statistical Association, Washington, D.C., pp. 169–
180 (reprinted in Ref. 7).

car purchases, these large differences are not entirely satisfactory. The number of people who do not expect to buy a car is so much larger than the number who do that only one-third of those who bought a car in a given year were found to have expressed the intention to do so a year earlier.[8] The problem of the fulfillment of expressed intentions as well as the analysis of subsequent purchases by individual optimists and pessimists, who are determined by attitude studies, are both very complicated. A variety of extraneous factors enter into individual decision making; they average out when changes in the proportion expressing intentions or in the sentiment of all people are compared with the changes in aggregate purchases (see Ref. 2, pp. 254ff.). Therefore even a relatively low fulfillment rate is not necessarily damaging to the major task, which is the prediction of prospective market trends. Contrariwise, high fulfillment rates on the part of individuals would not suffice to make the study of buying intentions acceptable for aggregate forecasting.

Buying intentions represent a relatively late intercept in the process of decision making. As one of several tools for the study of prospective consumer behavior, they are useful. But detailed analysis of those intervening variables that are the basic determinants of purchasing behavior remains indispensable.

ON METHODS OF FORECASTING

The psychological studies of short-range economic fluctuations described in this chapter conform in many respects with a variety of other economic studies. This may be best understood if we review, briefly, the theory and practice of economic forecasting.

In business life and in planning economic policy, forecasting is inevitable. Since decisions by business firms and the government relate to the future, they contain an assumption about future trends. The assumption may be implicit and imprecise, or it may be explicit and even expressed in one precise numerical value, e.g., "Next year GNP will be X billion dollars." With the availability and widespread use of a variety of statistical data relating to the past performance of the economy and the prevailing high esteem of quanti-

---

[8] For instance in 1960 among 100 people 16 expected to buy a car and 84 did not. In the first group 10 bought a car (60 per cent), in the second group 17 (20 per cent). Thus of the 27 car purchases, only 10, or 37 per cent, were explained by intentions expressed a year earlier.

fication, scholars and businessmen have become increasingly dissatisfied with forecasts based on hunches. Objectivity, that is, replicability and precision, represents the scientific method. The call for scientific forecasts has not remained unheeded. Numerous techniques have been developed. Most, if not all, of them can be grouped in one of three categories. (Some fall into more than one category.)

In the first category of economic forecasts fall those which are based on GNP models. The economy is divided into the three broad sectors—consumer, business, and government. The relations among the sectors are expressed in structural equations. Some major variables are projected on the basis of regression equations which express the most appropriate relations between those variables and explanatory variables—for instance, the relations between business investment and profits or consumer expenditures and income. The major and fully justified function of solving several such equations simultaneously is to make quantitative estimates of how certain assumed changes in one variable would influence other variables or the entire system.[9] Thus the repercussions of an increase in income or in tax rates on consumer expenditures or on the rate of unemployment can be calculated with the assumption that there are no other disturbances. In addition to this use, regression equations commonly serve to predict GNP and other broad aggregates. These projections are often called *standard forecasts*. The exactitude with which these forecasts can be, and often are, expressed blurs the fact, at least in the eyes of some readers, that the projections are valid only if the past relationships continue to prevail.

The business-cycle indicators compiled by the National Bureau of Economic Research constitute a second category of economic forecasts. Having identified past business cycles and the timing of peaks and troughs, a large number of statistical series are sorted into leading, coincidental, and lagging indicators according to their usual past performance. When most leading indicators show a decisive change, a similar change in the cycle is predicted. This prediction is valid if it is possible to rely on the analogy of the forthcoming cycle with the average past cycle. The statistical indicators represent a valuable tool in analyzing the large amount of data

[9] Methods of simulation may also be used to accomplish this important objective. See Guy Orcutt and collaborators, *Microanalysis of Socioeconomic Systems*, Harper & Row, Publishers, Incorporated, New York, 1961.

available every month, but they do not provide an assured method of forecasting, as the compilers of the indicators themselves emphasize. The mechanical use of changes in some leading indicators to predict other economic changes appears hardly warranted.

The third category of economic forecasts is based on *ex ante* variables.[10] The simplest and best-known example of such variables is residential building permits. A statistical agency collects information on these permits which represent past facts, solid and reliable as any other series of past data on, for example, sales or prices. While an upward or downward trend of past sales or prices does not necessarily signal the future trend—if this were the case, economic series could never alter their direction—building permits issued are causally connected with subsequent building activity. To be sure, construction during the next period will be based not only on past but also on future permits, and some permits may even be canceled. Nevertheless, trends in building permits do usually foreshadow future trends in residential construction.

Unfilled orders, say, for steel or machinery, likewise represent *ex ante* variables. Over the past twenty years much work has been done to extend the availability of this type of information. Collection of data on budgets and plans, as well as on intentions, appears worthwhile, even though the probability is much higher that contracts entered into will be carried out than the probability that plans either approved by boards of directors and committees or existing only in the minds of business executives or consumers will be realized. The statistical series of capital-expenditure plans collected by the SEC and the Department of Commerce, as well as, separately, by McGraw-Hill's Economics Department, represent forecasts based on *ex ante* variables. These series were found to be successful predictors of aggregate trends during the postwar years. The conceptual basis of collecting data on consumers' buying intentions is quite similar to that of studying business investment plans.

Ex ante data can be combined with predictions based on methods which have been classified in the two other categories. For instance, business investment plans and consumer buying intentions can be and are sometimes included as explanatory variables in the re-

10 They have been discussed before by G. Katona, "Business Expectations in the Framework of Psychological Economics," in M. J. Bowman (ed.), *Expectations, Uncertainty, and Business Behavior,* Social Science Research Council, New York, 1958, pp. 59–73.

gression equations that form the backbone of forecasts based on GNP models.

The Survey Research Center's Index of Consumer Sentiment may be viewed in the same light as data on consumer buying intentions. If consumers appear more optimistic today than three, or six, or twelve months ago, it is assumed that discretionary purchases will increase because optimism makes people step up their expenditures, provided other things are equal. This conclusion is justified in the same sense that predictions based on leading indicators or projections are justified. In view of past experience with these statistical series, the probability of the fulfillment of predictions is far better than chance. This is true because some aspects of the economic processes do repeat themselves, and there is a repetitive component in each successive business cycle. But in a very important sense each business cycle is unique. It is affected by new developments and shaped by new forces. Also human beings, the economic decision makers, are capable of learning, so they may react to the same stimuli today differently from the way they reacted to them yesterday.

Mechanical forecasting methods are useful and represent great progress over hunches and guesses. But they do not suffice. Forecasting has a scientific basis but is not a science. It is and will remain an art. Scientific research provides ingredients of forecasts. The study of changes in consumer attitudes and expectations may provide such ingredients, for consumer attitudes contribute to answering the crucial question of why. They may provide a better understanding of changes that have taken place in the recent past and of factors that make for incipient changes. Through better diagnosis of the current situation, the prediction of future changes as well as the introduction of remedial measures may be facilitated. Forecasting in this sense, to be discussed in the next chapter, represents a more complex task than the use of the mechanical forecasting methods thus far described.

10

Understanding Short-range Fluctuations

The comparison over time of changes in attitudes and expenditures on durables was described in the last chapter as the method of testing the predictive value of data on consumer attitudes and expectations. In that test the attitudinal variables are used in the same way at all times, in upswing and downswing, as well as in successive cycles. Unique features that shape economic trends at any one particular time are not given due consideration. Traditional economic research registers such unique features after the fact. It may show, for instance, that in one cyclical recovery automobile sales soared earlier and to a larger extent than other sales, while in another recovery the automobile industry lagged behind. Inferences can then be made about the factors responsible for the divergent developments.

Psychological economic research is in a position to attack the question of why directly. Several forces or vectors influence the decision makers and therefore the economic trends at all times. Information can be obtained about these forces and the direction in which they push businessmen and consumers which would provide an understanding of incipient trends. The collection of data on changes in consumer opinions, motives, attitudes, and expectations serves, then, the purpose of explaining what has happened. Not only the fluctuations of consumer sentiment itself, as shown in the Index in Chart 3, but also the fluctuations of specific attitudes that constitute its parts can provide insights into the economy. New questions must constantly be added to shed light on new developments. The attitudes elicited by certain questions may merit great weight in analyzing the prospects at one point of time, while at other times they may play no role at all.

THE RESEARCH TECHNIQUES

What are the techniques of survey research that help us to understand economic fluctuations? To some extent such understanding may derive from answers to the same questions that are used to make economic predictions. For instance, after the 1958 recession, short-range business expectations were found to have recovered to a similar extent as after the 1954 recession, while longer-range business expectations had not. Significant conclusions could be drawn on the basis of this simple comparison in the movement of components of the Index.

Some of the most important questions used specifically to reveal the forces that influence economic trends may be used in unchanged form in several successive cycles. The first among these are the why questions. Following the expression of optimistic or pessimistic expectations, respondents are asked, "Why do you think so?" Replies to these questions not only clarify and sometimes even rectify the answer originally given but also yield quantifiable data, of which the changes from one period to the next may be most revealing. Quantification proceeds by first determining the frequency of answers in three categories: (1) the mention of favorable substantive developments; (2) the mention of unfavorable substantive developments; and (3) the absence of substantive explanation. ("I heard business was improving" or "I was told so" are included in the third group.) The first two categories may be scrutinized to determine the frequency of references to prices, government measures, political events, and the like. Such data point to developments which at a given time are so salient that they are mentioned without direct questions about them.

Related but somewhat more specific is the following question regularly asked in the Research Center's quarterly surveys: "During the last few months, have you heard of any favorable or unfavorable changes in business conditions?" More people answer this question in the affirmative than are able to reply to the follow-up question, "What did you hear?" (The answer "I forgot" or "I don't recall" helps those respondents who do not wish to appear ignorant.) The proportion of American people who give a substantive reply to this question and mention economic developments is in itself an interesting indicator. We shall comment later on the fact that the proportion is usually much higher in bad times than in good times. The ratio of favorable to unfavorable news reported by respondents represents a major factor in the analysis of people's perception of business-cycle trends.

A fair number of other questions that are asked quarterly in unchanged form are also relevant for an analysis of short-run prospects. Questions on unemployment may be cited as an example. The surveys find out what people know about recent changes in unemployment and ask about expected changes as well. Opinions about the likelihood of a depression ("like the one we had in the thirties") or of a recession ("similar to that of 1958") as well as opinions about when the next recession may occur are also collected. Finally, reference should be made to questions relating to specific consumer decisions. Regarding purchases of houses and automobiles, much more is needed than information about intentions to buy and about consumers' evaluations of market conditions. Questions eliciting reactions to new automobile models (asked by the Survey Research Center in the late fall every year) and a variety of questions about compact cars are examples of ways in which further explanations of changes in opinions and expectations are sought.

In a somewhat different category fall the topical questions inserted in surveys because of specific developments that take place at given times. Such questions will be especially timely if the investigator is aware of the problem in advance. Once every four years this is an easy matter: Questions are regularly inserted in the quarterly surveys conducted prior to and following the presidential elections to determine the economic impact people expect of the person they think will be elected President or the person just elected President. At the other extreme are new developments that can hardly be foreseen. Questions about the stock-market break that occurred in late May, 1962, and its perceived influence on the economy were inserted in the August, 1962, survey but not the May, 1962, survey, since the questions for the latter had been formulated and sent to the printer early in April. Similarly, questions about the U-2 incident or the Cuban crisis could be formulated only after the events, while studies of information about and reactions to changes in interest rates, the long steel strike of 1959, or the proposal to reduce income taxes were conducted while these developments were under way. The purpose of these studies was to contribute both to an understanding of short-run changes in consumer buying inclinations and to the analysis of how consumers think.

Forecasting of short-term trends, as they emerge from a scrutiny of data of this kind, differs from forecasting that may be classified in any of the three categories described in the preceding chapter. In the usual forecasting models past and future are clearly differentiated; past data are taken from records, while data about the future are predicted by the economist or statistician. However, forecasting based on an understanding of the factors shaping economic developments does not separate the past from the future. The forecaster tries to explain why certain favorable or unfavorable changes have taken place and studies whether the forces have exhausted themselves or are likely to remain effective. After recognizing two or more forces that operate in opposite directions, the forecaster tries to assess the respective strength of each force. Finally, he may point to certain impending developments—such as international tensions, change in tax rates or interest rates—and predict how these changes, should they occur, would affect economic trends. The end result is less precise and less definite than the outcome of some other forecasting methods, since the forecaster is primarily concerned with the probable direction, rather than the exact magnitude, of the influence of various factors.

THE POSTWAR CYCLES

Whether or not such studies are worthwhile may be revealed by past experience. Forecasts in the terms just discussed have been made by the Survey Research Center since 1948, first only occasionally and later at quarterly intervals. The analysis of the factors making for changes in consumer demand has been published promptly following each survey. Prompt publication was necessary from a practical point of view—if the studies were not useful to business and government, they could not have been financed!—and it was indicated in the interest of scientific research. Predictions represent the best test of scholarly hypotheses. If the prediction is made explicit, the test becomes rigorous. There are risks involved in this procedure: Following erroneous forecasts, the researcher may lose his financial support. From the point of view of scientific research, what the researcher risks is his reputation. But he gains new insights which serve to improve his hypotheses both when his forecast is contradicted and when it is confirmed.

One major "prediction" made in the early studies was that the consumer was important and was in a position to influence business trends. As we mentioned earlier, in 1945 there was not yet sufficient evidence for this assumption; therefore the conclusion, from the very favorable prospects of consumer expenditures, that a recession shortly after the end of the war would be avoided was not drawn. But a prediction of this kind was made in 1948 and 1949 when optimistic consumer attitudes proved to prevail despite some cutbacks by business firms; within a few months business changed direction to keep pace with consumers rather than consumers changing to match the pessimism of business.

The major attitudinal findings of the postwar period, published previously in detail, will be recapitulated here with emphasis on the early indications they gave of cyclical turning points. This is done in order to illustrate the usefulness of the method which seeks to determine not simply what may happen but also why it may happen. For quantitative data the reader is referred to other publications.[1]

• Shortly after the end of the war and in 1946–1947, surveys showed consumers to be in an optimistic mood. Optimism was associated with the great desire for new durable goods by many consumers. Consumers did not feel that their liquid reserves, accumulated during the war, were excessive and should be reduced; they did feel that a slower rate of adding to financial reserves was justified. Thus runaway inflation that would have arisen from the simultaneous use of income and reserve funds did not threaten, while consumer purchases increased greatly.

• Contrary to widespread predictions of a recession, optimism endured in 1948–1949, even on the part of people whose income did not increase. Expectations that the inflation would end, or even

---

[1] For quantitative data, see Ref. 1, Chap. 13; G. Katona and E. Mueller, *Consumer Attitudes and Demand*, Survey Research Center 1953; G. Katona and E. Mueller, *Consumer Expectations*, Survey Research Center, 1956; Ref. 2, Chap. 13; and the volumes published annually since 1960 by the Survey Research Center on the *Survey of Consumer Finances* (Refs. 5 to 8). The latter volumes reproduce verbatim the quarterly reports issued in the last few years.

that prices would decline, contributed to optimistic attitudes. (There was no decline in consumer purchases in 1948–1949.)

• The outbreak of war in Korea in June, 1950, and news of military reverses shortly thereafter gave rise to an expectation of rapid price increases and shortages. Recollection of World War II experiences induced many consumers (and business firms as well) to stock up, even though disposable income did not rise.

• Beginning with early 1951 people differentiated sharply between a cold war or isolated conflict on the one hand and world war on the other. It was believed possible to produce guns for a cold war and butter too. Resentment of inflation developed. Even though their income remained the same or even increased, people subjectively felt worse off because of rising prices. (Purchases of consumer durable goods declined and remained low during most of 1951 and 1952.)

• Habituation to prices developed slowly in 1952. The presidential election in that year gave rise to some optimism. In 1953, however, consumers did not lead the economy—the downturn in that year must be attributed to business and government actions.

• In the spring of 1954, a period of stagnation on a fairly low level, consumer optimism showed marked improvement. Consumers were aware that there was a recession, and yet most of them did not feel hurt personally. Experience with stable prices gave rise to satisfaction. Buying conditions were evaluated most favorably partly because of the spread of discount houses. Attitudes toward the automobile market improved greatly in 1954. (The year 1955 was the year of the automobile boom, stimulated to some extent by a lengthening of installment credit maturities.)

• While optimism increased steadily from late 1953 until June, 1955, in the following twelve months attitudes remained on a favorable level without rising further, and intentions to buy automobiles declined. (Prosperity in 1956 was stimulated primarily by extensive business investments.)

• As early as toward the end of the year 1956, consumers were found to be unaware of any good business news, although the economy registered new records quarter after quarter. By June, 1957, consumer attitudes deteriorated sharply. Failure to see anything that might sustain good times, plus resentment of rising prices, caused many people to express concern in spite of rising incomes. Unfavorable business news was given great attention; the widely noted increase in interest rates was considered an unfavorable factor. Dissatisfaction with the assortment offered by the automobile industry spread in the fall of 1957. (Toward the end of the year 1957, the sharpest postwar recession began; demand for automobiles declined greatly in 1958.)

• In spite of rather pessimistic notions about the short-term outlook, early in 1958 people in general expected good times to return sooner or later. There was no evidence of consumers being saturated with goods; unfilled wants and desires remained substantial. In the fall of 1958 better economic news brought forth slow and hesitant gains in confidence and optimism. The American people remained conscious of the threat of unemployment and of the likelihood of recessions recurring at short intervals. (Recovery from the recession began in the summer of 1958 and does not appear to have originated in the consumer sector.)

• Disappointment about rising prices and concern with inflation were pronounced in 1959. The long steel strike adversely affected consumer confidence in the fall of that year. Many people were well informed about the strike and argued that inflation would ensue in case of a labor victory, while purchasing power would be insufficient to sustain the economy in case of a management victory. After the settlement of the steel strike, consumer attitudes improved again. (In spite of the steel strike, 1959 and most of 1960 were fairly good years.)

• The rise of consumer attitudes from their 1958 low levels was terminated, and they began again to deteriorate sharply, in the spring of 1960, long before the previous high of 1955–1956 had been reached. Least satisfactory among the attitudinal indicators was the long-range economic outlook of the people; they were concerned with the possibility of a recession. In 1960, they saw no factor that in their opinion might serve to sustain continuous good times. Worries about international tensions were also pronounced. (The new recession began late in 1960.)

• News about the election and the plans of the new President were considered the most important news in the fall and winter of 1960–1961. Just as in 1952, the majority of the people derived optimistic conclusions regarding business-cycle trends from the fact that a new man had been elected President. Although they were aware that a recession had begun and that unemployment was rising, consumers expressed no greater pessimism in the fall than in the summer of 1960. Thus their attitudes pointed to a short and mild recession (which actually developed) rather than to a catastrophe.

• Recovery from the recession of 1961 was accompanied by a recovery of consumer optimism. Yet the improvement of attitudes remained sluggish and within a year had reached its peak (February, 1962). The major and most significant exception was provided by attitudes toward automobile buying, which advanced sharply in May, 1961, and remained very favorable during the following year. (A long period of high demand for automobiles began toward the end of 1961.)

• In the spring and summer of 1962 people were found to be concerned with the threat of a recession. They were aware of the apparent inability to cope with unemployment and derived an uneasy feeling from the prevailing international tensions. At the same time there was satisfaction with personal financial trends as well as with the relatively stable prices. Buying intentions for automobiles were so strong that, considering all indications jointly, an early downturn in consumer demand was not indicated. The sharp decline in stock prices did not induce consumers to expect a recession or to postpone their purchases. (Economic conditions in 1962 can only be described as fair, that is, neither bad nor very good.)

• In November, 1962, substantial gains in optimism were registered. Income gains; better business news; and above all, the quick and, in the opinion of most Americans, favorable solution of the Cuban crisis made for an improvement in consumer sentiment. Attitudes toward the automobile market improved further, indicating a high level of sales during the forthcoming spring season. (Business was better in 1963 than in 1962 with the automobile industry making the best showing.)

• Signs of a possible reversal of the favorable trend were apparent in the spring of 1963. In the absence of new stimuli, there was pronounced concern about how prosperous times might be sustained. In the fall of 1963 confidence in a favorable economic outlook was again strengthened under the impact of an apparent relaxation of international tensions, an optimistic appraisal of the automobile market, and the expectation of a reduction in income taxes.

One underlying principle of studying business cycles in the manner just described was stated earlier: Attitudes shape decisions on major expenditures, and therefore changes in attitudes serve as advance indicators of the volatile elements of consumer demand. There exists a second underlying principle as well: Consumer attitudes do not fluctuate irrationally. Attitude change is the result of the perception of economic and political developments and can be understood as a sensible reaction to perceptions of what is going on in the world.

One may then ask: Why should one bother with attitudes; why not rely on the information which results in changes in attitudes? Would it not be simpler and more efficient to consider the underlying factors about which factual information is available rather than to interview samples of people about their perceptions and attitudes? These questions must be answered in the negative. Even complete information about all events and developments would represent nothing more than a listing of possible stimuli. From such a listing we would not know which items of news were salient or how they would be apprehended. The situation is different when we *start* our studies with the attitudes. Only after we know of the changes in attitudes are we in a position to relate them to events and developments; only then can we select the relevant stimuli.

Finding out which factors are crucial at any given time contributes, then, to the ability to predict forthcoming developments. The predictions are of course dependent on future events which, if they change in an unexpected way, may nullify them. But even in such instances, which probably occur infrequently, survey studies may provide considerable assistance. They may point to those future developments that must be watched and may even indicate what consumers' probable reactions will be if one or another contingency should materialize. For instance, in December, 1962, the Survey Research Center's quarterly report on changes in consumer attitudes stated: "Whether the next few months will bring a new international crisis, similar to the recent Cuban crisis, or a rapprochement between the U.S. and the Soviets, is not known. Should the former be the case, it would unfavorably affect consumers' discretionary demand. Should the latter be the case, favorable effects are probable." With statements such as these, however, we transcend the topic of this chapter. Understanding consumers and their reactions is the topic of the next part of this book.

PART FOUR

Consumer Psychology

11

Attitude Change over the Longer Run

Two arguments have commonly been used to disparage the introduction of psychological variables into the study of economic processes: Some economic theorists have asserted that expectations would exert a short-range influence only; and others, that changes in attitudes and expectations would depend on so many diverse factors that they would not lend themselves to rigorous scientific analysis.

An impact on short-range developments is often considered a temporary or passing influence. For a while, it is thought, pessimistic consumers may postpone their purchases, or optimistic consumers may buy in excess of their needs; but "real" needs and market forces will in time reassert themselves. Over the long run, then, the trend line of sales would have the same form it would have had if it had not been changed by "ripples" due to psychological factors. Even though short-range developments commonly have long-range effects, as pointed out in Chapter 4, the argument about psychological factors influencing short-range processes only may be thought to be reinforced by our own finding presented in Chapter 9: The predictive value of attitude changes, as measured by the Survey Research Center's Index of Consumer Sentiment, extends to six to nine months only. A study of the longer-range influence of consumer attitudes is therefore called for.

As to the second counterargument about the difficulty of scientifically analyzing attitudes and expectations, we must recognize that scientific analysis involves abstraction and generalization. The present inclusion of a large number of variables, as described in Chapter 10, represents only a preliminary step with which we cannot remain satisfied, though it has served us well in promoting our understanding of changes in consumer discretionary purchases. Should we find it possible to create order out of diversity and formulate generalizations about consumers' modes of thinking and acting, we would at the same time derive long-range implications from the analysis of short-term trends.[1]

Two considerations make our task difficult. First, there are numerous individual differences among people, and there are also great differences among groups of consumers. Yet the diversity should not be exaggerated, especially if one does not consider differences in the expectations of different groups of consumers at any one given time but rather the changes in attitudes and ways of thinking over a period of time. To be sure, statements made about the American consumer relate to the modal group of consumers only. Numerous exceptions do occur, but they do not negate the possibility of making generalizations which are valid for very many people.

The second difficulty stems from the fact that we are studying human behavior rather than human nature. The empirical findings made during the last twenty years in the United States are applicable, in a strict sense, to this period and this country alone. Even regarding prospective American developments, there is no assurance that we can learn from the past. But one fundamental lesson that emerged from our studies, which will be explained in the following chapters, minimizes this problem. This lesson stated briefly, is that social learning is a slow process. Unless influenced by great events that disrupt old and fixed stereotypes and opinions, the masses of consumers do not change their ways of thinking substantially from one year to the next; comparisons over four or five years are needed to discern even relatively small changes. Great events, such as the outbreak of a war or a major depression, are rare by definition. Therefore it can be postulated that what has been learned about consumer attitudes will remain significant for quite a while, especially the functional relationships established between patterns of attitudes and behavior; they are expected to remain valid in the

----

[1] In Chapter 28 we shall return to a discussion of the argument that behavioral economics must necessarily fail because of its consideration of a large number of variables and the conditional nature of its generalizations.

United States over several years. And to some extent at least, they
are also applicable to those foreign countries in which mass consumption prevails.

Our studies of common modes of thinking and of long-range
tendencies have been based, on the whole, on the same data that
have been used for understanding short-range developments. But
the data were used in a different way. For the sake of understanding
short-range fluctuations, we studied changes in the distributions
from one quarter to the next, or from one year to the next. In the
next few chapters we shall look at the same distributions and discern characteristics that have remained constant over many years;
we shall also study differences in the distributions in the early sixties
as compared with the early fifties, in good as well as in bad times.
For instance, earlier we pointed out fluctuations in income expectations that are included in the Index of Consumer Sentiment; in the
next chapter we shall show that, regardless of any short-run changes,
the opinion "We shall be better off a year from now" was much
more common than the opinion "We shall be worse off" in all the
postwar years. Likewise, in this part of the book we shall concern
ourselves with similarities and differences in the business outlook of
consumers during several cycles rather than with prospects of
upturn or downturn at any given time.

The reasons people give for their personal financial expectations
or their general economic outlook yield some information on their
way of thinking. So also do the answers to questions about certain
specific events that occurred at the time of one or another survey.
Studies of the impact on people's economic attitudes of presidential
elections, incidents in the cold war (Berlin, Lebanon, Congo, Cuba,
etc.), large strikes, violent movements in the stock market, to mention some important examples, may yield conclusions that are valid
for a period when the events themselves are almost forgotten. Of
particular importance will be findings about the kinds of information received by consumers—we have already referred to differences
between information transmitted and information received—and the
effect of that information on consumer behavior.

Social cognition may be viewed on two levels, both of which will
be considered. First we shall take up the major issues separately
and study consumer opinions and attitudes toward them—namely,
how future income trends, recession and inflation, the role of government in the economy, and the economic consequences of international tensions are typically perceived; or how saving money,

investing in common stock, and buying on the installment plan are viewed by the American people. We shall then undertake an analysis that cuts across specific issues and yields psychological principles of generalization, polarization, and habituation. Studies of the second level may enable us to draw conclusions about how consumers might react to new developments as they occur.

A fundamental question confronting us may be pinpointed by finding out which of the economic developments during the postwar period made the greatest impact on the American masses. This information cannot be obtained from direct questions asked of consumers. It would be of little use to ask people, even highly educated people, what in their opinion the main characteristics of the post-World War II economy were or how they differed from earlier times. Such an appraisal might help to indicate which of several developments was particularly salient at a given time but would not answer the question of their impact on the masses, which necessitates a summary view of a period of ten or twenty years. But a reader of thousands of detailed interviews, in which the free answers of people in all walks of life are recorded verbatim, may be permitted to summarize his general impression.

The threat of nuclear war and the economic impact of cold war and rearmament, satellites and space exploration, represent major new developments since the end of World War II and thus possible answers to the question. People's awareness of and concern with these issues cannot be doubted and will be discussed shortly. Inflation, loss of purchasing power of the dollar, and price increases may be thought to be further possible answers. The increased economic role of the government, with the variety of new functions it has assumed—not only old-age security and unemployment compensation, but also the task of arresting recessions and stimulating economic growth—form an additional area of consideration which may have impressed the American people greatly. Yet, in one observer's opinion, all these significant new developments have been overshadowed by another one: The awareness of increased well-being and satisfaction with living standards, coupled with higher aspirations and growing confidence in personal financial prospects, may represent the most significant difference between the American people's views of the postwar and the prewar economies. We shall, therefore, begin our analysis of consumer psychology by presenting, in the next chapter, recent findings on people's views about their personal financial situation and prospects.

12

Optimism about Personal Finances

During the entire post-World War II period the expectations expressed by most Americans regarding their own financial well-being fell into one of two categories: Many people thought that a year later, or five or ten years later, they would be better off than at the time of the inquiry, and many others believed that their personal financial situation would remain unchanged. Only a small minority expected a deterioration in their financial situation.

Most cyclical fluctuations were marked, therefore, by shifts between respondents' saying "better" and "same." Even in answer to questions about the preceding year, reports that their personal financial situation had worsened were infrequent, although somewhat more frequent than the expectation of reverses. This can be seen from the following tabulation of answers received in 1962. (Data from, say, 1950 or 1960 would give substantially the same picture.)

Table 3. Frequency of Unfavorable Attitudes
(Average of Four Surveys Conducted in 1962)

Personal financial situation	Among all consumers	Among consumers with incomes over $7,500	Among consumers 35–54 years of age
Worse now than a year ago	22%	13%	22%
Worse a year from now	6	5	9
Worse five years from now	10	11	6

INFLUENCE OF AGE AND EDUCATION ON
INCOMES AND EXPECTATIONS

Variations in the extent of optimistic attitudes among different groups of the population are of great interest. Optimism is largely a function of age and income. This is not simply a matter of well-to-do people or young people having optimistic *predispositions*. The differences in the extent of personal financial optimism among major population groups are founded in past experience. The question whether "you and your family are financially better or worse off than you were a year ago"—which, to be sure, asks for a subjective appraisal of experience—invariably provides a steady diminution of optimistic answers as we proceed from upper-income young family heads, among whom almost 60 per cent reported improvement in 1962, to low-income older family heads, among whom only 5 per cent reported improvement (Table 4, section A). Both age and income make for great differences. Similar data were obtained in each of the postwar years.

It is also true of personal financial expectations that the younger a person and the higher his income, the more optimistic he is. Age may play a bigger role than income in shaping expectations. Short-range expectations are somewhat more favorable than past experience in the age groups between twenty-five and fifty-five. It also appears that the optimistic outlook was somewhat more pronounced in the early 1960s than in the early 1950s.

Data occasionally collected about perceptions of change in an individual's personal financial situation over several past years and about expectations extending five or ten years in the future present a similar pattern. When asked about expected income trends "during the next ten years," by far the largest proportion of people say their income will rise. Only two other answers have been frequent among respondents under fifty-five years of age, namely, "Our income will remain the same" and "Our income will fluctuate." Section C of Table 4 shows that confidence in rising income trends is very widespread among both the young and the middle-aged. These data are also shown in Chart 4.

In appraising the significance of the data on people's optimistic outlook as related to age, it should be kept in mind that close to one-half of all family heads are under forty-five years of age, and

CHART 4

Relation of Income Prospects to Age and Income

(Columns indicate proportion of heads of spending units who said in 1962 that their income will rise during the next ten years.)

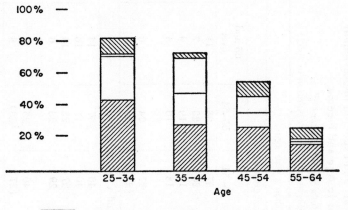

Age

 Opinions of spending units with less than $3000 income.

Opinions of spending units with income between $3000 and $4999 (lower part) and $5000-$7999 (upper part).

 Opinions of spending units with income of $7500 and over.

Proportions are cumulative; thus the proportion of high-income younger people who expect their income to rise is 81 per cent, etc. For precise data, see Table 4

close to two-thirds under fifty-five years of age. Since the majority of American family heads under fifty-five have an income of more than $5,000, it follows that optimism is widespread among the discretionary-income groups.

Optimistic income expectations are in line with people's notions about when they will reach their top income. When asked at what age they expect their highest lifetime income, some people in the labor force profess not to know or say that age makes no difference in their income. Among the 60 per cent who specified an approximate time, one-half said that their peak income would be reached

Table 4. Relation of Recent Past and Expected Improvement in Personal Finances to Age and Income

(Per Cent of Spending Units Saying "Better Off" or
"Will Be Better Off" in Various Subgroups of the Population in 1962)

A. Better off than a year ago

Income groups	Age groups					All age groups	
	25–34	35–44	45–54	55–64	65 and over	1962	(1954)
$7,500 and over	59	42	37	38	11	42	(40)
$5,000–7,499	52	30	26	23	7	34	(42)
$3,000–4,999	40	31	14	19	9	28	(32)
Under $3,000	31	20	18	16	5	18	(19)
All income groups:							
1962	49	33	27	24	6		
1954	(47)	(31)	(23)	(25)	(6)		

B. Will be better off a year from now

Income groups	Age groups					All age groups	
	25–34	35–44	45–54	55–64	65 and over	1962	(1954)
$7,500 and over	50	53	46	37	14	47	(39)
$5,000–7,499	56	40	40	17	10	41	(36)
$3,000–4,999	47	39	37	22	13	39	(37)
Under $3,000	50	51	29	23	6	26	(20)
All income groups:							
1962	51	46	40	25	8		
1954	(48)	(36)	(27)	(23)	(8)		

C. Income will rise during next ten years*

	25–34	35–44	45–54	55–64	All age groups 1962
$7,500 and over	81	69	51	21	62
$5,000–7,499	73	69	40	16	58
$3,000–4,999	72	46	34	16	47
Under $3,000	43	28	25	16	34
All income groups, 1962	73	60	43	18	

* Not included are such answers as "First it will rise, then fall" or "Will fluctuate, but will be higher ten years from now than it is now." Data for 1954 are not available.

SOURCE: Surveys of Consumer Finances, conducted by the Survey Research Center.

just before retirement or when they were over sixty. Among professional, managerial, and clerical people, the proportion who expected to receive their peak income when they were over sixty was higher still, and among blue-collar workers much lower. As expected, in answer to the question about what their peak income would be, most people gave estimates that were higher than their current income. The differences were very large on the part of professional and managerial people (median estimate of peak income was over $12,000 as compared with median income at the time of inquiry of under $8,000). People with a college degree—another classification in which most people expect income increases almost up to the time of retirement—mentioned an expected peak income of close to $15,000 (median value of estimates) as against a current income of somewhat over $9,000.

These estimates are optimistic but hardly out of line with prevailing conditions. When the income received in 1962 was tabulated according to the age of the family heads, professional and managerial people in their early fifties were found to have earned more than older and younger people in the same occupations. Blue-collar people earned on the average as much in their thirties as in their forties. For all people the peak income was reached at about forty-five years of age. The income gains with increase in age are most dramatic when tabulated according to the extent of education. Those with no more than grammar school education reveal a flat income curve which starts declining around forty-five years of age. Those with a college degree earn twice or even three times as much in their fifties as in their twenties.[1] When the proportion of those who have had income increases is tabulated by education, it has been found year after year that college-educated people have fared better than people with less education. Interruptions of rising trends by years in which income remains stable or even declines are least frequent among those with college education.

It appears, then, that the American people are aware of certain newly developed trends and believe that they will continue. Very many people know that income rises with age. And many people also know that the income of educated people rises most with age.

These opinions give rise to an optimistic outlook. They are the

[1] These as well as the earlier data are from the Surveys of Consumer Finances. See also J. N. Morgan and M. H. David, "Education and Income," *Quarterly Journal of Economics*, vol. 77, pp. 423–437, 1963.

basis of confidence in one's own power to influence one's fate: It is possible to improve one's standard of living through education. If it is too late for oneself, optimism and confidence are not necessarily impaired; people trust that their children will accomplish what they themselves are unable to do.

Let us not forget that the picture presented of the average American is severely marred by the existence of poor people who do not have an "American standard of living" and cannot even aspire to ever having it. We pointed out in Chapter 2 that these are, to a large extent, special groups—people who are discriminated against because of physical handicaps, old age, absence of a male head of the family, or race. In addition, lack of education or skills makes for poverty. Whether the recent rapid spread of high school education will help reduce the injustice of poverty in the midst of plenty is a difficult question, the answer to which depends on many considerations. Excess demand for certain types of workers does not help the people who do not have the necessary qualifications. Some hope may be derived from the finding that many young people do believe that education represents a method of improving their standard of living. Table 4 shows that young people are fairly optimistic even if their income is quite low. Generally, younger people are much better educated than middle-aged or older people.

The fortunates in our population greatly outnumber the unfortunates. A brief reference to unemployment may illustrate this. When a representative sample was asked early in 1961—that is, during a recession which followed closely on the recession of 1958—whether they had *ever* been unemployed, 62 per cent of wage- or salary-earning family heads answered in the negative.[2] About one-half of those with some unemployment experience reported that unemployment was something quite unusual for them; they do not count on its recurrence and are confident of being able to find employment should they lose their job. There remain close to 20 per cent of families with unfavorable past experience who live under continuing threat. They represent a much too high proportion of American families. Their existence causes misgivings even among the more fortunate 80 per cent.

The belief that education or the acquisition of skills makes it possible to increase one's income is probably not unrelated to peo-

[2] See E. Mueller and J. Schmiedeskamp, *Persistent Unemployment, 1957–61*, W. E. Upjohn Institute for Employment Research, Kalamazoo, Mich., 1962.

ple's confidence that their income gains over the past years have been due to their own efforts. This last conclusion was derived from direct questions addressed to representative samples of heads of families. Respondents were asked first how their income compared with that of five years earlier, in order to identify the great majority of people who in the inflationary years of the 1950s and early 1960s were aware of higher incomes. These respondents were then asked to explain why they were making more than five years earlier. Although some people were puzzled by the question, most of them found an answer after some hesitation. Only two kinds of answers were given frequently. The majority said, "I do a better job," "I deserve more," or "I advanced in my job," and indicated by these and similar replies that they had made progress in their careers. In their opinion, their own work was responsible for their higher earnings. A minority explained their income gains by saying that they were lucky or had good breaks. Ego involvement and personal accomplishment are reflected in the first answer but not in the second, in which chance and unexpected favorable happenings are emphasized. (Income gains are seldom attributed to inflation, as we shall point out in Chapter 14.)

Confirmation of these findings was provided by a different kind of inquiry. Members of representative samples were asked about their income expectations for the following twelve months and were reinterviewed a year later to find out how their income had actually changed. Two-thirds of the gains in income from the first year to the next were found to have been expected; only among lower-income people were there many whose earnings had advanced unexpectedly. With income declines, the findings were different: overwhelmingly they were contrary to expectations expressed a year earlier.[3] The major reasons for making more money than the year before were increases in wage rates, salary, or profit. These are matters for which many people strive and work. Making less money than the year before was attributed primarily to working fewer hours (because of loss of overtime, layoffs, unemployment resulting from loss of job, or illness) and also to unforeseen adverse business developments or bad luck—that is, to matters for which outside forces are thought to be responsible.

Inquiries about surprising or unexpected developments yielded

[3] See J. N. Morgan, "The Anatomy of Income Distribution," *Review of Economics and Statistics*, vol. 44, pp. 270–283, 1962.

similar conclusions. Survey respondents were asked, "Looking back over the past twelve months, did things work out pretty much as you expected financially, or did anything unexpected happen?" Somewhat more than 30 per cent answered in the affirmative to the second part of the question. (This is an average from several surveys conducted in the early sixties; the figure fluctuates little.) When asked further, "What was that?" 27 per cent reported unfavorable and 4 per cent favorable surprises. Even though the majority had experienced favorable income developments, they were not reported as surprises. Being laid off, losing one's job, as well as illness and accidents are, however, reported as unexpected. Most people who had changed their jobs during the preceding year for a better job did not report this as an unexpected event; getting a better job is thought to be due to one's own effort.

Answers to survey questions also reveal that the majority of younger and middle-aged people believe they are able to "make quite definite plans for their lives for the next few years." This is a reflection partly of confidence in job security and partly of trust in one's own ability to shape one's future. Job security alone cannot explain the findings because many people expect to change their job.[4]

STRIVING FOR EXTRA INCOME

Standard of living is not determined by income in a given week or month. The regularity of work influences it to a large extent. Pessimistic conclusions may be derived from the finding that during each of the years 1958 to 1962 more than 20 per cent of families received income for less than fifty weeks because of unemployment, temporary layoffs, or the seasonal nature of their work. (Self-employed families and those whose head is not in the labor force are excluded.) This is, however, not the whole story. In each of these years approximately one out of every ten family heads had a second job and another one out of every ten did some paid work in addition to his main job. A large part of the second jobs or of additional work is done regularly. They add to family income and push it to higher brackets. But if the earnings from second jobs or

[4] In 1960, 40 per cent of employee spending units had had their current jobs for less than five years. One in every four respondents expressed the expectation of having a different job in a few years.

additional work are deducted from family income and then related to earnings from the main job, it is evident that it is not the poorest who supplement their income. In the early 1960s second jobs and additional work were most prevalent among families in which the main job brought $5,000 to $10,000 income. Possibly low-income people do not have the education or skills required for finding additional earnings. Possibly many of them live in labor surplus areas in which unemployment is high and additional work not available. In addition, it appears that the most ambitious people are not the poorest people.

Similar conclusions emerge when the return of wives to work is studied. Between the time of finishing school and marriage, or the birth of the first child, most girls are in the labor force. Until their youngest child reaches kindergarten age, most women are fully occupied in their homes and unable to seek work. Returning to work when the children were in school increased in frequency during the 1950s, together with growing affluence. The proportion of wives working doubled between 1940 and 1960, and the increase was much greater among older than among younger women. In 1959, when seven out of every ten heads of spending units were married, close to 40 per cent of their wives earned some income. In that year close to 12 million married women aged thirty-five or over and with husbands present were in the labor force; ten years earlier only 5 million, and ten years before that only 2 million women in that category were working.

Middle- and upper-middle-income families show the greatest proportion of wives working. The highest proportion—50 per cent of complete families in 1962—is found in the $7,500 to $15,000 income group. Even in the $15,000 to $25,000 group one-third of complete families had a working wife. The income of the wife greatly contributed to the family's living standard. Again it is not easy to differentiate between cause and effect. Yet some major considerations underlying the American families' decisions were explored in many interviews.

Having acquired some of the good things of life whets the appetite for more and better things. Having advanced a little arouses the desire for further advances. Well-educated women, whose husbands are usually in the middle- or upper-income brackets, are the most dissatisfied with staying home when their youngest child reaches school age. They are also in the best position to find remunerative employment. Emotional and psychological needs must be emphasized; money does not represent the only incentive to seek work. But the role of money should not be forgotten either. Unfulfilled wants and desires abound among these people, as we shall have opportunity to show later in the book. What additional income can buy is important, and women, just as men, take the initiative toward satisfying family wants.

Beside determining the number of household heads having a second job and the number of wives working, efforts to increase income were also studied (by the direct-question method). When a representative sample of families (excluding the retired) was asked in 1962 whether anybody in the family was making a "special effort to add to their income," close to 30 per cent answered in the affirmative.[5] Among people with incomes under $3,000, the proportion was lower; the proportion also declines with age. To a follow-up question, three kinds of answers were frequently received—the special effort consisted of the head's having a second job, of the head's occasionally taking on extra remunerative work, or of the wife's working. Although the question made no reference to wives, in close to one-half of the cases in which the wife was working, full- or part-time, this was mentioned as a special effort. Thus not only second jobs, but also in many instances, the wife's work is acknowledged as stemming from the desire to increase the family's regular income. Some women interviewed explained their return to work by their desire for money to send their children to college.

Since women usually must give up gainful employment after the birth of their first child, the most striking data supporting the widespread optimism prevailing among young Americans are found in statistics on childbirth. It is well known that Americans marry young. In 1959 the median age for first marriage was 22.7 years for males and 20.2 years for females; that is, half of the men and half of the women were younger than those ages when they married. In 1920 the respective ages were 24.6 and 21.2 years. These are much smaller changes than those found in other far less well-known statistics. The time between marriage and the birth of the first child has shortened very substantially since the 1930s and even during the 1950s.

[5] The question was: "Are you people making a special effort to add to your income, for example, by trying to earn money outside of your (head's) regular job?"

Married for the First Time	Number of Children Born per Thousand Women within 12 Months after Marriage
In 1955–1959	444
In 1950–1954	348
In 1945–1949	329
In 1930–1934	242

SOURCE: *Current Population Reports,* U.S. Bureau of the Census, No. 108, July 12, 1961.

Since some women have twins, the number of marriages in 1955 to 1959 which produced children within twelve months is somewhat lower than 44.4 per cent. Within three years after marriage, 1,016 children had been born to every 1,000 women who had married in the years 1950 to 1954 compared with 732 children to every 1,000 women who had married in the years 1930 to 1934.

Having children not only detracts from family earning power but also involves additional expenses. If families must make a choice between having children and acquiring material goods and choose the latter, children are postponed. The data indicates that this took place much more rarely in the late 1950s than at earlier times.

Decisions about having children therefore reflect increasing prosperity as well as an optimistic outlook. Very many young people believe that they will be able to have children as well as acquire the many things which they feel they must have for their children (a nice home, a car, a refrigerator, a washing machine, etc.).

THE EXTENT OF SATISFACTION

The extent of the prevailing optimistic outlook may be illustrated not only by answers to questions about expectations but also by answers about satisfaction with the current situation. It was shown in an earlier publication that in 1954, 74 per cent of urban families expressed satisfaction with their occupational progress, 68 per cent with their standard of living, and 58 per cent with their income (saying, in the last instance, that their income was about what they ought to be getting). I argued at that time that such sentiments were characteristic of the climate in which prosperity flourishes (Ref. 2, Chapter 11). In the years following those measurements, the United States underwent two recessions, but the degree of satisfaction with personal financial progress remained unchanged. A few illustrations will be presented here.

In 1962 about two-thirds of all people said they were satisfied with their standard of living. They were told that "The things we have—housing, car, furniture, recreation, and the like—make up our standard of living; some people are satisfied with their standard of living, while others feel that it is not as good as they would like." In reporting then how they themselves felt, 64 per cent said that they were satisfied, and 32 per cent that they were not fully satisfied and would like to have a better standard of living (4 per cent were undecided). Satisfaction was more pronounced among the wealthy than among the poor, but the differences among different income groups were moderate: satisfied among those with less than $2,000 incomes—51 per cent; among those with income between $5,000 and $7,500—64 per cent; among those with an income of over $10,000—78 per cent.

Similar questions were also asked about satisfaction or dissatisfaction with housing. Here are a few illustrations of findings:

If you could do as you please, would you like to have more space in your home (apartment), less space, or is it about right? Present space about right: 53 per cent.

If you could do as you please, would you like to live close to the center of the city, further out in the country, just where you are, or what? Just where we are: 60 per cent.

Are you fully satisfied with the neighborhood, fairly well satisfied, or dissatisfied? Fully or fairly well satisfied: 70 per cent.

Most people are also satisfied with their retirement prospects. When asked whether they will get along all right financially when they retire or whether they think that retirement will cause financial problems, more than one-half of all heads of families in the labor force (thirty-five years of age and over) say they will get along all right.

Two major questions arise in connection with these expressions of satisfaction. First, it may be questioned whether the expressions are honest; perhaps they represent polite assent and unwillingness to criticize or complain rather than an expression of true feelings. Secondly, satisfaction with existing conditions may be deplored rather than considered as a sign of progress. We reported before that in the opinion of some scholars and writers, satisfied people lack incentive and do not strive to improve their situation.

A variety of survey findings have been presented in this chapter in which the answers "good" or "better" far exceeded in frequency the answers "bad" or "worse." May these findings be attributed to biases or survey errors? The errors may take different forms. It is conceivable, for instance, that people would hesitate to express out-right pessimism when asked about their personal financial expectations. If this were the case, the table at the beginning of this chapter showing the low frequency of people's expectations of being worse off should not be given much weight. But the emphasis in this chapter has been placed on the high frequency of optimistic replies in comparison to noncommittal replies (such as "unchanged" or "same"). It can hardly be argued that well-to-do survey respondents would find it difficult to answer, "Things will remain as they are."

It is not true that expressions of satisfaction are more frequent than those of dissatisfaction in reply to all survey questions. It will be shown, for instance, in the next chapter that in the early 1960s the number of pessimistic answers in reply to the question about the general economic outlook during the following five years was as high as the number of optimistic answers. Earlier we mentioned that when people are asked about unexpected developments, they mention in overwhelming proportion unfavorable rather than favor-able ones. Complaints about the performance of one's car or electric appliances are verbalized more easily and more frequently than satisfactions. Important also are the answers received about satis-faction with savings (as will be shown in Chapter 20 more people expressed dissatisfaction than satisfaction with the size of their financial assets). It is nevertheless possible that there is an optimistic bias in some of the data presented in this chapter. Information on the relation that prevails between variables is more reliable than information on the proportion of people who expect to be better off at any given time. But even if the percentages cited are higher than justified, the overall finding that there was widespread opti-mism about personal financial matters in the 1950s and early 1960s cannot be attributed to survey errors.

The relation of satisfaction to incentives and behavior will occupy us in several later chapters. In the discussion of housing, for instance, we will find that satisfaction with housing does not impair resi-dential mobility. We shall also find that ownership of many durable goods in satisfactory condition does not bar the purchase of new ones. Similarly, satisfaction with expected retirement income does not detract from the exertion of effort to add to it. Satisfaction does not represent saturation and may even stimulate additional desires and wants.

In this chapter one aspect of the problem will be taken up,

Table 5. Expectations about Future Standard of Living*

Future standard of living will be	Age				
	All	25–34	35–44	45–54	55–64
Better	46%	76%	64%	43%	19%
Same	43	19	31	45	62
Worse	4	1	1	4	7
Depends; don't know, not ascertained	7	4	4	8	12
	100%	100%	100%	100%	100%

	Income			
	Under $3,000	$3,000 –7,499	$7,500 –9,999	$10,000 and over
Better	32%	50%	59%	48%
Same	54	40	32	42
Worse	4	4	3	4
Depends; don't know, not ascertained	10	6	6	6
	100%	100%	100%	100%

* The question was: "During the next five or ten years, do you think your standard of living will be better, or will it remain about as it is now, or what?"

because it supplements our discussion of optimistic expectations. What is the relation of satisfaction with the prevailing standard of living to expectations about the future standard of living? When asked how their standard of living in five or ten years would compare to their present standard of living, people said either that it would improve or that it would remain unchanged. Only a few people expressed expectations that their standard of living would worsen (see Table 5). Expectations of improvement were most frequent among young people, while the notion that the standard of living would remain unchanged was most frequent among older people.

Expectations of improvement were more frequent among those who were not satisfied with their current standard of living (63 per cent) than among those who were satisfied (39 per cent). Especially among younger people, dissatisfaction with the current situation and an expectation of improvement was frequent and is understandable. With some people dissatisfaction may have a stimulating effect. But it should not be forgotten that two out of every five people who expressed satisfaction with their standard of living foresaw an improvement. Satisfaction does not necessarily mean that things are so good that they cannot be better or that it is no longer necessary to work to make them better.

The price of affluence is not saturation and absence of incentives. Yet there may be a price to pay for the experience of substantial progress and the expectation of further progress. When expected progress is not achieved, we feel disappointed or even frustrated. What we have today, even if it is much more than that which we had and which gave us full satisfaction yesterday, is no longer enough tomorrow. These dynamic attitudes, while they form the backbone of our progress, may under certain circumstances lead to emotional instability. Insecurity and uneasiness exist and may even be augmented in a mass consumption society in which greater desires follow close on the heels of greater accomplishments and in which people who have accomplished much have much to lose.

13

People's Economic Outlook

The average American consumer is well informed about prevailing economic trends. Although he does not follow business statistics or read technical reports on the state of the economy, he knows whether business activity is improving or deteriorating. When questions are asked about business trends from representative samples of all American households, the answers indicate close correspondence between people's notions and the available statistical data.

THE EXTENT OF ECONOMIC INFORMATION

Consider, for instance, the following question asked in the quarterly surveys of the Survey Research Center: "Would you say that at present business conditions are better or worse than they were a year ago?" I myself, who have studied the fluctuations of the answers to this question over many years, was surprised when some years ago a friend sent me a version of Chart 5. One curve represents the difference between the proportion of respondents who thought business conditions had improved and the proportion who thought they had deteriorated. The other curve shows year-to-year changes in the Index of Industrial Production, prepared by the Federal Reserve Board. This Index represents the best available measure of the quantity of nonfarm commodities produced in the entire economy. Measures of opinions, including those of people with little education and no interest in economic affairs, obtained from consumers who live in urban and rural areas, as well as in towns where special circumstances make for good or bad times irrespective of the business cycle, bear an amazingly close resemblance to complex statistical data.[1]

CHART 5

Fluctuations of Public Appraisal of Business Conditions and of the Production Index

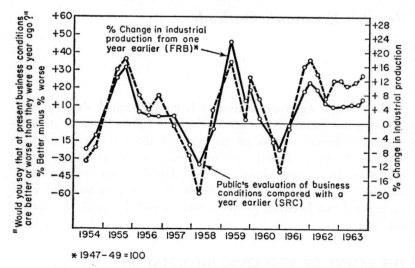

1954 1955 1956 1957 1958 1959 1960 1961 1962 1963

* 1947–49 = 100

In most people's minds, past and future trends are not clearly differentiated. Answers to questions about business trends in the near future are given as easily as about the recent past. The relation between opinions about past and expected trends is rather complex. The statement that "What has happened in the past will happen in

[1] Obviously, many individuals do not judge correctly whether business trends are upward or downward. Some people express no opinion; others express opinions that are contrary to the trends indicated by the statistical data, but these opinions are less frequent than the conforming opinions. There is no evidence that people's notions about past business trends "predict" the changes in the Production Index. In the Chart the two curves are drawn for the same dates. To be sure, at the time the interviews are conducted, the Federal Reserve Index data for the same period have not yet appeared in print.

the future" does not represent the key to an understanding of opinion formation. People do perceive continuous trends, as indicated, for instance, by their saying that business conditions are better now than a year ago and will be better still a year from now. But this type of opinion is far from being the rule. People often report on an improvement or deterioration by saying that it has run its course. Sometimes they expect a past movement to be followed by a movement in the opposite direction.

The opinion about the direction in which the economy is moving is usually affect-laden. People express their satisfaction or, alternatively, their concern and uneasiness rather than make a rational judgment about business trends. Many people answer the question of "what" promptly and unequivocally, while they have no answer to the question of "why." Others, when asked why business conditions have improved—if they have made such a statement—repeat in different ways what they have just said. "More goods are produced," "Retail sales have been increasing," and the like, are frequent answers. Similarly, those who have said that business is worse than a year ago give such explanations as "Factories are producing less" or "People are not buying as much as last year."

Praising or blaming business or government for having brought about better or worse business conditions is rare; citing statistical data or economic theories is rarer still. And yet, many people have notions about the economy which reflect some understanding. The first indication was obtained shortly after World War II, when many respondents explained that "Things are different from what they were before the war," "A depression like we had before the war is no longer in the cards; the tragedy of the 1930s can't happen again." In the early 1950s slightly over half and in the late 1950s three-quarters of all people expressed this opinion without any reservation. (Only 10 to 15 per cent replied at that time, in answer to a direct question, that a depression "like we had in the 1930s" was likely to happen again; the remaining 10 to 15 per cent had no opinion.)

Why do people think a depression cannot happen again? The majority have a prompt answer to this question. It is expressed in many different ways but usually contains the word "government." About one-third of all people and one-half of high-income people point out that the government is in a position to act to avert a depression. The second most frequent answer contains the expres-

sion "We have learned" (to cope with depressions, to avoid cata-
strophic turns in the economy); the experience of the 1930s need
not be repeated because now we know better.

When asked further about what we have learned or how the
government may avert a depression, most people are unable to
answer. The opinion that we know how to cope with a depression
is often based on an indistinct feeling rather than on any economic
argument. References to defense spending, inflation, taxes, and the
like, are made by a rather small proportion of people.

In the late 1950s the American people learned something new.
In 1955–1956 the majority thought that the next five or ten years
would be good years, not interrupted by periods of unemployment
and bad business; after 1958 the majority thought that recessions
were likely to happen again. On the average, according to frequently
repeated measurements, between 1959 and 1962, 62 per cent of all
people and 69 per cent of high-income people thought that a
recession "like we had in 1958" was likely to occur during the next
five years. The answers to this question did not differ much in good
times or bad times. (But the answers to a follow-up question,
"When do you think it will happen?" varied greatly according to
when the question was asked.) Again most people could not explain
their opinion in a manner that would satisfy an economist. "We
just don't know how to keep the economy on an even keel" summarizes what very many people said, in different words.

The change in people's opinions about the recurrence of recessions may be attributed to the experience of early 1958. For most
people the worsening of economic conditions came suddenly and
appeared substantial. It was a shock with lasting effects. This can
be seen most clearly in the answers people gave to the following
question: "Looking ahead, which would you say is more likely—
that in the country as a whole we'll have continuous good times
during the next five years or so, or that we will have periods of
widespread unemployment or depression, or what?" This question
is rather puzzling to many people, and some highly sophisticated
as well as some uneducated people refuse to commit themselves.
They say that one cannot look so far ahead or that economic
developments during the next five years depend on many things
(war, international situation, prices, etc.). But about 70 per cent
of all respondents did give an opinion at all times. In 1956 the
opinions were distributed as follows:

```
Good times ...........................   47%
Pro-con .............................   16
Bad times, widespread unemployment .....   10
Can't say, depends .....................   27
                                        ____
    Total ...........................  100%
```

Compare this with the following distribution obtained in 1961 and 1962:

```
Good times ...........................   26%
Pro-con .............................   19
Bad times, widespread unemployment .....   25
Can't say, depends .....................   30
                                        ____
    Total ...........................  100%
```

The frequency of optimistic views declined and that of pessimistic views increased following the recessions of 1958 and 1961. What do people have in mind when they speak of recessions that will recur during the next five years? They speak, first of all, of high rates of unemployment. Recessions also mean low rates of production, slow retail trade, difficulty or even inability to obtain a job. In the opinion of most people, however, bad times do not last long, no more than a year or even less.

Frequently it appears to the reader of interviews that there is little understanding among the American people of what makes the economy move or what is lacking when it does not move. But occasionally, under the impact of certain events, millions of people —as indicated by the answers of large proportions or even the majority of representative samples—seem to know a lot and to understand certain basic features of the economy. I obtained such a glimpse in the fall of 1959. There was a strike in the steel industry lasting several months, and almost everyone was aware of it. People in all walks of life agreed that the strike was very bad and would produce bad effects even after it was settled. They disagreed about how it should or would be settled. If industry should win and labor receive no wage increases, some people said, there would not be enough buying power in the country to sustain good times. If labor should win and get sizable wage increases, others argued, prices would go up and that would bring bad times. The overall opinion—namely, whatever the outcome, it will be bad—served as an indicator of short-term prospects at that time. The prevalent opinion that inflation makes for bad times will be discussed in the next chapter. Here it suffices to call attention to the degree of economic sophistication indicated by the common answers. Irrespective of whether one agrees with one or the other opinion, it appears that very many people have some notion of what makes the economy move.

Questions about unemployment likewise yield the conclusion that the average consumer is fairly well informed. When people were asked whether unemployment had been increasing or decreasing during the previous few months, the changes in their answers corresponded in most periods with the direction of change in the rate of unemployment as indicated by government statistics.[2]

According to survey findings people in general were aware that during the recovery from the 1958 recession, and again during the recovery from the 1961 recession, the rate of unemployment did not decline as much as it should have. Respondents said that times were good but also said that it was hard to find jobs. Unemployment and the government's inability to reduce it represented a persistent concern during the years 1958 to 1963. This was found to be true among people who were threatened with losing their jobs, as well as among those with steady employment or businessmen and professionals who were immune from unemployment. The optimism of people with rising incomes was dampened by the cloud they saw over the economy. Even when respondents argued that the rate of unemployment was intolerable, their opinion nonetheless reflected some of their underlying optimism. They confidently believed that government or business was in a position to cope with many of our economic problems and therefore found failure to deal with unemployment especially distressing.

When the level of information—regarding changes in unemployment as well as changes in business trends—of the well-educated or the high-income people is compared with that of people who have little education or low incomes, some substantial differences

[2] It is worth noting that to some extent economic attitudes appear to predict prospective changes in unemployment, and to some extent they are explained by past changes in unemployment. L. R. Klein, University of Pennsylvania, found that the Survey Research Center's Index of Consumer Sentiment forecast 46 per cent of the fluctuations in the rate of unemployment during the half year following the attitude measurement in the period 1952 to 1962. For a discussion of unemployment as an explanatory variable of the change in attitudes, see Eva Mueller (Ref. 4).

are found. But when the change in the opinions of the two groups is compared—how many more respondents say "times are better" or "unemployment has declined" in any one survey than in earlier surveys—both groups are usually found to have moved in the same direction. The amplitude of the changes was, however, greater among the well-educated than among the poorly educated. Indications of cyclical turning points by shifts in answers, from, say, "unemployment has been increasing" to "unemployment has been decreasing," were more frequent among the former than among the latter, although they occurred at the same time in both groups.

BUSINESS NEWS HEARD BY CONSUMERS

We mentioned in Chapter 10 that one of the questions asked at quarterly intervals is whether respondents have heard of any favorable or unfavorable changes in business conditions during the previous few months. As might be expected, more high- than low-income people answer in the affirmative. But the relation of reports of favorable to unfavorable business news—studied on the basis of answers to the follow-up question "What did you hear?"—are quite similar among different income groups.

The frequency with which respondents report the news heard represents in itself an indicator of some interest. In bad times more people speak of news they have heard about business conditions than in good times. During the years 1954 to 1963 the highest frequency of such reports was recorded in the spring of 1958 when 60 per cent of all people spoke of some business news they had heard; the second highest was recorded in the spring of 1961 when 56 per cent did so. Both of these times were, of course, times of recession. In 1956 and again in 1963—periods of prosperity—the proportion of those able to report on some news heard was less than 40 per cent. Bad news is more salient than good news. News about increased unemployment, strikes, or a recession attracts more attention and is recalled more frequently than good news about employment or an increase in production. Similarly, an increase in the cost of living receives more attention than price stability, and naturally, there is greater public awareness of acute international conflict and threat of war than of peaceful developments on the international front.

According to indications derived from counting the frequency with which respondents could recall news they had heard, consumers appear to lag behind developments. The frequency rose early in 1958, that is, *during* the recession, and not in 1957, when the recession threatened. But when the relation of favorable to unfavorable news is studied, consumers do appear to signal economic changes in advance.

In 1955 most Americans were aware of the improvement in business conditions and reported having heard favorable news; rising incomes, sales, and production were news, salient to many people. In 1956 the same information was noticed by many fewer people; record levels in income and production were an old story rather than news. Even when specific questions were asked, only a few people could recall any unfavorable news in 1955, while such news was reported spontaneously by a sizable proportion of the people in 1956. In the first nine months of 1957, when economic statistics on GNP, national income, retail sales, and the like, chalked up further high points, they did not constitute salient news. Even isolated and rare unfavorable items were, however, widely noted. At that time the sharply increasing proportion of people reporting unfavorable news served as an important indicator of the impending downturn.

Only what is new is news—this is the first principle governing the impact of information on masses of people. In bad times or shortly after a recovery has begun information on improved economic conditions is big news. When, however, the good news continues over a year or more, habituation sets in. Whether newspapers, TV, and radio played down the good news in 1956 or early in 1957 by giving it less coverage, by no longer featuring it on the front pages, or by giving it smaller headlines, we do not know. But even if it were true that there were changes in the manner in which the information was transmitted to consumers, there still remains the psychological factor: In a survey conducted in February, 1957, people who revealed an awareness of favorable economic trends when reminded of them by the interviewer had spontaneously reported adverse factors in an earlier phase of the same interview.[3]

When late in 1957 bad news became the rule, it was big news, and, as we have said, the degree of awareness increased. But some habituation to bad news was also observed, coupled with a further

[3] The first finding resulted from a true-or-false test, the second from asking whether respondents had heard any economic news.

phenomenon that had previously been noted in 1954: Anxiety about layoffs, unemployment, reduced income, and the like, slowly gave way on the part of many to satisfaction that they had not themselves been hurt. Since even in the worst postwar recessions the majority maintained stable incomes, and some even had income increases, people slowly began to derive satisfaction from a comparison of their own situation with the news about the economy.

It took a while, after the recession of 1958, before respondents' reports on favorable news exceeded in frequency the reports on unfavorable news, and in the following years the relation of the two measures never did regain the lopsided distribution of 1955. As early as May, 1960, and, following the next recession, as early as May, 1962, reports of unfavorable news were again more frequent than those of favorable news. We may follow the impact of economic news in 1962: The ratio of reports on favorable to unfavorable news deteriorated in the spring and summer and improved toward the end of that year. Only a very small proportion of people could cite data or authorities, but still the survey measure of news reported corresponded, at first, with the sluggishness of the recovery and then with some newly won vigor.

Only the direction of economic trends is indicated by the relation of favorable to unfavorable news reported by consumers. The news itself which consumers recall is seldom of interest. Many people talk in generalities, saying, for instance, that production or sales have increased. Prices and employment represent the two topics most often noted. Sometimes business trends in one's own community are discussed, often with personal references. Statistics are very rarely cited, and economic terms are seldom used.

We may conclude that a tendency toward counteracting extreme trends is inherent in the manner in which consumers take note of information. Good times do not develop into booms because good news does not persist. Bad times likewise stop short of catastrophes because unfavorable news tends in time to lose its impact. Surely this is no law of human nature—in 1930 to 1933 people's reactions may well have been different—but it is a major feature of post-World War II behavior and will be cited later, together with other stabilizing features of consumer thinking and reacting.

14

Inflation

Overwhelmingly, the American people believe that inflation is bad. This notion has prevailed, substantially in the same form, ever since the middle 1940s. What is inflation, in the opinion of the people, and how do we know that they consider it an adverse development?

PERCEPTIONS OF AND ATTITUDES TOWARD INFLATION

Indirect methods of questioning yielded the most important evidence, although direct questions also provided useful information. In nationwide surveys conducted with representative samples of consumers, respondents were asked whether in their opinion "this is a good time to buy or a bad time to buy (automobiles, household appliances, houses, or various other consumer goods)." Whichever opinion a respondent expressed, he was asked, "Why do you say so?" Although some answers referred to special conditions in the markets about which the inquiry was made, only one kind of reply common to all goods was given frequently: reference to prices. Those who thought that it was a bad time to buy spoke of price increases. "Prices are too high," "Prices have been going up," and "Prices are going up" are some of the ways respondents expressed themselves, making no distinction between past price trends and expected price trends. Those who judged buying conditions to be favorable spoke of stable prices and also of discounts, bargains, and special opportunities to purchase. Many people said, "Prices didn't go up last year" or "Prices won't change," in explanation of their opinion that it was a good time to buy certain major consumer goods.

Particularly informative were reactions to automobile prices, because it was possible to observe how these reactions changed. In 1956, 1957, and 1958 most people thought each year that it cost more to buy a new car than a year earlier and that prices would go up further. Whether people's notions about past trends were correct is hard to determine, since for most people the price paid for a new car depends on the trade-in value placed on their old one. We are concerned here with people's opinions and attitudes. In those years, people considered the price increases which in their opinion had taken place unjustified and reacted to them in an unfavorable manner. In the early 1960s, however, automobile prices were judged to be stable by the majority of respondents who expressed an opinion. This was to a large extent the result of the introduction of compact cars, which we shall discuss further in Chapter 23. Here it suffices to say that attitudes toward car purchases became much more favorable when most people thought the prices were stable.

During the twenty years 1943 to 1963 people in all walks of life became aware of rising prices. They were asked, in the Survey Research Center's studies, about price movements "during the past year" of food, clothing, appliances, and automobiles. In order to avoid the impression that the interviewer was testing respondents' knowledge of economic trends, the question was usually put in the following form: "We'd like to know what has happened to prices of things you buy here in . . . (name of community) during the past year; have they stayed about the same, gone up, or gone down?" The proportion of people saying "Prices have gone up" always exceeded the proportion saying "remained the same"— practically nobody reported price declines—and the difference between the two answers proved to be a fair indication of the prevalence of larger or smaller price increases. In the conversational type of interviews conducted by the Survey Research Center, few people reply by simply choosing an alternative. The usual answers included expressions of disappointment or even anger about price increases or satisfaction about price stability.

The term inflation is frequently used in answers to questions about prices. It has become a common word with which people in all walks of life are familiar. To them it means price increases of many things over an extended period of time. Speaking of business decisions on the prices of a specific commodity, people rarely use the word inflation except when they point to the probable consequences of such decisions which will influence the prices of many products—for instance, "The higher steel prices will make for inflation." It must be an upward price trend of a general nature extending over several months at least, rather than a one-time increase in the price of one item, in order to qualify in the public mind as inflation.

The fluctuations in people's price expectations recorded between 1956 and 1963 may be classified as minor. In the late 1940s and again in the early 1950s, many more people said that prices (of things they bought) would go up during the next year than said they would go up during the next five years. "What goes up must come down" was an opinion frequently voiced. It was thought that price increases over a short period would in time be reversed. Later in the 1950s the distribution of answers to the question about what prices would do during the next five years changed. In the late 1950s and early 1960s, the majority of people felt that prices would rise "permanently."[1] But the extent of expected price increases was small. Most people thought that prices would advance by less than 10 per cent in five years, and many even put the increase at 5 per cent or less.

These conservative and at the same time rather realistic notions were connected with definite affective undertones. We reported in Chapter 9 that survey respondents, after expressing their opinion about what would happen to prices of things they would buy during the next twelve months, were asked, "Would you say that these (rising prices, unchanged prices, etc.) would be to the good, to the bad, or what?" Most people did not hesitate to give a definite

[1] During the years 1956 to 1963, we find that the highest proportion of people expecting prices to go up within the succeeding twelve months was 70 per cent and the lowest 50 per cent. Five-year price expectations varied still less; 50 to 60 per cent of the respondents expected increases. In the late 1940s, on the other hand, there were several periods when only 10 per cent of representative samples said that prices would advance during the following five years. At the same time, the majority expected prices to rise during the next year. One-year price expectations likewise fluctuated more sharply in the earlier years than in the later years.

answer, although the formulation of the question was intentionally vague. What most people had in mind and could report was not a careful judgment about the advantages or disadvantages of inflation for the country or for themselves but an emotional reaction to it. The findings, averaged from several surveys conducted in a more recent and a more remote period, were as follows:

Expected Price Increase*	1956–57	1961–62
To the good	14%	11%
Undecided	18	22
To the bad	68	67
	100%	100%
Expected Price Stability*		
To the good	61%	72%
Undecided	24	17
To the bad	15	11
	100%	100%

* Expected price declines, expressed by relatively few people, were usually considered "to the good."

In 1961–1962 the number of respondents who expressed a positive evaluation of price stability and a negative evaluation of price increases appeared even more pronounced than in 1956–1957. In 1957 some people who called stable prices a bad thing explained that prices were so high that it would be bad if they remained unchanged. But the differences between earlier and later findings are of much smaller significance than the consistently unfavorable appraisal of inflation.

People's reaction to the steel strike of 1959, as described in the previous chapter, may also be cited to indicate that people generally consider inflation to be bad. Further evidence comes from a study of the perceived effects of rearmament on the economy. It will be shown in Chapter 16 that according to the beliefs of many people, an increase in armament expenditures has unfavorable effects on the economy. Among the reasons with which people support their opinion, one is relevant at this point: The more the government spends on defense, the more probable is inflation; therefore the ultimate effect of rearmament is detrimental.

There can be no doubt that millions and millions of Americans experienced the best years of their lives in years of inflation. On the average, income not only kept pace with price increases but even exceeded them so that there were gains in the purchasing power of the population. Among individual families, of course, there were many for whom the income-price relationship deteriorated and, by the same token, many more for whom it improved. It appears also that owners of fixed assets who found no compensation for the loss in purchasing power of their assets constituted a minority (see Chapter 20). But personal experience does not appear to have determined opinions about inflation.

Are people then influenced by articles or news they read about the ravages of inflation? Since what is gathered from reading matter usually does not overcome personal experience, the explanation must lie elsewhere. The persistant condemnation of inflation may be connected with the fact that people relate it only to higher prices and not to their higher incomes. We reported in Chapter 12 that people who said they were making more than they had been five years earlier were asked why that was so. In reply to the puzzling question, "How come you make more than five years ago?" only a very small proportion of people referred to inflation. Even blue-collar workers with union contracts specifying cost-of-living increases attributed their gains over five years much less frequently to inflation than to what they themselves deserved to get. People consider inflation bad because higher prices detract from the enjoyment of their higher incomes, which in their opinions, are the well-deserved fruits of their labor.

It appears that many people's feelings go far beyond the notion that inflation is bad. They resent inflation. It should not have happened and it need not have happened, they argue. Only a few people explain in detail that they feel that during an all-out war price increases might be justified, but that in a cold war one can have guns and butter as well; therefore, since there are no shortages, there should not be any price increases either. But even if this rational argumentation is not very common, its affective tone is widespread: There is clearly no justification for peacetime inflation in the opinion of most Americans.

Nevertheless, most people do not place the blame for inflation on any group of our society. There are, of course, survey respondents who say that labor or trade unions having the power to push wages up year after year have caused the inflation. Other respondents blame big business or speculation, and others again say that the excessive spending by the government or the deficits are the causes of inflation. But even though such replies can be elicited through direct questioning about the causes of inflation, the answers are not salient in people's thinking. Most people resent inflation, but very few resent the activities either of trade unions or big business or government. Inflation, like recession, is viewed as one of the evils which we have not yet mastered. We should be able to do without inflation but we have not or have not as yet learned how—this is how many people leave the problem. Yet their attitudes toward inflation do influence their behavior in spending and saving.

INFLATION AND SPENDING

How do people react in terms of purchases when they expect price increases? The traditional answers to this question are simple, most convincing, and supported by a multitude of observations gained over several centuries in a variety of countries. When people expect prices to go up, they tend to buy in advance of the price increases—they try to stock up and hoard in order to beat inflation. Since some people will always be in a position to react in this manner, inflationary expectations are supposed to stimulate demand; the greater demand, in turn, drives prices up. Thus the expectations are thought to be self-justifying.

Does it follow from this theory that inflation results from people's attitudes toward it? In past publications I have pointed to certain weaknesses of the theory of self-justifying expectations (Ref. 2, pp. 236ff.). On certain occasions, for a short time, people did behave as just described. But even in times of galloping inflation in Germany, France, and China, it was found that millions of people were aware of what they considered valid reasons for inflation. Had this not been so, they would not have maintained strong inflationary expectations over long periods of time. Inflation came about as a joint effect of what were perceived as the causes of inflation—for instance, a great increase in the amount of money in circulation or in the amount of bank credit extended—and of inflationary expectations. Although sometimes repeated severe inflationary shocks have created mass hysteria and led to steadily and rapidly increasing prices, usually inflationary trends have been interrupted by plateaus of stable prices. Expectations are not necessarily cumulative and self-supporting. It has been observed in many countries at different times that people have felt that the causes of inflation have exhausted themselves, that prices have risen as much as the perceived causes warranted. Inflationary expectations were then supplanted by expectations of stable prices.

In principle, then, it is necessary to distinguish between two types of expectation. Some are cumulative and elastic—they are strengthened by the fulfillment of what one expects. Others are inelastic and not self-reinforcing. Accordingly, one attitude toward inflation may consist of viewing it as a break with the past, in which case it results in buying in excess and in advance of needs; in the extreme instance, this attitude results in flight from money. Inflation is then seen as something inevitable and rapid. People's perceptions and expectations are very different, however, when inflation is seen as a development which is not inevitable under the given conditions. Then people's time perspective continues to extend both backward and forward; unfavorable reactions to and resentment of past price increases exert the major influences on people's purchases. If the expectation of further small price increases persists under such circumstances, people will not be induced to buy in advance of their needs.

The *stock-up* theory of inflationary expectations must be contrasted with the *postpone* theory. In the United States during most of the postwar years of creeping inflation, consumers on the whole reacted to inflationary experience and expectations by buying less rather than by buying more. Inflation was considered a bad thing, and this was true both of price increases that had occurred in the past and those that were expected to occur in the future. A development that is viewed as unfavorable does not stimulate but rather deters one from the satisfaction of needs and desires.

People's notions about the relation of income trends to price trends may again be cited in this connection. Questioning about future prices and about future income indicated that both were expected to go up. But the two increases were not seen as being related. When asked specifically, in the late 1950s, the majority of people said that they were not sure whether their income would keep pace with the price increases. One thing many people were sure of: When there is inflation, they have to spend more on necessities. Expecting expenses for food, children's clothing, and other things they could not do without to rise, they believed that spending on things they would like to have, but could do without, would have to be cut. It was found in many interviews over several years that many people argued, "With prices going up, our expenses will increase and we'll have to postpone buying a new car (or an electrical appliance, etc.)."

Once only during the postwar period were the American people's reactions to inflation quite different. In 1950, shortly after the outbreak of war in Korea, rapid price increases as well as shortages of civilian goods were anticipated, under the influence of adverse military developments, by people who still had a vivid recollection of World War II and rationing. At that time they did stock up with goods. But over the years that followed this experience, the attitudes and reactions of masses of consumers underwent a change. Doubts arose about the strength of the forces making for price increases. As reported above, at all times between 1955 and 1962 the majority of consumers, in reply to a direct question, said they thought prices would go up, but they were not very sure about it. Also they expected relatively small increases.

Basic to the general reaction to price changes was that people found stable prices to be a reassuring feature in the economic picture. When automobiles, home furnishings, clothing, or food appeared to be priced as they had been several months or a year earlier, people felt reassured. They believed that the prices were right. Buying is stimulated by such notions as it is stimulated by the perception of unusual opportunities (clearance sales, discounts, and the like) which are considered temporary. When prices have been rising, that reassurance is missing. Confidence that one is paying the right price and absence of uncertainty are strengthened by expectations of price stability; these conditions create "good times to buy."

Statistical data on aggregate trends of consumer demand support these conclusions about the effects of people's attitudes. It may suffice to refer to Part Three of this book, where we had frequent occasion to cite inflationary expectations, or their absence, as factors that contributed to the explanation of business-cycle trends. There are also some data available concerning the relationship between individual consumers' attitudes toward inflation and their subsequent purchases. Eva Mueller has shown that people who expected prices to go up and considered this an unfavorable trend made fewer purchases of durable goods in the following twelve months than people who expected prices to remain stable or go down and considered this favorable.[2] Similar results were also obtained when, between 1960 and 1962, a sample of consumers was interviewed three times in succession. The statistical analysis was complicated by the fact that the proportion of those who were constantly inflation-minded[3] in those years was highest among high-income people and lowest among low-income people; it was the other way around among those who did not have any inflationary expectations. Among families with an annual income of $7,500 or over, it was found that more than twice as many of those who did not expect inflation than of those who were inflation-minded spent as much as 30 per cent or more of their income in 1960 and 1961 on consumer durables and home improvements. In the two groups the proportions of large spenders were 32 and 15 per cent respectively. (Among lower-income people no relationship was found between expenditures and expectations of inflation.)

INFLATION AND SAVING

The American people appear to have reacted to inflation in a sensible manner rather than to have gone overboard. Additional evidence for this contention comes from a study of the influence of inflation on saving and investing. In this respect again, inflation did not result in a break with past behavior and had little effect on opinions and beliefs that must have prevailed for a long time. We may start by citing the answers of one respondent; similar replies were obtained in many cases. In an interview conducted by the Survey Research Center in the early 1960s, a foreman in an airplane plant was asked, "What have prices of the things you buy done during the last few years?"

"Everything's gone up," he said.

"What do you think prices will do during next year?"

"Shoot up further. Seems like there's no limit."

Then the questioning turned to saving. "It is important to have some savings," the foreman explained. "Something unexpected may happen; you've got to save for a rainy day." Asked whether he had

[2] Eva Mueller, "Consumer Reactions to Inflation," *Quarterly Journal of Economics,* vol. 73, pp. 246–262, 1959.

[3] These are the respondents who said in both the first and the third series of interviews that prices would be higher "a year from now" as well as "five years from now."

saved and in what way, he explained that for over ten years he had had an account with a savings bank and that the account had been growing year by year. "Banks are safe, mighty convenient, and they pay interest besides," he added.

"You spoke of inflation—does that have anything to do with how you feel about your savings account?" he was then asked.

"Oh, I know what you mean," he replied. "The $100 I put in the bank ten years ago aren't worth that much today. Maybe inflation has dropped them to something like $80. But what if I hadn't ever put the $100 in the bank at all? Then I'd have spent the money. . . . Believe me, $80 is a lot better than nothing!"

U.S. government bonds (war bonds) were the most popular form of saving during World War II and the first few postwar years. Savings accounts with savings and loan associations, mutual savings banks, and commercial banks served as the principal outlet for the majority of savers in later years. Such saving, which did not provide protection against inflation, was not based on ignorance. Many savers knew the score; but they were not 100 per cent sure of price increases, expected small price increases at the most, and knew of no other convenient savings outlet, devoid of risk, which they could have chosen. And, in spite of inflation, the savers were not unhappy about their experience. Except for top-income people, the majority in each income group expressed their preference for fixed assets during the entire postwar period.

In Part Five of this book we shall discuss saving practices in greater detail and point to the paramount importance people attach to safety, that is, the absence of risk and any speculative element for reserve funds that are meant for future contingencies. We shall also show the desire for diversification. This latter widely felt need led an increased number of people to put money both in fixed-asset savings and in investments not tied to the value of the dollar. The large increase in the number of stockholders in the late 1950s and early 1960s will be shown to have been the response to diverse motives and desires rather than to fear of inflation alone.

Economists have often spoken of money illusion. A dollar is a dollar, so people are supposed to think, irrespective of the deterioration of its purchasing power. No doubt there are people under the influence of such an illusion. No doubt the illusion plays a role with some people who are aware of inflation and makes them complacent about rising prices. But the economic intelligence of most American consumers should not be underestimated. They spent and saved with open eyes in the late 1950s and early 1960s. To most of them inflation represented an inevitable evil of which they were aware but with which they were unable to cope. Because of increases in income and in the value of one very important asset, homeownership, the majority of people suffered no substantial net losses from inflation. There was no need for a radical reorganization in their thinking, their spending, or their saving.

In some other countries, but not in the United States during the past twenty years, inflation has meant the beginning of a new era in which old values were overthrown. In this country inflation has been just one of many factors shaping modern life rather than a factor of overriding importance. Inflation was seen by many people as an adverse development, because it detracted from the enjoyment of a good life; but the enjoyment was still there, since to detract did not mean to destroy.

We concluded in the previous chapter that because of their reactions to news and their attitudes toward business fluctuations, consumers exert a stabilizing influence on the economy. A similar conclusion emerges from the study of inflation. Purse strings are drawn tighter when prices go up, while money flows more freely when prices are thought to be stable. Thereby consumers counteract inflationary forces. To be sure, they did not succeed in arresting inflation. But without the given attitudes and reactions of consumers, inflation would have been more rapid.

The last conclusion is reinforced by numerous observations about business behavior. Business managers appear to be familiar with consumer reactions to price increases. For the past twenty years they have hesitated to raise prices, fearing adverse consumer reactions. When increases appeared to be inevitably necessary, business firms tried to conceal them as much as possible. Rather than raising prices directly, they frequently resorted to such practices as cutting discounts or introducing new products at higher prices, or occasionally even to such questionable tactics as reducing sizes and lowering quality. As a last resort, businessmen apologized for raising their prices.

It is the essence of the *traditional* psychology of inflation that demand under its influence becomes independent of the price level or even increases with rising prices. The essence of the *new* psychology, as it has developed in the United States since the end of the war, is that price increases are resented, and the expectation of price increases creates uncertainty and lack of confidence and thus reduces discretionary demand. There is no assurance that the new psychology will continue to prevail. Conceivably, new developments might revive the traditional psychology, or people might eventually learn to view creeping inflation without misgivings. What is sure is that in the future we shall not be able to rely on the traditionally postulated simple relation between inflation and spending or saving. We now know much more than we once knew of the complex influence of the intervening variables.[4]

[4] In Chap. 28 we shall characterize what has been concluded about inflation in this chapter as a "conditional generalization" and shall discuss the significance of such generalizations.

15

Attitudes toward the Government

There is much controversy about the role of the government in the economy. Party politics as well as differences in philosophy are reflected in the arguments of experts. Individualism has a long and highly valued tradition in America; yet the economic functions of the government have grown immensely in our lifetime. The economic history of the post-Depression era may be described, without much exaggeration, as an uninterrupted increase in what its opponents call statism. This is true of the ever-increasing role of the Federal government not only in dealing with the unemployed, the disabled, and the retired but also in fighting recession and inflation. The American consumer cannot be understood without an analysis of his attitudes toward the government. We shall describe recent findings on how consumers felt about and reacted to a variety of government measures. The data can be presented without regard to controversial issues of philosophy or politics, because they reveal an unexpected uniformity and agreement among most Americans.

Three attitudes which prevail rather uniformly among all segments of the population are: (1) confidence in the government and the belief that the government is very powerful in economic matters; (2) support of most domestic economic programs of the government and readiness to accept increased government spending for diverse purposes; and (3) feeling that deficits, large government debt, and high taxes are undesirable, coupled with habituation to all these "evils." Understanding of how taxes and government spending influence economic developments is limited. Lack of congruence and even some dissonance characterize some aspects of public

142

thinking about the government's role in the economy. This is an indication of thoughts and attitudes being in a state of flux rather than of their being governed by selfish considerations or rigid stereotypes.

ON THE GOVERNMENT'S POWER

Whenever unfavorable developments in the economy are discussed, the American people speak of the responsibilities of the government. The remedies for unemployment, recession, or inflation are to be found, in the opinion of most people, in the government's "doing something." People in all walks of life, including the majority of top-income people, agree that the government has the power to influence the economy.

In Chapter 13 we became acquainted with the conviction shared by most Americans that a depression such as we had in the 1930s could not happen again. Lesser fluctuations, however, and even frequently recurring recessions, were considered probable. The main reason for these notions was found in the belief that the government has it in its power to avert a depression but does not seem to know how to cope with recessions or how to create full employment. Our surveys have revealed only a few persons who understood how "automatic stabilizers" function or who even mentioned that taxes take a larger bite from income and profits in prosperous times than in times of recession. Yet many people had the feeling, which experts may not characterize as inaccurate, that the character of the postwar business cycle differed from that of the prewar cycle (specifically, from what had prevailed in the 1930s).

Many people believe that the government can bring about good times if and when it really puts itself to the task. Reactions to the election of new Presidents in 1952 and 1960 provided insights into these attitudes. The election of General Eisenhower made for optimism in the business outlook. When asked whether the election had any significance for business prospects, most people replied that there would be an upturn. The arguments people used differed. Some opponents of the new President said the new government was a business government; it was the function of such a government to bring about good times, and it would certainly do so. Some supporters of the new President argued that business confidence would improve under the new administration, and this would do the trick.

Fundamentally similar were people's reactions eight years later. The election of Kennedy to the presidency was greeted by friend and foe alike with the notion that times would improve, and the impending recession would soon be overcome. Some people, to be sure, spoke of temporary improvement due to, in their opinion, inexcusable government spending; others praised the end of a period of government inaction. Whichever was the case, the reactions indicated many people's belief that it was in the government's power to do something about economic activity.

Surveys conducted shortly after the end of the recessions of 1958 and 1961 yielded similar conclusions. People who, in October, 1958, or in June, 1961, knew that recovery had begun—a substantial minority at both times—attributed the turn to government action. Respondents were asked whether in their opinion the Federal government had done a good job, a fair job, or a poor job in dealing with the problems of recession and unemployment. Only about one in five, in representative samples, said at both dates that they did not know. In October, 1958, 23 per cent of all people and 21 per cent of high-income people thought that the government had done a poor job or had not done enough; in June, 1961, 11 per cent of all and 14 per cent of high-income people expressed these same negative opinions. At both dates, then, the majority agreed that the government had done a good or a fair job in bringing the recession to an end. Criticism of the government's antirecession policies was quite rare, even among its political opponents.

It should be noted, however, that the findings do not indicate identification with the government. In reply to the question about the likelihood of another major depression, many people answered, "*We* have learned something." But in talking of prospective actions by the new President, it was *he* who was expected to do something to help *us* or to help the economy. In discussing the recessions of 1958 or 1961, most people spoke of the impersonal government which should act for the benefit of the economy.

IN FAVOR OF THE GOVERNMENT'S ECONOMIC PROGRAMS

A large majority of the American people have favorable attitudes toward several major domestic economic programs of the government. In a number of surveys conducted in the early 1960s, respondents were given cards on which eleven domestic programs, not including national defense but involving sizable federal expenditures, were listed. Respondents were asked whether in their opinion the government should spend more money, less money, or about the same amount as at present on those programs. The most frequent answer consisted of a request that the government spend more. Regarding five programs this answer was given by the majority; regarding four additional programs this answer together with the answer, "same amount," represented the majority; and only regarding two programs did the answer "less" exceed the answer "more." (Space exploration and support for agriculture were the two exceptions.) Increased spending was favored

For none of the programs	by 6% of the sample
For one program only	by 8% of the sample
For two or three programs . . .	by 22% of the sample
For four or five programs	by 29% of the sample
For six or seven programs	by 20% of the sample
For eight or more programs . . .	by 15% of the sample
	100%

The popularity contest was won by three programs identified as "help to older people," "help to needy people," and "education." More than 60 per cent of all people favored increased spending on each of these three.[1]

The findings quoted thus far were obtained in answer to questions in which no reference was made to the problem of financing the government expenditures. After respondents had expressed their attitudes toward each government program, the interviewer asked: "You said the government should spend more money on . . . ; if the government had to raise taxes to finance the additional expenditures, then for which of these things would you favor spending more money?" In other words, people were asked to reconsider their previously stated preferences. It was suggested to them that they might not have thought of the necessity of raising taxes to finance

[1] The other programs were, in the order of their popularity, slum clearance, hospital and medical care, public works, support for small business, highway construction, unemployment benefits, parks and recreational facilities, space exploration, and support for agriculture. See Eva Mueller, "Public Attitudes toward Fiscal Programs," *Quarterly Journal of Economics,* vol. 77, pp. 210–235, 1963, for detailed data on this question as well as several other issues discussed in this chapter.

the additional expenditures; they were then asked whether in that case they would still stick to their previous opinion.

Many people revised their opinions in response to the new question. They listed considerably fewer programs on which they favored additional spending, but they still expressed a desire for the expansion of several of them. Half of all respondents said they would be willing to pay more taxes for two or more expanded programs, while only 14 per cent were unwilling to pay higher taxes for any government program. Yet no single program was so popular that a majority of all people were prepared to pay higher taxes for it. Education ranked highest in this respect, with 41 per cent of American adults favoring greater outlays for education, even if they would mean higher taxes.

Although the questions about government programs were formulated in as unbiased a form as possible, there is no denying that they could have been asked in such a way as to produce different results. If, for example, people had been asked first about the programs for which they would be willing to pay higher taxes and only second about programs for which they would spend more if free funds were available, the answers might have been different. But then these short questions were not designed to provide specific advice to lawmakers. The problem of supporting specific expenditures through taxation is far too complicated to be studied through brief survey questions and is hardly suitable for a plebiscite. People were asked to express their attitudes toward specific government programs even if the programs would involve tax increases simply to permit us to study the intensity of those attitudes. The findings justify the conclusion that many people are strongly committed to several domestic programs involving large amounts of money. The replies in support of government expenditures cannot be explained away by contending that respondents did not want to appear to be opposing education or aid to older and needy people.

Attitudes toward programs involving large government expenditures did not differ much among different income groups. The notion that upper-income people, who must bear the brunt of government expenditures by paying the highest taxes, would be less favorably disposed toward the programs than low-income people was not confirmed. Overall, the differences between income groups were negligible, although some programs were preferred to a greater extent by upper-income people, while others were particularly popular among lower-income people. Aid for the needy as well as hospital and medical care fall in the latter category.

Increased support for the aged is advocated to a similar extent by the elderly, the middle-aged, and the young. Similarly, people with and without small children favor Federal expenditures for education to an equal extent. Irrespective of their personal situation, millions of Americans have learned during the last few decades that it is the task of the Federal government to provide aid to individuals not only when they need aid (for instance, because of unemployment) but also in order that the rich and the poor should have equal opportunities (for instance, by access to education).

Even though most people are in favor of at least some government programs and approve spending for what they consider good and worthy purposes, they are against spending itself. It is an easy matter to formulate survey questions which elicit replies in which the virtues associated with frugality and thrift become apparent. When, for instance, it was suggested that expenditures for national defense and the cold war might increase, close to two-thirds of all people argued that the government should spend less on other things then, rather than raise taxes or go into debt.

Being opposed to government spending but, at the same time, in favor of spending for education, highway construction, or medical care represents just one of several inconsistencies which we shall describe in this chapter. People often show themselves inconsistent in their answers about what belongs in the public and what in the private domain. But in one respect there are no indications of conflict or dissonance: The desire for the extension of government services is not felt to be in contradiction with people's preoccupation with private consumption. Affluent people appear to be in favor of both private and public spending.

DEFICITS, DEBT, AND GOVERNMENT SPENDING

When people are asked direct questions about deficits, they almost unanimously condemn them. That deficits are bad is a long-prevailing belief, apparently unchanged for several decades, and in this respect similar to the previously discussed belief that inflation is bad.

The great majority of people cannot see any difference between the budget of the government and that of business firms or individuals. Prudent people are supposed to balance receipts and expenditures by adjusting the latter to the former. Relatively few people realize that the government, in contrast to firms or individuals, may also use the reverse procedure, namely, to increase revenues when spending increases or must be increased. Deficits are accepted when there is an emergency. The resulting debt is viewed as a burden which must be repaid sooner or later.

While many people explain the evils of deficits and the evils of inflation in similar terms, the basis for their attitudes toward them differs in certain respects. First and foremost, information about inflation is extensive and fairly accurate, while information about deficits is rare, limited, and inaccurate. Even when asked directly, "Do you happen to know whether the Federal government is now operating with a deficit?" which question may be suggestive and asks for the simplest memory function of recognition, about one-half of all people answered incorrectly at a time when the deficits were fairly large (fall of 1961). When asked about the effects of deficits, most people were unable to reply; a minority said that because of deficits taxes would have to be raised or inflation would be the result.

The reaction to deficits is, then, primarily emotional. Most people are not greatly concerned with deficits. The absence of real concern was demonstrated when attitudes toward reducing government debt were studied. In surveys conducted in 1960 and 1961 questions were asked about the possible impact of disarmament and a reduction in defense expenditures. "Some people say that there will be disarmament and our government will spend less on arms and defense," respondents were told. "Suppose this is the case, what would you say should be done with the money saved?" Only 14 per cent of all people and 22 per cent of people with over $10,000 income suggested that the government debt should be reduced. The need to do away with high debt is not salient to very many people. When, following the spontaneous answers, respondents were given five choices and asked to assign priorities to them, debt reduction was the first choice of only 24 per cent. Larger expenditures for various domestic programs—welfare, schools, highways—were chosen by more people.[2]

In 1962, in discussing arguments against a tax reduction, rela-

[2] For complete data, see Eva Mueller, *op. cit.* It should be noted that respondents appeared to pay little attention to the introductory phrase about disarmament. Most of them answered the question according to their preferences among the various alternative policies, rather than in terms of replacement for arms expenditures. The following were the first choices of respondents

tively few people (8 per cent of all and 11 per cent of high-income people) cited deficits as a reason for not cutting taxes. As we shall soon see, other reasons were voiced more frequently.

Deficits and government debt represent technical matters with which few people are fully familiar. Not really understanding them is not a matter of personal concern. Government expenditures, on the other hand, relate to many aspects of everyday life and do not appear to represent a technical problem that requires expert knowledge. Most people are much more personally involved in questions of government spending on welfare or schools or medical care than in the problem of government debt or deficits.

Absence of personal involvement may help to explain the persistence of erroneous notions. Studies of attitudes toward war bonds conducted during World War II were the first to reveal them. "Bonds must be bought so that the government may pay for arms, tanks, and planes," said many respondents at that time. Many people believed that war expenditures would have to be curtailed if the government did not receive enough money from the people to pay its expenses. The most extreme form of this rationale was encountered toward the end of 1945. A sizable minority of Americans, when asked why they were buying war bonds, replied, "To bring the boys back home." People who wanted their loved ones returned quickly from Europe or the South Pacific thought they could contribute to their goal by buying bonds; they thought to supply the government with the funds needed for transportation expenses.

Similar attitudes, held even by many college-educated people, were evident in 1962. About one-fifth of all people, when asked about a possible reduction of income taxes, argued, "It can't be done." Some people said, "Cuba, Berlin, and the cold war cost money; the money has to come from somewhere." Others said

---

among five suggested uses of money saved through disarmament:

Surveys Conducted in 1960–1961	*Ranked as First Choice*
Increase public welfare programs	30%
Build schools, highways	23
Reduce government debt	24
Reduce income taxes	16
Increase foreign aid	3
Not ascertained	4
	100%

simply, "We can't afford a tax cut," the reason being the necessity for large defense as well as domestic nondefense expenditures. The extreme point of view is represented by one respondent who said that the tax reduction plan "jeopardizes national safety." Usually, references to vital obligations of the government were voiced in less emotional tones.[3]

Since government budgets are viewed as subject to the same rules as private budgets, the true relation between government spending and private spending is often not seen. We may refer to survey findings made as early as during World War II (see Ref. 1, pp. 45ff.). "Suppose taxes are raised, what will happen to prices then?" survey respondents were asked at that time. Relatively few people saw that higher taxes meant taking money away from people and therefore tended to reduce the demand for goods. According to a more common view, taxes were seen as items of costs; the higher the taxes, the more business would have to charge for its products. The most prevalent view, of course, was that there was no connection between taxes and prices.

On the whole, people do strive for some understanding of the manifold effects of government expenditures, but frequently they are not successful. It does not follow, however, that concentrated efforts to bring forth a better understanding must remain unsuccessful. It may be difficult but surely not impossible to provide the public with some understanding of the fundamental differences between government budgets and private budgets. As I argued in 1962, "If a tax cut is enacted, the government has the added task of informing and educating the public about the reasons for its action."[4]

ATTITUDES TOWARD TAXES

A situation that prevails for a long time is rarely considered burdensome. We get accustomed even to bad things which, at the beginning, gave rise to complaints and opposition. This process of habituation characterizes attitudes toward taxes. Although the

[3] The proportion of people mentioning this type of argument was somewhat lower in 1963 than in 1962. Extensive public discussion of the tax cut led to some reduction in the number of people who said, "It can't be done."

[4] Testimony by George Katona before Joint Economic Committee of Congress, Aug. 8, 1962. *Hearings on the State of the Economy and Policies for Full Employment*, p. 73.

American people do grumble about taxes, especially when filing their tax reports each spring, there was very little dissatisfaction with taxes in the late 1950s, even on the part of upper-income people. When, for the first time during the recession of 1958, survey respondents were asked about a reduction in income taxes,[5] favorable reactions to the plan could be elicited on the basis of one argument only—to overcome the recession and reduce unemployment. But the notion that the high tax rates represented an enduring brake on economic growth had few adherents at that time. In the summer of 1961, approximately one-half of all people called a tax cut a good idea in reply to a direct question, again primarily as an anti-recession weapon. Yet one-half of the people thought it a bad idea either because in their opinion a recession did not threaten or because we could not afford lower taxes. The idea of lowering taxes did not originate with taxpayers in 1962. When President Kennedy proposed it and many people became aware of the experts' approval of the proposal, people's attitudes and opinions underwent some change.

When asked in 1961 what should be done if government expenses on arms and defense should decline substantially because of progress toward international disarmament (a question cited above), only 10 per cent of all respondents thought spontaneously of reducing income taxes. When such a reduction was proposed as one of five possible measures, only 16 per cent ranked it as their first choice and an additional 21 per cent as their second choice (see footnote 2). In the same year, in a different survey, close to 30 per cent advocated an increase in income-tax rates in answer to a question in which the need for increasing defense expenditures was suggested. Acceptance of the *status quo* appeared even more pronounced regarding taxes than regarding the government debt; at that time more people considered it urgent to reduce the debt than to reduce taxes.

On the other hand, there is some evidence from surveys conducted in 1951 that shortly after a tax increase many people complained about the new level of taxes. Changes in opinions also became apparent in 1961–1962. After President Kennedy proposed a general tax cut, in the fall of 1962, 74 per cent of people with some opinion (and 64 per cent of all people) called a tax cut a good idea

[5] See the author's proposal of tax refunds, made in 1958, in Ref. 2, pp. 224ff.

as against 47 and 42 per cent, respectively, a year earlier. In 1962, in contrast to the summer of 1961, relatively few people argued that a tax cut was needed to help the country get out of the recession. A somewhat greater number, but still only a minority, said that a tax cut was needed to raise purchasing power. But the majority of those who called the tax cut a good idea made no reference to its possible effects on the economy. They explained their opinion by saying that taxes were too high or by giving selfish reasons (for instance, "I would be glad to pay less taxes"). The sharp increase in replies of this kind between 1961 and 1962 indicates that a desire for lower taxes could easily be aroused by public discussion.

Probably as a result of continuous public debate, there was some small change in people's understanding of the relation of a tax reduction to economic conditions in 1963. In the fall and winter of 1963 the following questions were asked in the Survey Research Center's nationwide surveys: "In your opinion, will a cut in income taxes have any effect on business conditions or employment?" (If "Yes") "What kind of effect?" In reply, 44 per cent of all people and 57 per cent of people with incomes over $10,000 said that the effect would be beneficial, and hardly anyone said that it would be harmful. However, many people answered "no effect" or were unable to give any reply, illustrating the widespread lack of understanding of the proposal. Again, the idea that the tax cut might raise demand and purchasing power was the most frequent reason given by those who believed that it would improve business conditions.

In attempting to summarize public attitudes toward taxes, deficits, and government spending, it is possible to argue that relatively few people are well informed. The opinions of many people lack firmness and stability, and even consistency. There are many people who in one context opt for tax increases—for instance, in discussing heightened international tensions—and in another context say they want lower taxes.

Yet there are also indications of striving for understanding of the budgetary problems of the government. The relationship between deficits and private spending poses difficult technical problems. Conflict between valuing thrift and mistrusting those living beyond their means, on the one hand, and believing that increased spending is beneficial to the economy, on the other hand, increases the difficulties of understanding. Conflict between individualism and statism may also play a role, albeit a smaller one. Under these circumstances it is not surprising that full cognitive congruence is often not achieved. Nevertheless, many people appear to have learned something during the postwar years about the function of government spending. Also, lack of stability and of congruence is not necessarily disadvantageous; in some cases, flexibility reflects the first step toward the acquisition of better understanding.[6]

[6] We shall return to the discussion of the reduction of income taxes in 1964 in Chap. 28. It may suffice to recall here that positive action on the part of the government, such as the tax cut, is viewed favorably by very many consumers, who feel that the government has the power to improve economic conditions.

16

Cold War and International Tensions

Inflation has an adverse effect on the economy—this was found to be an almost unshakable conviction held by the great majority of the people. That deficits are bad is held by somewhat fewer people, since concern with deficits is much less widespread than concern with inflation. A third general value judgment of an enduring nature is that heightened international tensions have an adverse effect on domestic economic trends. This opinion is of more recent origin, but in the 1950s and early 1960s many more people were convinced of it than of the contrary.

These three beliefs are related to what most people see as the essential feature of good times: Times are good when standards of living are rising and when people can look forward to still higher standards of living in the future. The results of work and effort on the part of individuals are thought to be hampered by the three adverse developments: Inflation is seen to entail loss of purchasing power; deficits mean to many people that sooner or later they will have to pay, probably through higher taxes; war and international conflict are viewed as deterrents to planning ahead and improving one's life.

Two general roots of the belief that international conflict has an unfavorable economic impact may be distinguished. One is the abhorrence of uncertainty about the future. We pointed out before that for most people uncertainty represents a disturbing situation in which they are threatened by disagreeable surprises and cannot plan ahead. The cold war, for example, means for many people that our future depends on or is greatly influenced by what the Soviet leaders will do. Periods of heightened international tensions occur when uncertainty about the unpredictable adversary increases, and periods of relaxation in international affairs occur when the future course of Soviet action seems somewhat more predictable.

Secondly, people distinguish sharply between defense production and civilian production. The total capacity of the economy is thought to be limited—if the production of guns increases, the production of butter declines, and vice versa. Relatively few people are aware of underutilization of productive facilities or think of the possibility of expanding those facilities. Other more sophisticated people speak of disruption of civilian production by increased defense production and of higher taxes or inflation as a result of large defense expenditures. In either case, the chances of acquiring more and better consumer goods appear to worsen.

There exist contrary views, too. Relatively few people subscribe to the opinion that defense production makes the American economy move or is responsible for American prosperity. Some do, however, point out that "more money is put into circulation" by defense expenditures. Favorable effects of the cold war are recognized most frequently in such statements as "Defense production makes for more jobs." This answer was quite frequent in times of recession and in certain special areas of the country in which defense production predominates.

In addition to the minority who see favorable economic effects of the cold war, there are those who see no connection at all between the domestic economy and what happens on the international scene. As a rule, the proportion of those who see no connection has been relatively small when adverse foreign news has made headlines. When new conflicts arose—Berlin, Lebanon, Congo, etc.—or when Stalin or Khrushchev made threatening speeches, the opinion that the cold war made for bad times increased in frequency.

It was in the summer of 1951 that the question about the effects of "the way things are going in the world today, I mean the cold war and our relations with Russia, on business conditions here at home" was asked for the first time, and the frequency of the answer about the cold war making for bad times became apparent. Late in 1952, when the danger associated with the war in Korea was deemed much less threatening, favorable effects on the domestic economy were mentioned by an increased number of people. In later years the relation of the two answers varied according to the climate of international tensions.

In the fall of 1957 Russia's orbiting of the first Sputnik was viewed as unfavorable news. People were surprised and disturbed by the technical proficiency of the Soviets. It occurred to very few people that Russian achievements would stimulate great American expenditures on missiles and satellites and would thus bring forth scientific advances as well as employment for many people.

The opinion that the cold war affected the economy adversely was predominant over the opposite opinion to the largest extent in the summer and fall of 1960. Following the U-2 incident, the breakdown of the Paris summit conference, and Khrushchev's outburst at the UN meeting, there was much talk about increased defense expenditures, and yet many more people spoke of bad rather than good economic effects. Some people mentioned that they were worried about the international situation, and these worries were associated with reluctance to spend. In 1961, however, the proportion which said that the cold war made for "good times" increased, and the proportion which said that it made for "bad times" decreased. At that time, some people acknowledged that America's defense preparations had contributed to the quick recovery from the recession of 1960–1961. On the average in 1961–1962, prior to the Cuban crisis, 33 per cent of all people said that the cold war made for bad times, 20 per cent that the cold war made for good times, 27 per cent that they didn't know or were undecided, and 20 per cent that the cold war had no effect on domestic business.

No data are available on how the American people felt about this issue during the fortunately short period of the Cuban crisis in October, 1962, when the possibility of an atomic war loomed large. Whether or not this period had any similarities with the period after the outbreak of the Korean War, we do not know. But in a survey conducted in November and December, 1962, that is, after the settlement of the crisis, there was an increase in the proportion of people who said that the way things were going in the world had a favorable effect on the domestic economy. According to interview data, the majority of people not only felt relieved by the withdrawal of Russian missiles from Cuba but also spoke of a victory in the cold war and of improved prospects of peace. Improvement in people's economic outlook and even in personal financial expectations could be traced directly to the news about Cuba.

In August, 1963, at the time of the signing of the treaty banning atomic tests, 25 per cent of all respondents said that the world situation made for good times and discussed the favorable economic effects of the relaxation in international tensions. A similar proportion maintained the old position and spoke of adverse economic effects of the conflict with the Soviets. In the latter group the largest number were lower-income people. Among people with an annual income of over $7,500, 36 per cent said "good times" and 21 per cent "bad times" in reply to the question about which of the two conditions our relations with Russia would tend to produce.

Overwhelmingly, the American people approve of defense expenditures. Economizing has adherents in many fields, including space exploration, but hardly when defense is concerned. Many people say they are willing to make sacrifices and suggest tax increases should it be necessary to increase defense expenditures further. Defense is considered something we must have and for which we must pay. As such, it is differentiated sharply from things we like to have and for which we pay willingly. Although they are accepted as necessary and even approved, increased defense expenditures still remain an evil. Even people who recognize that defense spending relieves unemployment or helps to overcome recessions deprecate these good effects by saying that they provide only temporary good times or temporary improvements in the economy.

Scholars have given some thought recently to the economic effects of disarmament. No doubt a substantial reduction in armament expenditures would give rise to great problems in the domestic economy, although the experience with reconversion in 1945–1946 is most reassuring. In one respect the prospects are clear and anxiety may be allayed. The American people would not lose their heads and would not turn pessimistic in the event of a sizable cut in arms expenditures. As mentioned in the last chapter, when asked directly, people proposed a variety of urgent civilian expenditures by the government which they felt should take the place of defense expenditures. The proportion of those who would like the savings to be used for debt reduction is not insignificant but hardly large enough to exert much influence. The fact that prosperity is not associated by the people with high defense expenditures augurs well for the time when a cut in those expenditures may be possible.

Public attitudes toward the economic effects of defense expenditures may be viewed as a process of the generalization of affects. Unfavorable and threatening developments, such as heightened international tensions, are seen to have unfavorable consequences. Because of its hold on people's emotions, this generalization appears to influence people's thinking to a larger extent than news about increases in production and employment due to rising armament expenditure.

We conclude that the feeling of security which makes for increased consumer spending results not only from a confident assessment of personal financial prospects, closely linked with the prospects of the entire economy, but also from what transpires on the international scene. International conflict and uncertainty about international prospects make for hesitation, postponement of cherished plans, and waiting for better times. When, on the other hand, a relaxation of international tensions is seen, many people feel ready to proceed with their spending plans. This last reaction was particularly pronounced after the solution of the Cuban missile crisis, when American action provided relief from frustration.

17

Social Cognition

In the last five chapters we have discussed consumers' modes of thinking regarding some major issues of our times. Views about personal financial prospects, the general economic outlook, inflation, government spending, and the cold war were studied separately as is appropriate for each of these important aspects of public opinion. Yet the subjects whose views on differant issues were studied were the same—the American people in the late 1950s and early 1960s. Unifying principles of organization should then emerge, irrespective of what issue is analyzed. In this chapter we shall search for such principles of public apprehension of major issues.

Scientific psychology developed originally as the psychology of the individual. When, more recently, social psychology emerged, it evolved primarily as a psychology of the group. In small face-to-face groups—the family or a work group, for instance—as well as in larger social groups—such as the employees of a corporation—the relation of the individual to the group and problems of group belonging and group influence were studied. Demographic groups, such as all businessmen or all young people, remained on the whole the object of sociological rather than psychological studies. Concern with the dynamics of perceiving, learning, and reacting by unorganized masses was noticeably absent in most studies. The psychology of all the people in a country remained for a long time in the realm of literature or was the subject matter of nonquantitative essays consisting of the observations of imaginative thinkers and writers rather than of measurements by scholars. More recently public-opinion research, making use of the survey method, has provided some data of this type; yet in analyzing the factors shaping economic attitudes, we are treading fairly virgin soil.

Learning and cognition are concepts of individual psychology. In a certain sense these terms are rightfully restricted to the individual. He alone is capable of learning. Saying that a group learns is a metaphor, implying that there is some uniformity in the learning of all individuals belonging to the group. This statement indicates a special province of sociopsychological studies, namely, the examination of the similarities and the differences in the information acquired by group members. We shall be concerned mainly with the uniform features of the learning process among millions of unorganized consumers.

Cognition is the process of acquiring information and knowledge. The term *knowledge* is used in the sense of knowing what has happened in the environment rather than in the sense of exact or scientific knowledge. In the original sense of the term, cognition is contrasted to emotion and volition. It is commonplace to say, however, that there is hardly any knowledge lacking affective connotations. Most significant information we acquire, we usually either favor and approve or oppose and disapprove. Still the cognitive processes have a specific meaning. These are the processes through which an individual or a people acquire their image of the environment both in fairly general terms regarding the relation of a person to his world and in specific terms regarding the meaning of, say, prosperity, depression, inflation, or deficits. These images result from a selective crystallization of past experiences as influenced by attitudes and expectations.

The principles of social cognition regarding economic matters that will be enumerated and illustrated in this chapter are far from final. They represent a first attempt to bring order to a difficult and much neglected area. The findings discussed here are mostly the same as those presented in the previous chapters. What is new is the organization of the findings. Therefore in presenting each of the principles of social cognition, we shall refer to instances of supporting evidence which we have already discussed.

1. Generalization of Affect

The first principle of social cognition concerns the spread of affect. The operation of this principle was first noted in 1945–1946, when surveys indicated that most people considered it inconceivable that the wonderful news—the end of World War II, victory—could have anything but favorable economic consequences. In simplest terms, what is considered to be good is seen as having good effects, and what is considered to be bad is seen as having bad effects. More specifically, under the influence of good developments, spirits rise and gratification of wants becomes easier; contrariwise, unfavorable developments make for caution and postponement of purchases.

In listing examples of generalization of affect we start with very big news but mention developments of lesser importance as well.

A. The end of World War II was seen as something which would have to produce good consequences and could not cause such bad things as recession and unemployment.

B. The threat of war, heightened international tensions (e.g., the U-2 incident, Berlin, Congo) are seen as unfavorable developments that cannot stimulate prosperity. On the other hand, the relaxation of international tensions (e.g., the end of the Cuban crisis late in 1962) results in greater reassurance and the feeling of being able to plan ahead or to carry out one's plans.

C. In the fall of 1957, the first Sputnik was seen as a great achievement of our enemy and, therefore, as unfavorable news. The reaction was one of pessimism rather than optimism that the Sputnik would lead to increased American space efforts and thereby contribute to prosperous business conditions.

D. Inflation is thought to be bad; therefore, in the view of most people, rising prices must have unfavorable effects on one's own as well as on the country's development.

E. News about rising interest rates was seen in 1957 as bad news, because for many years easy money had been associated with good times and because interest charges were considered by some people as cost items. Therefore the widely noted news about rising interest rates contributed to pessimistic attitudes.

F. The long steel strike in 1959, definitely bad news, gave rise to pessimistic expectations.

We do not argue that every person is subject to the principle of generalization of affect. In 1945–1946, for example, most economics experts predicted recession and unemployment, and they did have some followers. Also, as noted in Chapter 16, there were always some people who envisaged favorable economic effects of rearmament, although many of them spoke of the favorable effects as being temporary. Nevertheless it remains true that the emotional connotation of news spreads and appears to be contagious. Uniformity of action results primarily from many people feeling the same way about new developments. Thus many people felt that the increase in interest rates represented an adverse development, while knowledge of what had actually happened and how it would affect business was limited.

2. Organization and Polarization of News

Isolated items of information are rarely influential and are quickly forgotten. Information that is influential with many people over longer periods is organized around some major issues or around their affective tone. Rarely do many people mention both favorable and unfavorable business news at the same time; according to whether they feel that business conditions are improving or deteriorating, only good news or only bad news are salient to them.

In studying public notions about the complex problems of government finance and fiscal policy, we mentioned some instances of absence of resolution and congruence. But in most areas, and especially in evaluating business trends or in recongnizing recovery or recession, the picture is colored by only one hue at a time.

Instead of noticing a number of diverse economic developments, people usually organize the news around a central point. There were times when inflation served this purpose, and economic news was salient only when it had that as its focus. At other times unemployment had the organizing function. International tensions or presidential elections, when in the center of attention, tend to suppress other news. Such a polarization effect was clearly noticeable in the fall of 1960 when Kennedy's election, rather than the impending recession, was the most salient news; the economic expectations of consumers did not deteriorate at that time.

3. Habituation

One form of change in attitudes or opinions, that is, one form of learning, is getting accustomed to things. Habituation to higher prices was first observed in 1951–1952. In the first half of 1950 and early in 1951 rising prices were big news and were reacted to by hoarding; after a while, when prices did not continue to advance rapidly, people got accustomed to the new price level and ceased to complain about "high prices." As we said, only what is new is news, and when the same kind of news continues over prolonged periods, it ceases to be news. Examples of habituation noted at different times were:

A. *To higher price levels.* Observed in 1952 as well as in 1962–1963.

B. *To good business news.* Records in GNP, national income, sales, etc., were not salient in 1956–1957.

C. *To bad business news.* The threat of unemployment loomed much larger in the public mind in the winter of 1957–1958 than in the spring of 1958, although actually it had hardly lessened by then. (There is much stronger support from survey data for A, B, and D than for C.)

D. *To taxes.* Following an increase in tax rates people say, "Taxes are too high." Some years later spontaneous complaints about taxes cease to occur, and people no longer seem aware of being hurt by taxes. What is with us for many years becomes the normal thing. (To be sure, it was shown in 1962 that it was possible to reawaken the old feeling about taxes.)

4. Slowness and Gradualness of Social Learning

We have encountered significant instances of the absence of social learning: The notions that inflation is a bad thing and that international tensions have unfavorable economic consequences have hardly changed over two decades. Sudden learning, through an abrupt reorganization of people's "cognitive map," may also occur both in individuals and among masses of people. Under the impact of very great events (e.g., outbreak of war), consumer thinking may change both suddenly and radically. Also several severe shocks may, and have in the past in many countries, disorganize and radically alter consumer behavior. Think, for instance, of the bank runs in the United States during the Great Depression. But on the whole, and especially in times of peace, masses of people change their opinions and attitudes very slowly and gradually. The development of new stereotypes is a long-drawn-out process. The slowness and gradualness with which masses of people become cognizant of important information represents one of the most important characteristics of social learning. It can be illustrated by many examples that are significant in a mass consumption economy:

A. *Expected price movements.* As reported in Chapter 14, during the first years after World War II the majority of consumers expected prices to rise for a short while but to return later to their original level. The reasoning that "what goes up must come down" was characteristic of that period. Public attitudes changed gradually between 1952 and 1959, and slowly the new notion of an inflationary age developed. People learned that they were living in a period in which prices were advancing, that five years from now prices would be higher than now, ten years from now higher than five years from now, etc. Slowly people became aware that, not temporary factors associated with the war, but rather certain enduring features of our age kept pushing prices up, even though it was not clearly understood what those features were.

Similarly, the relative price stability (lessened inflationary pressures), evident to the experts after 1959, has only very slowly and gradually begun to influence public opinion and indeed has not yet made a great impact on consumer thinking. For instance, at a time when the President of the United States stated in his Economic Report that "Prices have been essentially stable for five years; this has broken the inflationary psychology" (January 21, 1963), relatively few consumers agreed with him. Learning by the masses of such new developments appears to be much slower than many experts believe.

B. *Impossibility of a deep depression.* It took from 1945 to 1955 before American consumers acquired the conviction that a depression like the one we had in the 1930s could not happen again. Gradually more and more people learned that the government was able to cope with a deep depression. Since 1955–1956, when over three-fourths of the people held this conviction rather firmly, there has been no substantial change in belief.

C. *Probability of recurring recessions.* After the recession of 1957–1958 consumers learned, quite rapidly in this instance, that "recessions are with us" and that "we don't know how to avoid them." The relatively short intervening time before the 1960–1961 recession and the fairly high rate of unemployment between the two recessions, as well as after the second one, accelerated the learning process.

D. *Income expectations and education.* We reported in Chapter 12 that in our society income is a function of both age and education; young people may look forward to income gains over approximately three decades, and these gains are much larger for well-educated people than for people with little education. The people themselves have learned of these relationships. During the last decade more and more people slowly became convinced of the influence of education on incomes.

E. *Attitudes toward installment credit.* It will be shown in Chapter 22 that the American people's attitudes toward installment buying became increasingly favorable from 1947 to 1960. This change was partly the result of having had a good experience or of knowing about others who had had good experiences with buying on credit. Partly it was the result of opponents of credit dying out—older people were always least favorably disposed toward debt; but, as those who approved of credit buying became older, they usually maintained their favorable attitudes. In 1950 opposition to buying on the installment plan was quite common among people fifty years of age; in 1960 a similar preponderance of opposition began at around sixty years of age. The notion that installment credit was the best way of acquiring certain kinds of goods when they were needed spread slowly and gradually.

F. *Popularity of investment in common stock.* Here again we refer to data that will be presented later (Chapter 21). Right after World War II people overwhelmingly considered common stock risky, speculative, and suitable only for the rich or for insiders; the recollection of the crash of 1929 was still quite vivid. These attitudes changed slowly, primarily under the influence of rising stock prices. The change was not radical; most of the many people who acquired common stock for the first time in the 1950s remained cautious in their attitudes. Stock ownership was favored first of all for the sake of diversifying one's assets. Thus stocks became suitable for only one part, and usually the smaller part, of one's assets. The newly acquired opinions and attitudes gradually influenced people's actions.

G. *Attitudes toward compact cars.* According to survey data, people's attitudes toward compact cars were favorable right from the time of their introduction. But many people with favorable attitudes hesitated for quite a while before they actually purchased compact cars. It was some years before satisfaction with the available models and their prices expressed itself in sustained large demand.

To summarize, change in the attitudes of the masses is slow and gradual. The acquisition of higher income, and of more consumer goods or financial assets, is also a gradual process for most people. The development of new wants and desires likewise follows gradually, because people's level of aspiration, when raised with achievement, is somewhat higher but not much higher than their present level of living.

5. Search for Understanding

As we said in connection with the organization of news, what comes to people as an isolated piece of information rarely exerts great influence on them. Real learning does not take place in the absence of some framework within which to place the new information. People try to understand what is going on, and they acquire new opinions and attitudes when they feel they know why the new way of thinking is "right."

In speaking of the masses' understanding of economic developments, we do not use the term in the sense in which an expert in the field would use it. As we have said, economists have no reason at all to be satisfied with what consumers in general have learned of economic principles. Understanding in our context means the acquisition of simple causal notions. Development A is understood if it is attributed to cause B and if that cause appears sufficient to justify the new development. Thereby, for most people the problem appears to be solved and closure is achieved. Business recovery is understood when it is attributed, for instance, to increased government spending; a slump in car buying is understood when the models offered are thought to be unattractive; inflation is understood when its "cause," for instance, large wage increases, is known.

The fifth major feature of social cognition, then, is not the understanding of economic developments or concepts, but rather the search for such an understanding. People constantly look for simple reasons which make for clarity, satisfy their curiosity, and reduce their feelings of uncertainty. They try to achieve what for them represents a solution of a problem, even if, from the expert's point of view, it represents a misunderstanding or at best a partial understanding.

A few further references to findings discussed in previous chapters may be in order. We have shown that a depression such as we had in the 1930s is generally thought to be impossible, *because,* in the opinion of the masses, government or business has learned how to cope with it. Recessions, however, are thought to recur at short intervals, *because* no mechanism exists to avert them. Or, as we shall show later, installment buying is considered a good thing, *because* paying for an article while using it makes sense.

Sometimes, however, masses of people are capable of rather remarkable feats of understanding. The American consumers thus arrived at a sharp distinction between runaway inflation and creeping inflation. To be sure, they have no knowledge of the variety of factors that create the difference, and most people are not capable of giving a precise account of it. They have been aided by the association between runaway inflation and war, on the one hand, and between creeping inflation and peace, on the other. Nevertheless, it must be cited as evidence for the sensible nature of consumers that they learned to distinguish a slow though distasteful upward movement of prices from inevitable and rapid price increases and responded differently to the two.

When the search for understanding is not successful, people fail to maintain an opinion. The major reason why people said in good times that an upswing would not last is that they did not see any factor that would sustain it. A peg is needed to which to attach one's notions; if it is not found, doubts arise about the validity of the notion.

Search for understanding represents, then, a mechanism aiming at congruence of opinions on diverse matters. Quite often, however, congruence is not achieved. In some of these instances, the people themselves are not aware that a number of their opinions do not fit with others. Since the process of search for understanding is not carried to its conclusion, conflicting notions may be maintained side by side. For instance, compact cars were greeted favorably, because they were seen as economical in performance. (Other factors relevant for appraising compact cars will be mentioned in Chapter 23.) At the same time, and unrelated to the interest in economy, desires for a variety of expensive features of cars remained pronounced. The public was aware of no conflict between the two.

The struggle to understand what is going on can perhaps be best illustrated by instances which to the expert represent misunderstanding. We mentioned before that in 1962–1963 the most common reason for opposing a tax cut was that, with reduced revenues, the government would not be able to meet its necessary expenditures (defense, welfare programs, etc.). The analogy between private budgets and government budgets is most powerful, because for many people it solves intricate, puzzling, and otherwise ununderstandable problems of government finance. The notion that the more spent on guns, the less can be spent on butter likewise represents a carry-over from the solution of familiar personal problems to the solution of a seemingly similar although actually somewhat different national problem. The closure having been achieved, it shapes opinions and attitudes and becomes difficult to alter by rational arguments.

The stock-exchange crash of May, 1962, was attributed by many people to speculation and manipulation by insiders (Chapter 21). Here again a simple solution was found for a dissonant situation, namely, a sharp decline in stocks at a time when the business outlook was seen as favorable: Stock-market developments were seen as not being related to business developments. From this solution of the problem followed notions and attitudes of importance.

CAUSES OF SIMILARITY IN ATTITUDES AND ATTITUDE CHANGES

American consumers are unorganized and, in contrast to business-men, do not constitute a specific group that is aware of common interests. Regional differences as well as differences in income or class and age should make for diversity of opinions and reactions. Absence of leaders and lack of specific information about how other consumers think and act make it improbable that uniformity in opinions or behavioral patterns should result either from group belonging or imitation and contagion. Nevertheless, opinions and attitudes toward personal financial prospects, the business outlook, inflation, government finances, and the economic consequences of the cold war were found to have been similar, and to have changed similarly, among very many people. Analogous findings will be presented in later parts of this book from studies of spending and saving patterns. Because of the existence of minority views and individual differences, the term uniformity is not used in any exact sense. But the existence of a very large modal group has made it possible for us to speak of *the* opinion of the American consumer, as, for instance, when we reported that inflation was considered to be bad or that severe depression was no longer deemed possible.

One important reason for this situation is to be found in the prevalence of the same dynamic principles of social cognition among masses of people. In the 1950s and the early 1960s the principles described in this chapter prevailed fairly generally among millions of people and shaped their opinions and attitudes. The extent of similarity in American consumers' behavior patterns must therefore be attributed both to the uniformity of stimuli, that is, to the fact that substantially the same information reaches very many people at the same time, and to the uniformity of their cognitive processes.

With this answer we have, of course, not solved the question of why the five principles of social cognition operate and result in similarity of attitudes and in changes of attitudes among masses of people at the same time. Yet we cannot pursue the problem further; psychology has made much greater progress in describing people's behavior than in explaining the causes of their behavior. Although we are far from having solved the problem, we have made progress. The principles of social cognition have a predictive value that exceeds the predictive value of data on consumer behavior alone. Knowing something about the origin of changes in consumer attitudes permits us to discern and predict probable reactions to new developments about which behavioral data are not yet available. Information on habituation and the slowness of social learning, for instance, yields conclusions about reactions to contemplated measures of economic policy, which conclusions do not emerge from a description of prevailing opinions and attitudes alone.

We have not yet finished the discussion of consumers' ways of thinking and acting. Patterns of consumer behavior must be explored in further areas. Up to now we have dealt with attitudes toward income and attitudes toward public issues. In the next two parts of the book we shall turn to private finance, that is, the allocation of consumers' money outlays to either spending or saving and among different forms of expenditures and saving. The principles of consumer behavior that will emerge from those studies will be similar to the ones set forth in this chapter. In public as well as private finance the consumer functions as a conservative, discriminating, and sensible person.

PART FIVE

Saving

18

To Save or to Spend?

Economists usually begin their analysis of consumer behavior with the equation $Y = C + S$: Consumer income is equal to consumer spending plus consumer saving. The equation implies (1) that there is an unequivocal difference between spending and saving, and (2) that the major consumer choice consists of deciding how much to spend and how much to save out of income. When we turn to the question of how consumers themselves see the alternatives available to them, we find that neither of the two assumptions seem to fit. From the point of view of consumers, a third proposition connected with the original distinction must also be contradicted. This is the proposition that saving consists of refraining from spending and represents therefore a form of abstinence.

WHAT IS SAVING?

Let us begin by listing the various major items that are usually included under *personal saving* in the presentation of the nation's economic accounts by the U.S. Department of Commerce and indicate what those items represent to the average American consumer.[1]

[1] In this discussion we shall disregard the "wealthy" people, who are primarily investors rather than savers. We shall study their attitudes in Chap. 20. We shall also disregard saving (and borrowing) on the part of unincorporated businessmen, who likewise invest and have strong incentives to plough back profits, although most of them are far from wealthy. And of course, personal saving, by definition, excludes corporate saving.

First there is *contractual saving,* resulting from contractual obligations entered into at a previous time. The payment of life insurance premiums and repayment of debts (mortgage debt, install-ment debt, etc.) are the major forms of those contractual obligations that are considered as saving. They are fulfilled as a matter of routine requiring no genuine decision making. To be sure, the consumer may default on his obligations, but this happens so rarely that it is not worth considering in a discussion of present-day con-sumer behavior.

The repayment of installment debt is viewed by most debtors as an expenditure. As we shall point out in Chapter 22, by buying a car on time people feel that they are paying for it out of income— to be sure, not out of the income of any one year, but out of the income of two or even three years. Life insurance is likewise viewed by the great majority of people as an expenditure rather than a saving, namely, as a fee paid for the sake of being protected against unexpected adversity. Only a small minority carry life insurance as a form of saving. Repayment of mortgage debt is seen by some people as equivalent to rent payments and therefore as an expendi-ture, although many are aware of the fact that by repaying their mortgage they enhance their assets. Even so, this accumulation of assets is usually distinguished in their mind from saving money.

When consumers buy a house with a mortgage debt, or durable goods on the installment plan, they make genuine decisions. Usually these are decisions to buy certain goods, that is, decisions to spend rather than decisions to borrow. In the national accounts, of course, the incurrence of consumer debt appears as negative saving. Since the value of durable goods bought is not added to savings, the result is that those years in which many cars are bought on credit, and credit extension exceeds debt repayment, show up in the national accounts as years of substantial dissaving.

Social security and private pension accumulations, whether paid by an individual or his employer, are rarely considered to be money saved. In most cases the employer's share is entirely disregarded when personal finances are considered. This is not generally true of the individual's share. Yet frequently the take-home pay, which excludes the amounts withheld from wages and salaries for taxes, social security, and pensions, constitutes the starting point for con-sidering how much money shall be spent.

There remains what may be called discretionary saving, which most people do consider saving. Additions to deposits in banks, savings and loan associations (which are seen as banks by most people), and credit unions, as well as income used to purchase bonds (mostly United States savings bonds) and stock, represent, in the view of most people, the means of accumulating reserve funds. Withdrawals from those liquid assets, for any purpose other than transfer to another asset, are seen as a diminution of reserve funds or savings.

In order to find out what people consider as saving, respondents in representative samples were asked: "During the last twelve months or so did you people save any money, or did you decrease your savings, or did you just break even?" Those who said they had saved or decreased their savings were asked what they had done. In reply, most people referred exclusively to what has been described in the last paragraph as discretionary saving. Very few respondents mentioned life insurance, repayment of debt, or incurrence of debt.

It does not follow, of course, that every addition to bank deposits is considered an amount saved. When survey respondents were asked what they would do with some "extra money" or when they were asked in 1962–1963 what they would do with additional cash resulting from a tax cut, their replies indicated that checking accounts, and sometimes savings accounts as well, are often seen as temporary depositories of funds, prior to their use. "I'd bank it until I decide what I want" was a fairly common answer to the question on the probable use of money from a tax cut in 1963. The use of the term *save* to represent a short-term action may be illustrated by such answers as: "We would save it toward a vacation next year"; "Leave it in the bank to use for travel to see my children"; "I need new teeth; I'll save the tax money for that."

Parts of checking and savings accounts represent, then, funds of maneuver rather than savings or reserve funds. Many people who are not familiar with the concept of liquidity nevertheless have some notion about not wanting to be without some readily available money. Others want to have their savings less readily available, so they will not be so easily tempted to spend. In whatever form the savings, a large share is subjectively earmarked for specific purposes and is therefore not considered liquid. These considerations have little to do with the technical definition of what is and what is not liquid.

THE PURPOSES OF SAVING

For what are savings earmarked, or what are the purposes of saving? People in all walks of life talk freely about the purposes for which they save, for which they would like to save, or for which they feel they ought to save. Although they express themselves in many different ways, most of the reasons they gave for saving may be classified in one of the following categories:[2]

1. *For emergencies.* Upper-income as well as lower-income people say that the future is uncertain; rainy days may come, something may happen which will impair one's earning potential or require large expenditures. Therefore reserve funds are necessary. But even when unemployment occurs or large medical expenses have to be paid, savings are used grudgingly, because the worse the current situation, the greater looms the need to maintain reserve funds for future emergencies.

2. *For retirement.* Concern with retirement or with money needed for one's old age is frequently expressed even by people in their thirties. The frequency does, of course, increase with age.

3. *For children and family needs.* Some people mention the education of their children specifically, while others say that in a family with children there are always years with large expenditures, and it is therefore necessary to have money in reserve. This third purpose of saving is mentioned less frequently than the first two; the fourth is mentioned least frequently.

4. *For other purposes.* Some people save to buy a house, to buy a business, to buy durable goods, or to pay for vacations and other trips.

Saving in order to earn additional income in the form of interest or dividends and saving in order to bequeath money to one's heirs represent purposes that are conspicuous by their absence in the discussion of the average consumer. It does not follow that people are not concerned with the interest or dividends they receive—we shall come back to this point later—but it is apparent that most

[2] Earlier data were reported in Katona, "Attitudes toward Saving and Borrowing," *Consumer Installment Credit,* part 2, vol. 1, pp. 450–487, National Bureau of Economic Research and Federal Reserve Board, 1957. See also Ref. 2, Chap. 7. Substantially the same findings were made in the early 1960s as in the 1950s.

people do not save for the specific purpose of enhancing their income in later years.

The accumulation of savings for the purposes mentioned constitutes a highly valued goal. The American people do not speak of saving as a negative act—as refraining or abstaining from using money. Savings are associated with important values and are seen as a goal for which it is worthwhile to strive. Not saving is regretted and sometimes considered morally wrong. The high value attached to thrift has puritan undertones that persist among many people despite the much-lamented "thing-mindedness" of our age.

SAVING VERSUS SPENDING

No one can deny that there is great concern with material goods in our society. We have stressed the prevalence of striving toward a better standard of living and shall later discuss the process of upgrading specific possessions. Are the new findings about the positive value attached to saving and the accumulation of reserve funds in conflict with the concern with more and better consumer goods? Not in the eyes of most American consumers. Larger reserve funds are viewed as part and parcel of a better standard of living. People strive for a better home and car, more durable goods, occasional travel, fun and enjoyment, as well as security through the accumulation of reserve funds. Most people are not aware of a sharp distinction between owning many things and owning financial reserves; they want both and take steps toward both goals.

Different ways of using one's money are often in conflict. Determining priorities among several goals constitutes crucial decisions, even on the part of affluent people. To buy a new car and to build a second bathroom, for instance, may both be urgent wishes of the family; or both a better and larger refrigerator and increased reserve funds may be pressing desires of another family. The point is that conflict between spending and saving plays the same role as conflict between two expenditures; the first type of conflict is neither more common nor more fundamental than the second type. Consumer thinking in general is not correctly described by asserting that people first decide how much to spend and how much to save, and later decide on what to spend.

Many people are not aware of a conflict between spending and saving, although they do want to increase their savings and are at the same time eager to acquire more and newer and better consumer goods.[3] They fail to see a conflict because, as they readily acknowledge (with regret to be sure), they believe they are unable to save. Not only low-income people, but also some people in good financial condition report that buying what is absolutely necessary for them exhausts all that they earn. Extensive contractual obligations, including repayment of mortgage and other debt and life insurance premiums, are included in the necessary expenditures.

For our purposes, more important than this pushing aside of the conflict are the other methods by which consumers resolve the problem of desiring both to save more and to buy more things. One resolution is to do both. This sometimes becomes possible through an increase in income. At other times it is made possible by paying for expensive consumer goods on the installment plan.

That a sizable proportion of American consumers purchase large durable goods and add to their reserve funds during the same year was shown in an earlier statistical paper.[4] Undertaking both activities was found to be associated with income gains as well as with optimistic expectations. Discretionary saving was found to be subject to the same dynamic influences as discretionary expenditures. Since increased reserve funds and better or newer consumer goods are both highly valued goals, successful, confident, and optimistic people proceed toward achieving both. The distinction inherent in con-

[3] The extent of the prevailing desire to save is indicated, not only by questioning people about their attitudes toward saving, but also by studying their expressed intentions. Regarding most large consumer goods, many fewer people say they plan to buy them in the following year than actually do buy them. (This is hardly surprising since advance planning is never complete.) Regarding saving money, the opposite is true—more people say they plan to save in the following year than report the next year that they actually did save.

[4] See reference in footnote 2, above. The widely quoted statistical data showing that negative saving is very common among purchasers of durable goods have nothing to do with the relation of discretionary saving to the purchase of durables. The findings result from the great amount of installment buying and from the practice of regarding installment debt as negative saving; at the same time, as we have said before, saving in the usual definition excludes the value of the durable goods purchased. Sometimes, to be sure, saving is defined to include both the value of durables bought and the debt incurred; sometimes both are excluded, as in our definition of discretionary saving.

The year 1963 was one of the years in which many people added to their savings accounts and also increased their expenditures on durables, often through buying on the installment plan.

sumer discretion, between what people want to do with their money
and what they feel they must do cuts across the traditional distinction between spending and saving.

The notion that there is an inverse relation between saving and
spending is derived, of course, from the simple equation that income
equals spending plus saving. If we rewrite the equation to read that
income equals the sum of (1) discretionary spending, (2) other
spending, (3) discretionary saving, and (4) contractual and other
saving, new possibilities arise. The share of income devoted to (1)
may then increase without a corresponding reduction in the share
of (3). In prosperous times, in response to income increases, both
discretionary spending and discretionary saving may increase, while
in times of recession the response may be the opposite.[5]

In one important respect, however, there is validity to the view
of those who see the present-day thing-minded society as having an
adverse influence on saving. The result of the perceived urgency of
numerous wants for consumer goods, as well as for such services as
travel and recreation, is that the desire to save is frequently pushed
into the background and discretionary saving becomes residual.
Some people wait to see how much remains after diverse other
wants have been satisfied before they save. Because some motives
to spend are more immediate than the motives to save, saving is
postponed, and the postponement may be repeated over and over
again. But it should not be forgotten that there are other people
who carry out their plans to save. Much of discretionary saving is
not residual.

We shall show in Chapter 20 that dissatisfaction with the amounts
of savings or reserve funds is widespread—much more so than dissatisfaction with the standard of living. In neither case does satisfaction or dissatisfaction depend exclusively on what one has. Many
people with fairly large assets are found to be dissatisfied, and many
with quite small assets satisfied with the size of their reserve funds.
Felt needs and levels of aspiration may rise after an improvement
in one's living standards as well as after an accumulation of some
reserve funds. What has been called upgrading of consumer goods
has its parallel in savings.

[5] In contrast to the extensive information available on differences in consumer investment expenditures during different phases of the business cycle,
little is known about the influence of recession on saving behavior. For a discussion of this problem, see Ref. 2, pp. 109ff.

Thing-mindedness represents just one of several characteristics of our society that have been emphasized by the theorists who believe that in the post-World War II period Americans have not been concerned with saving and that therefore the extent of personal saving has been too small compared to the investment needs of the economy. Five additional and more specific arguments in support of the alleged insufficiency of saving will be discussed, and will be found wanting, in the next few chapters. It has been maintained that saving is curtailed because of

1. Widespread collective retirement arrangements (Chapter 19)
2. Inflation (Chapter 20)
3. The practice of buying on the installment plan (Chapter 22)
4. Low interest rates (Chapter 20)
5. The prevailing wealth (Chapter 20)

A study of each of these arguments will contribute to the understanding of consumer motivation.[6]

In this chapter, in which saving has been considered from a broad point of view, just a few words remain to be said about the relation of saving to the desire for security. The critics who argue that in today's allegedly materialistic society saving loses out forget that at the same time other critics assert that the society is security-minded and lacks ambition, risk taking, and entrepreneurship. The distinction between achievement orientation and security orientation has a weighty psychological foundation, and people of both types, as well as of many mixed types, are to be found in present-day American society. In analyzing motives to save we have pointed out that saving for a rainy day, which reflects concern with security, is ubiquitous. Yet the meaning of security has undergone some changes during the last few decades. At present most American families have extensive contractual obligations. A substantial share of their income

---

[6] Simon Kuznets, who is concerned about the adequacy of the rate of personal saving in relation to investment needs, presents an additional argument in support of the validity of this concern. He argues that because of persistent international tensions, "there is a continued sense of insecurity about the future." "Savings are essentially a stake in the economic future, and such stakes become less important when non-economic factors make the future uncertain" (*op. cit.*, p. 456). This argument is far from convincing. The empirical studies cited in Chap. 16 indicate that heightened international tensions most commonly result in the postponement of large discretionary expenditures; in consequence, residual saving might well be increased rather than decreased as the result of international crises.

is earmarked—either legally or by subjective commitment—for specific expenditures. Installment payments on a car or other goods must be met, and rent or mortgage debt as well as a variety of dues and fees must be paid every month. Most people are aware of these compelling needs which, together with necessary expenditures for food, use up a very large part of their income. Decline in income, then, is not just an inconvenience but a tragic occurrence. Security represents assurance that one will be able to meet the contractual obligations; insecurity represents a threat to the continuation of the way of life which is considered standard and normal. Security and savings are closely related, because the availability of some liquid reserve funds provides the assurance that contractual obligations will be fulfilled. Very frequently, then, concern with security does not represent a desire for a soft and easy life, or for relaxation and the enjoyment of good things, in preference to striving for improvement. Feeling secure about one's standard of living constitutes the basis for aspiring toward a better and more abundant life.

19

Saving for Retirement

The extension of collective security plans to provide retirement income represents one of the important economic changes introduced during the postwar years. By the early 1960s practically all members of the labor force participated in old-age, survivors, and disability insurance and were entitled to receive pensions during their retirement. At the same time, rather than becoming less valuable because of inflation, old-age insurance payments were made somewhat more adequate. In addition, private pension plans, quite rare before World War II, covered approximately 22 million people in the early 1960s and provided additional, sometimes substantial, benefits during retirement.[1] (In the majority of cases, however, some of the benefits, and at times all of them are lost if the employee changes employment.) We want to note here that some improvement has taken place in the situation of retired people,

[1] R. F. Murray, in the 43rd Annual Report of the National Bureau of Economic Research, 1963, pp. 20ff., summarizes the increase in private pension plans as follows:

	1950	1960	1970 (*Est.*)
Number covered in millions	9.8	21.6	34.0
Number of beneficiaries in millions	0.5	1.8	3.9
Assets accumulated in billion dollars	11.7	49.9	127.3

In 1960 old-age, survivors, and disability insurance and other federal, state, and local plans covered more than 80 million individuals. Most people covered by private pension plans were also covered under social security.

even though in the early 1960s there was still a sizable number of older people who had retired without the benefit of social security or pensions. Therefore, in the future, we may expect much greater improvements in the economic situation of older people than have yet occurred. Our present concern, however, is not with those who have already retired but rather with the impact of the greatly improved retirement prospects on the economic behavior, particularly regarding saving, of those people who are still working.

HYPOTHESES REGARDING THE IMPACT OF COLLECTIVE SECURITY PLANS

It has frequently been postulated that the growth of collective security arrangements retards individual saving and adversely influences individual incentive. This argument has been expressed, for instance, by L. J. Kalmbach, chairman of the board of the Massachusetts Mutual Life Insurance Company, as follows:

> It is very difficult to assess fully the long-range impact of this giant welfare program on savings habits and individual initiative. But I think we can assume, first, that, as the level of benefits has increased, more and more individuals have taken the attitude that it is not necessary for them to carry on savings programs, and, second, that this attitude would become more widespread with further increases in the general level of benefits. Anything of this nature which reduces the incentives for people to acquire a competence of their own, that spreads the feeling that the future is secure without any unusual efforts on their part, is something which can have adverse effects on our economic growth.[2]

Let us note that Mr. Kalmbach is not primarily concerned, nor am I, with changes in the aggregate amounts of savings. Individual saving in bank deposits, bonds, stocks, and life insurance might well be reduced in response to collective security arrangements; yet the total amounts saved each year might increase if the reserves from social security taxes and employers', as well as employees', contributions to pension plans exceed the reduction in personal saving.[3] The question at issue in the present context is whether dis-

[2] *Michigan Business Review*, p. 5, July, 1962.
[3] Benefits paid out by federal old-age insurance differ little from social security tax receipts; private pension plans, however, take in much more than they pay out because the beneficiaries represent, and will continue to represent

cretionary saving in banks, securities, and the like, has been reduced, or is bound to be reduced in the future, because collective security arrangements are substituted for it. That this is a question of people's motivations is clearly recognized by Mr. Kalmbach, who wrote of changes in individuals' *attitudes,* of reduced *incentives,* and of the *feeling* that the future is secure.

In our research we studied the problem as it relates to present-day American realities. The question of how people's motivations and behavior would be influenced if collective arrangements provided, after retirement, most or all of the income earned before retirement did not concern us. In the United States in the early 1960s insured people with private pensions expected to receive, on the average, less than one-half of their current income after retirement. This may be viewed as sufficient for minimal needs. People thus provided for may feel assured of not being destitute after retirement, even if they do not have private means or do not earn extra money through occasional work during retirement. Living with one's children or depending almost entirely on their help was the common fate of retired people as recently as a few decades ago. There is no argument that collective security plans have made it possible for many people to avoid this undesirable situation. The question is whether, in addition, collective security has influenced individual saving and individual incentives.

We may reformulate Mr. Kalmbach's conclusions in simpler terms and present them as Hypothesis No. 1 regarding the impact of collective security arrangements on the spending and saving practices of people not yet retired:

> Being assured of some resources after retirement, people spend more freely on the good things of life and concern themselves to a lesser extent with saving for retirement.

This is not the only possible hypothesis on the impact of improved old-age benefits. Hypothesis No. 2, postulating the opposite behavior, may be formulated as follows:

> Being assured of some, for most people insufficient, funds after retirement, the provision of adequate funds during old age no longer

---

for at least another ten years, a small proportion of the number of people covered (see footnote 1, above). The National Bureau estimates that saving through pension funds amounts to almost 3 per cent of personal income. A sizable proportion of the asset accumulation by pension funds has in recent years been invested in common stock.

appears an insurmountably difficult problem; being closer to the goal stimulates people to work harder to achieve the goal, and therefore collective retirement plans promote individual saving.

This hypothesis is derived from the goal-gradient hypothesis which assumes that effort is intensified the closer one is to one's goal; psychology has provided extensive support for this thesis through experiments with animals and humans. A related principle that is also pertinent and that has been found to prevail in economic behavior concerns the realistic, rather than fanciful, nature of common wants and desires. Goals that are believed to be attainable stimulate us to a much greater extent than improbable dreams. The confident expectation of reward makes for sustained effort to a much greater extent than fear or punishment. Finally, the theory of levels of aspiration must be cited in this context. Even if the amount of the pension offered by a private pension plan seemed enough for one's needs prior to participating in the plan, it may not appear so after it has been assured; aspirations may grow with success.[4]

Obviously the two hypotheses do not represent the only possible ones about the relation of collective retirement plans to individual saving. It is also conceivable, and is no doubt the case with some people, that retirement prospects have no impact whatsoever on spending and saving behavior, at least over short periods of time. Short-term considerations may be so powerful that they alone determine decisions about spending and saving.

It is probable that substantial differences prevail among different individuals and perhaps also among different groups of the population. Some individuals may be influenced by considerations subsumed under Hypothesis 1, while with others the motivational factors expressed in Hypothesis 2 may be more influential. Such complexities of human behavior make for difficulties in testing the hypotheses.

Certain findings, available for some time, seem more in accord with Hypothesis 2 than with Hypothesis 1. The first one, mentioned in the last chapter, is the frequent reference made by survey respondents to providing for old age and retirement as a purpose of saving. Just as many people called retirement an important reason for saving in the early 1960s as in the early 1950s, despite the spread

---

[4] The second hypothesis is also related to findings on the influence of wealth on saving, which will be discussed in Chap. 20.

of private pension plans in the intervening decade. Secondly, it has been found that all classes of the American people are concerned with how they will make out during retirement. This becomes true at an early age: Many people in their thirties speak of this as one of their worries or speak of making adequate provisions for retirement as one of their goals. The expression of this kind of concern becomes fairly general by the time the age of fifty is reached.

Until recently, very little evidence has been available concerning the impact of retirement expectations on people's saving behavior. Some data on the proportion of income put into life insurance by those people participating versus those not participating in private pension plans, as well as insured versus uninsured under social security, were collected by the Survey Research Center in 1957. The findings tended to support the second hypothesis or, at least, contradict the notion that improved retirement prospects are seen as substitutes for individual life insurance.[5]

Philip Cagan, of the National Bureau of Economic Research, utilized data collected in 1958 for other purposes (the sample was composed of subscribers to *Consumer Reports,* issued by Consumers Union, Inc.) to compare the savings of people who had with those of people who did not have private pensions. At the time of this writing Cagan's report has not yet been published—a preliminary and confidential draft was circulated in 1962—and therefore the following brief references are taken from the annual reports issued by the National Bureau of Economic Research. Comparison between the average saving ratios of people covered and people not covered under a private pension plan indicates that the former saved slightly more than the latter: On the average, saving in cash, savings accounts, and securities amounted to 2.8 per cent of income in the group with pension plans as against 2.1 per cent in the group without such plans; saving through life insurance, annuities, and equity in a house or other real estate amounted to 5.9 as against 5.7 per cent. These data do not prove much because there may be differences in the incomes of those people who have and those who do not have pension coverage, and that difference may account for the higher saving ratios of the first group. Yet other data appear to

[5] See the publication, *The Life Insurance Public,* issued in 1957 by the Institute of Life Insurance on the basis of Survey Research Center data. The findings were discussed by Katona in Ref. 2, pp. 98ff. It contains the first formulation of what has been presented here as the second hypothesis.

make it probable that the higher saving ratio is associated with coverage under a pension plan rather than with other characteristics that might cause a higher propensity to save. Thus no support is found for a substitution effect, and Cagan speaks of a recognition effect: "Realization of retirement needs and of the opportunities for financial independence opened up by a pension stimulate the motivation to save."[6]

In 1962–1963 the Survey Research Center, thanks to a grant from the Social Security Administration, undertook an extensive study to clarify the problem of the effect of retirement plans on saving behavior. The study was based on interviews with representative samples of all American consumers, consisting of close to 5,000 families. Of course, some of those in the sample are not relevant at all (for instance, the retired people), and others may not be truly relevant because they are young or because their behavior may be assumed to be atypical. (Single persons or people not in the labor force may think differently about retirement from family heads in the labor force.) There is ample reason for excluding also the lower-income people who have little discretion of action and rarely save. Therefore a *crucial group* was selected and defined as follows: Heads of complete families in the labor force, aged thirty-five to sixty-four (and not retired), with a family income of more than $3,000. The data reported in this chapter refer to this group.

HOW RETIREMENT PROSPECTS ARE SEEN

Before discussing the findings on the influence of retirement prospects, we must become acquainted with people's views and expectations about retirement. On the whole, consumers' financial expectations were found to be fairly short-range. When people were asked about future developments beyond about twelve months, in such financial areas as income, saving, or spending, it was most usual to get vague and imprecise expectations reflecting at best the direction of change, rather than precise data. Expectations about retirement appeared to be more definite than other long-range expectations studied in various surveys. Indecisive answers such as "don't know," "can't tell," or "never thought of this" were less frequent in response to questions about retirement than, for instance,

[6] *43rd Annual Report,* National Bureau of Economic Research, 1963, p. 23.

about the income people expected to receive in the following five or ten years.

In Chapter 12 we presented some data on the expected peak lifetime income, obtained by two fairly direct questions which implied strongly that the respondents should be able to answer them. And yet 35 per cent of the respondents replied that they could not tell when they would receive their highest annual income, and 40 per cent professed to be unable to say what the highest income they would ever earn might be. Similarly, when asked about what their income would be "ten years from now," the most precise answer obtained from a very large proportion of respondents was: "We shall make more at that time."

When the question was formulated in a more permissive form, the proportion that did not commit itself was larger still. The Survey Research Center asked, for instance, in 1961: "Nobody can be sure about his future income, but many of us have some idea about what we might be making; have you ever thought about what your family income might be, say, five years from now?" More than half of the respondents replied that they had never thought about the income they would earn in five years. To a follow-up question, "About how much do you think you will be making five years from now, that is, in 1966?" only 37 per cent gave a numerical answer that could be coded in broad brackets. By comparison, it may be mentioned that in surveys conducted each spring, a definite figure about the income expected during the following calendar year is obtained from more than two-thirds of the respondents.

It appears, then, that longer-range developments are surrounded by much uncertainty. It is not true that many people think in terms of lifetime earnings or of earnings over a span of ten or even five years. Lifetime planning is practically nonexistent on the part of younger people. Foresight is indicated regarding the felt need for savings—because, as we reported in the previous chapter, the future is thought to be uncertain—but not regarding the amount of savings needed or the allocation of income to either spending or saving in future years. Some foresight is, however, indicated regarding retirement: Many people in their forties and fifties appear to have given some thought, often considerable thought, to the questions of what they will do and how they will find the means to satisfy their needs during retirement.

To the question, "When do you expect to retire?" 10 per cent of respondents (in the crucial group) replied that there was no retirement in their kind of work or that they expected to work as long as possible. Another 10 per cent said they did not know when they would retire. But the remaining respondents answered the question precisely; about half of all respondents expected to retire at sixty-five to sixty-nine years of age.

"How do you feel about retirement; is it something to look forward to, or to be dreaded, or what?" was the next question asked in the surveys. Slightly more than one-half said they looked forward to retirement, while close to 20 per cent said they dreaded it. (The other respondents chose replies between the two extremes.) The answers were quite similar in different income groups and indicated that considerations other than financial played a major role in determining the answers.

The surveys also contained two questions about how the respondents expected to get along financially during retirement.[7] About one-half replied that they would have enough, and retirement would not cause them any financial problems. Only 14 per cent answered both questions pessimistically. It appears, then, that the proportion of people truly worried about retirement is relatively small. The higher the current income, the more frequent are confident expectations about the financial situation during retirement, but even among those with $3,000 to $6,000 income, 36 per cent said that they would have enough.

A number of considerations were found to make for an optimistic outlook. First, practically everyone in the crucial group believed that their expenses would be reduced after retirement. Housing played an important role in this belief; most homeowners expected to own their home free of debt by the time they retired.

Furthremore, the majority of people said that by the time they retired they would have some savings or larger savings than currently. This answer was in line with replies about the amounts people expected to save in the near future, which we mentioned earlier and which were found to represent aspirations rather than to predict future behavior. Only a minority looked forward to any income from life insurance or annuities; many more spoke of earning income by occasional work. About half of the respondents thought they would earn some money after they retired, but the income expected from a variety of part-time activities was usually quite small.

---

[7] The questions are reproduced in the Appendix to this chapter, p. 196.

Practically everyone in the crucial group expected social-security payments after retirement. (The question asked in the surveys lumped other government pensions and railroad retirement together with social security.) Coverage by private pension plans was acknowledged by 42 per cent of the families in the crucial group. The larger the income, the more frequent was such coverage—among those with over $10,000 annual income 52 per cent, and among those with $3,000 to $6,000 income 26 per cent, said that they participated in private pension plans. In the entire labor force the proportion covered is somewhat lower than in the crucial group, and among all families it is of course much lower. One-half of those covered said that their participation had begun during the last twelve years.

The question of how much money people expected to receive after they retired was studied in several different ways. Some people gave one definite figure when asked how large their total income from all sources would be during retirement. Other people gave numerical answers to questions about the expected income from different sources, and those answers were added up. Again, others who said they could not answer the questions about specific amounts could be prompted to estimate the relation of the expected retirement income to their current income. Altogether, data on expected retirement income were obtained from 85 per cent of the respondents.

The median income of the crucial group was $7,800 during the twelve months before the interview; the median expected retirement income was under $3,600, or less than one-half of current income. About 45 per cent of the respondents estimated their retirement income to be between 35 and 55 per cent of their current income. Only about 10 per cent thought that it would exceed 70 per cent, and less than 20 per cent thought it would be below 30 per cent. Especially among upper-income people the expected retirement income was considerably below the current income (see Table 6 in the Appendix).

Respondents were also asked to estimate how much they thought they would need during retirement. (This was asked before the question about how much they thought they would receive.) The amounts needed were estimated to be substantially lower than the current income. About 44 per cent of those with an opinion gave an amount which fell in the same thousand dollar bracket as the amount they expected to have, and 26 per cent thought that the needed amount would exceed what they expected to have, while

30 per cent thought they would have more than they would need. In this respect the situation was found to be quite similar in different income groups.

Possibly the expression ". . . how much you people will need each month (or each year) after retirement" was understood to mean minimum needs only. Even if this were the case, it appears that on the whole the American people view their retirement prospects rather favorably. For many people participation in a private pension plan was the cause for the favorable outlook, but there are others who expected relatively high retirement income without private pensions. Sizable differences were found in the expectations of different respondents; these differences made it possible to study whether people with more favorable retirement prospects differed in their saving behavior from people with less favorable prospects.

SUMMARY OF FINDINGS

The effects of retirement prospects on discretionary saving by people not yet retired may be studied in different ways. We may disregard private pension plans and determine what income people expect to have during retirement, or how they view their retirement prospects, without regard to the sources of retirement income. Alternately, we may focus attention on the effects on saving of either participating or not participating in a private pension plan. The first problem is of theoretical interest. It may shed light on the relative validity of the two opposing hypotheses formulated at the beginning of this chapter, one of which postulated that the assurance of sizable resources after retirement stimulates saving and the other that it retards saving. The second problem is of great practical importance. Even though some people not covered by a pension plan may have assured themselves of substantial retirement income, for instance, by having saved money during the recent prosperous decades, the great new development of the postwar years, which will exert increasing influence in the future, has been the spread of private pension plans. In addition, only a study of the effects of pension plans can clarify the significant policy question of what influence collective security arrangements may have on individual initiative.

Each of the two problems raised, the effects of more and less favorable retirement prospects and the effects of participation in private pension plans, was studied in several different ways. The description of the methods used and the presentation of the findings are somewhat involved and are therefore relegated to an Appendix.[8] Here we restrict ourselves to presenting the conclusions derived from the data found in the Appendix:

1. Hypothesis 1 was contradicted. Groups of people with unfavorable retirement prospects were not found to have saved more or to be more interested in saving than people with favorable retirement prospects. The results obtained through some of the methods used indicated that people in the two groups saved approximately to the same extent, while other findings obtained through different methods indicated that more of those with favorable prospects saved and were interested in saving than of those with unfavorable prospects. Fear and uncertainty about retirement do not constitute powerful incentives to save.

2. People who participated in private pension plans showed a greater saving performance than people who did not participate, in each of the three income groups considered. But, as shown in the Appendix, these findings do not suffice, since people who expected private pensions had, on the whole, much higher incomes than people who did not expect such pensions. Further analysis was therefore carried out by studying separately the saving performance of those with and those without private pensions among people who expected relatively high, medium, and low retirement income compared to their current income. These data likewise indicated superior saving performance and heightened interest in saving on the part of those who participated in private pension plans. Pending the use of further refinements in statistical methods, it appears probable that participation in private pension plans stimulates saving; under no circumstances does such participation result in reduced saving performance or in lesser interest in saving.

We have discussed here average data obtained for groups of people, because they tend to reveal aggregate trends, of significance for the entire economy. But these data mask the existence of substantial individual differences. There are individuals with favorable retirement prospects who save little, because they substitute their contribution to pension plans for saving in other forms—this pro-

[8] No technical appendix was prepared concerning other findings discussed in this book because those findings have already appeared in various scholarly monographs and papers which contain the technical details. The retirement studies, however, had not been completed at the time of this writing.

cedure has been made attractive to upper-income people through provisions of the tax laws—and there are also individuals with unfavorable retirement prospects who save a relatively high proportion of their income. Yet it appears that these people constitute a minority; the number of large savers with favorable prospects and of small savers with unfavorable prospects is greater. The differences between groups of people are relevant for the consideration of two major problems, namely, (1) the meaning of private pension plans in today's society, and (2) the dynamic principles of economic behavior revealed by studies of retirement prospects.

Pension plans, to quote the investigators at the National Bureau of Economic Research, "represent a major effort of a society seeking to translate gains in living standards into a degree of financial independence for the older members of society which will more adequately preserve human dignity" (*43rd Annual Report*, p. 24). The validity of this conclusion cannot be doubted. Yet we must add to it a further point. Society has not taken over in its entirety the task of guaranteeing financial independence and human dignity to older citizens. The new institutional arrangements contribute to this task without destroying individual initiative. Pension plans frequently help people to help themselves. By perceiving new vistas, people gain confidence in their own ability to provide for themselves and are sometimes stimulated to exert added effort. Concrete rewards that are thought to be attainable represent a major dynamic force that changes economic behavior.

Had our findings been restricted to an indication of higher saving performance on the part of people with more favorable retirement prospects, the explanation might have been that thrifty people, or people with the established habit of saving, judged their retirement prospects to be good, rather than that good retirement prospects had a stimulating influence on saving. But the data on coverage by pension plans do not lend themselves to that interpretation. It is improbable that a higher percentage of savers than non-savers was represented among those participating in private pension plans.[9]

---

[9] The continuation of the studies should yield further insights into the direction of causation, since information has also been collected on asset holdings and expected asset holdings of the respondents. For the moment, it may suffice to mention that those not covered by private pensions include most of the self-employed, who usually save much, as well as a relatively high proportion of unskilled workers, who usually save little.

The current situation need not persist. Collective security arrangements could have a different effect on discretionary saving if they, for instance, were to guarantee more favorable retirement prospects than they do at present. Aggregate saving, including saving through contributions to private pension plans, will also be affected in a different way when the time comes that beneficiaries of pension plans receive substantial payments. Yet for the moment, and for the next ten years as well, the conclusion is clear: The problem we face is not too little saving but rather too much saving because of the steadily growing importance of pension plans.

Appendix to Chapter 19

ON THE STUDIES OF THE INFLUENCE ON RETIREMENT PROSPECTS ON SAVING

In Chapter 19 we made a distinction between (1) the influence on saving of relatively favorable as compared to relatively unfavorable retirement prospects, irrespective of the sources of the retirement income, and (2) the influence of participation in private pension plans.

In seeking information on the first problem we used three methods of dividing the respondents into the two requisite groups—those with favorable and those with unfavorable retirement prospects. All three methods were based on the respondents' subjective appraisal of their prospects, although the first may be thought of as less subjective than the other two. In Method 1a we relied on the ability of respondents to estimate the income they expected to have during retirement. We first calculated the ratio of expected retirement income to current income for each respondent. Low ratios were more frequent in upper-income groups, and high ratios in lower-income groups (Table 6). Since expecting a retirement income of, say, 50 per cent of current income may mean something different to a person with $5,000 income from what it means to a person with $10,000 income, respondents were ranked in each of six narrow income groups according to their retirement-income to current-income ratios; they were then divided into three groups separately in each of the six income groups. Each of the three groups contains the same number of respondents with high and low income, i.e., the

Table 6. Expected Income during Retirement
in Relation to Current Income
(*Percentage Distribution of Crucial Group**)

| | Current income | | | |
Ratio of retirement income to current income	$3,000 to 6,000	$6,000 to 10,000	$10,000 and over	All
29 per cent or less	11%	15%	28%	18%
30–39 per cent	9	16	16	14
40–49 per cent	19	19	16	18
50–59 per cent	16	20	17	18
60–69 per cent	15	6	7	8
70 per cent or more	13	9	4	9
Not ascertained	17	15	12	15
Total	100%	100%	100%	100%

* The crucial group consists of heads of complete families in the labor force, aged thirty-five to sixty-four, with family income of over $3,000 in 1962.

income distribution of the groups is identical. Group 1, consisting of the one-third of respondents with the highest ratios, was then compared with group 2, consisting of the one-third of respondents with the lowest ratios. In this instance, then, favorable retirement prospects mean favorable in comparison to other people; members of group 1 expected to receive a much higher proportion of their current income during retirement than those of group 2.

The other two methods of separating those with favorable from those with unfavorable retirement prospects made no use of comparisons among different people's expectations; both left to the respondents themselves the task of evaluating whether their retirement prospects were favorable or unfavorable. This was done in two ways. In Method 1b we asked the respondents to estimate the amount they thought they would need each year after retirement. We then related the amount needed to the amount expected by the same respondent. Respondents who estimated their needs in the same thousand dollar bracket (e.g., $3,000–3,999) as their expected income were excluded from either group. Group 1 was formed of the 30 per cent of respondents who estimated their retirement income to be higher than they would need, and group 2 of the 26 per cent of respondents who estimated it to be lower than they would need. Income-wise, groups 1 and 2 were rather similar.

Finally, Method 1c relied on the following two questions, one of which was asked early and one late in the interview: "Do you think you will get along all right financially when you retire, or do you think that retirement will cause financial problems for you people?" and "Would you say that what you can look forward to will be enough or not enough for retirement?" Group 1, consisting of 51 per cent of the respondents, was formed of those who said that they would get along all right, in answering the first question, and that what they could look forward to would be enough, in answering the second question. Group 2, 36 per cent of respondents, contained those who were uncertain, or who said that they might not have enough, or who mentioned financial problems they might have during retirement. Current income was found to be related to this grouping: There were more high-income and fewer low-income people in group 1 than in group 2, as determined by Method 1*c*.

In seeking information on the influence of participation in private pension plans, our first obvious procedure, which we shall call 2*a*, was to divide the respondents into the two relevant groups—the 42 per cent who said they participated in a private pension plan and the 52 per cent who said they did not. (Six per cent who were uncertain or were unable to answer the question were omitted.) Among those participating in a pension plan, there were more high-income and fewer low-income people than among those not participating. This can be seen in Table 7, which also shows the differences in the retirement-income expectations of the two groups.

Table 7. Income and Expected Retirement Income of People Participating and Not Participating in Private Pension Plans

	Current income*		Expected retirement income	
	In private pension plans	Not in plans	In private pension plans	Not in plans
Under $3,000	—	—	26%	49%
$3,000–6,000	18%	38%	56	37
$6,000–10,000	45	38	18	14
$10,000 and over	37	24		
Total	100%	100%	100%	100%
Median in dollars	8,740	6,900	3,920	3,030

* Income of crucial group during twelve months prior to interview in 1962 or 1962–1963.

Finally, Method 2*b* consisted of making joint use of 2*a* and 1*a*. This permitted us to compare those with private pensions and relatively high, medium, or low retirement expectations to those without private pensions with similar retirement-income expectations.

The five methods provided us with five different independent or explanatory variables. What we wanted to find out was how differences in these variables related to saving. To obtain a measure of saving, we made use of three dependent variables. Since the retirement surveys consisted of only one interview with each respondent, we could not determine amounts saved by comparing assets at various earlier points of time. We therefore had to rely on memory questions for this purpose and asked the questions separately for checking accounts, savings accounts, government savings bonds, and common stock. Such questions concerning amounts saved could not realistically be asked for a time span beyond twelve months preceding the interview. Thus, the data obtained relate to a much shorter period than is desirable and cannot be judged to be fully reliable. Yet, there is justification for assuming that the different subgroups made similar errors in estimating the amounts they saved. Dependent variable 1 was considered to consist of the proportion which had saved $500 or more during the preceding year.

Secondly, we sought the respondents' opinions of whether or not they had saved any money during the preceding twelve months and also the preceding twenty-four months. The two questions asked were: "During the past twelve months or so, did you people save any money or did you decrease your savings or did you just break even?" and, following the determination of current assets, "Now taking all the financial reserves you have—stocks, bonds, bank deposits, and the like—how does the amount you now have compare to what you had two years ago?" Dependent variable 2 consisted of those respondents who said both that they had saved during the past twelve months and that they had either more or the same amount of savings as two years earlier. It also included those who said they had more savings than two years earlier and the same as one year earlier. These are the people who believed they had been saving some money at some time during the preceding two years.

Finally, respondents were asked, "Suppose you had some extra money—say, an amount equal to one week's wages or salary (income)—what would you do with this money?" Those people who said that they would save or invest the extra money and did not mention spending it at all were considered to be saving-minded. They represented dependent variable 3.

Several additional techniques were used in order to study the impact of retirement prospects and participation in private pension plans on saving or spending. In some of the methods we determined asset holdings; in some, the major consumer expenditures. (These methods, as well as multivariate analysis of the findings, will be discussed in a forthcoming publication devoted entirely to retirement prospects.)

The findings obtained from the five methods of inquiry we have outlined are presented in Table 8. Data are presented not only for all respondents in the crucial group,[1] but also separately for three income groups within that group. This is necessary, because the larger the income, the more frequent is saving and the larger the amounts saved. Statistically significant are those differences among all respondents that exceed 4 percentage points and those differences in the data relating to income groups that exceed 7 percentage points (both on the one standard-error level). Yet uniformity of change observed in the different groups adds to the reliability of the findings.

It appears from Table 8 that when respondents were classified by Method 1a no difference was found in the saving performance of those with favorable from those with unfavorable retirement prospects. When grouped according to Methods 1b and 1c, people with favorable prospects believed they had saved more and were more frequently saving-minded than people with unfavorable prospects. Among the eighteen comparisons presented in Table 8 in the three income groups by using Methods 1b and 1c, fourteen show that favorable prospects made for increased saving (thereof ten are statistically significant); two, for equal saving; and two, for slightly decreased saving.

The differences in the results obtained through the use of different methods of classifying the respondents, as well as through the use of different dependent variables, were subjected to further analysis. This analysis suggests that favorable retirement prospects exert the strongest stimulating effect on people's desire to save and inter-

---

[1] The crucial group, as defined in Chap. 19, consists of heads of complete families in the labor force aged thirty-five to sixty-four (and not retired) with a family income of over $3,000. For reasons explained in the text no others were included in reporting our findings.

est in saving. Yet such desires do not insure a substantial addition to bank deposits or securities in every twelve-month period.

One part of Table 8 which is not fully satisfactory is 2*a*. In view of the substantial income differences among people who were and who were not participants in pension plans, as shown in Table 7, it is possible, and even probable, that among those with pension

CHART 6

Saving by Middle-Income People ($6000–9999) with Favorable and Unfavorable Retirement Prospects

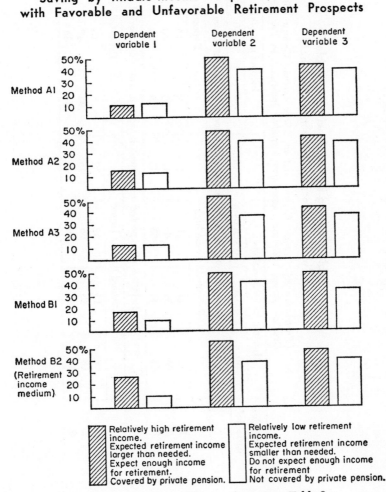

For explanation of dependent variables, see footnote to Table 8.

Table 8. Saving by People with Favorable and with Unfavorable Retirement Prospects

(Proportion of Crucial Group, and of Three Income Groups within Crucial Group, with the Dependent Variable Indicated in Per Cent)

Dependent variable*	Income in 1,000 dollars				Income in 1,000 dollars			
	3–6	6–10	10 and over	All	3–6	6–10	10 and over	All
	1a. Relation of expected retirement income to current income							
	Expected income high				Expected income low			
1.	11	11	19	14	9	12	29	17
2.	28	51	60	47	29	40	61	44
3.	38	43	55	45	36	39	51	42
	1b. Relation of expected retirement income to amounts needed							
	Expected income larger				Expected income smaller			
1.	9	15	32	22	6	13	18	12
2.	18	48	65	48	23	40	58	40
3.	31	41	59	46	34	38	46	38

1c. Estimate of situation during retirement

	Will have enough				Will not have enough			
1.	7	13	32	19	7	13	25	13
2.	30	52	66	53	21	37	51	34
3.	39	44	56	47	31	38	48	37

2a. Participation in private pension plan

	Covered				Not covered			
1.	8	16	33	22	5	9	23	12
2.	27	49	63	51	24	41	60	39
3.	43	49	57	49	32	36	47	37

2b. Pension and expected retirement income jointly considered

Retirement income:	High		Medium		Low	
Pension plan:	Have	Don't have	Have	Don't have	Have	Don't have
1.	15	13	26	10	25	13
2.	51	44	56	38	49	39
3.	48	41	48	40	52	35

* The dependent variables are defined as follows:
1. Saved $500 or more in past twelve months
2. Say they saved during past two years
3. Would use extra money for saving or investing

plans in the, say, $6,000 to $10,000 income group, there were more people with $9,000 or $10,000 income and fewer with $6,000 or $7,000 income than in the same income group without pension plans, and similarly in the other income groups. These differences might reduce the differences in the saving performance shown in part 2*a* of Table 8. (A similar argument also applies, to a lesser extent to be sure, to Method 1*c*.)

Method 2*b* is much less subject to the objection just raised, since those with relatively high retirement income, and those with middle or low retirement income as well, were chosen in equal proportions from each narrow income group. Thus Method 2*b* suggests that people with pension plans save more and are more saving-minded than people without pension plans; this finding needs to be confirmed through multivariate analysis.[2]

The findings obtained for respondents with $6,000 to $10,000 income are presented graphically in Chart 6. It is apparent that while Method 1*a* yields no difference between those with favorable and those with unfavorable retirement prospects, according to the other methods favorable prospects and coverage by pension plans are associated with somewhat higher saving performance than unfavorable prospects and absence of coverage. Similar differences appear in the proportion of people who are saving-minded.

The conclusions drawn from Table 8 and Chart 6 were presented in the last section of Chapter 19.

---

[2] Such confirmation was obtained after the completion of this manuscript and will be published shortly.

20

Consumer Assets

Having found that a very substantial proportion of the American people are highly motivated to save, we turn to a study of the results of their saving activity. Through saving money some people acquire wealth; most people acquire some reserve funds which they consider less than adequate for their purposes. Consumer assets are highly concentrated—relatively few families own the major share of all financial wealth in private hands. If we exclude the approximately 15 per cent of families whose net worth amounts to more than $25,000—most of these cannot be called wealthy—and if we exclude the roughly 30 per cent of families who have practically no financial assets, we find that in the early 1960s the average family had assets (minus debts) approximately equal to their income in *one* year.

Statistical data on amounts saved by individuals in a given year and on financial assets owned by them are subject to considerable error. This is true not only of survey data on individuals' assets but of aggregates as well, even though the latter are derived from records. Great difficulties prevail in separating savings of unincorporated businesses, trust funds, estates, and pension funds from personal savings. Sample interview surveys represent the only source of information on the distribution of savings among families. In order to answer questions about the relation of income or age to assets, for instance, the perusal of records does not suffice, and it is necessary to turn to the savers themselves. In the usual cross-section sample surveys, however, very wealthy people tend to be underrepresented. Therefore total assets and their rate of concentration are usually underestimated. In addition, reporting errors regarding amounts of savings occur even in the best-conducted surveys, primarily because of failure of memory and a tendency to underreport certain assets. The statistics on savings that will be reported in this chapter have benefited from repeated surveys, each of which made use of identical methods, as well as from a survey conducted with a special sample of wealthy people, in which it was possible to make some checks on reporting errors. The data can, of course, not claim to represent entirely accurate information. They are presented simply to indicate the probable order of magnitude of certain important relationships.[1]

According to the survey data, during each year in the early 1960s, about one-half of all spending units saved some money, about one-third dissaved, and the rest broke even. Saving is defined here as the increase in bank deposits, securities, and investments in real estate and business and the decrease in installment and personal debt.[2]

The relatively great proportion of individuals who dissave each year results both from occasional diminution of liquid reserves and from borrowing. As reported in Chapter 18, years in which major durable goods are purchased, either on the installment plan or by paying cash out of liquid assets, commonly appear as years of dissaving for the purchaser. In addition, even among families who are highly motivated to save, unusually large expenditures result in a net reduction of reserve funds, and years of saving are often inter-

---

[1] The findings presented in this chapter are based primarily on work by the Survey Research Center. See "1953 Survey of Consumer Finances" in *Federal Reserve Bulletin*, September, 1953; chap. 7 of Ref. 5; chap. 6 of Ref. 7; and the article, "The Wealth of the Wealthy" (Ref. 3). See also R. J. Lampman, *The Share of Top Wealth-Holders in National Wealth, 1922–56*, National Bureau of Economic Research, Princeton University Press, Princeton, N.J., 1962. Extensive studies were carried out by the Inter-University Committee for Research on Consumer Behavior, of which I am a member, on errors in measurements of savings and on methods to improve such measurements. Robert Ferber, the director of those studies, will publish the findings soon. More recent and presumably more accurate asset data are expected to result from new studies carried out by the Federal Reserve Board and the Inter-University Committee.

[2] Excluded are such forms of contractual saving as life insurance premium payments, repayment of mortgage principal, and social security and private pension accumulations.

rupted by years of dissaving. In 1960 to 1962 the middle-most person in the income group under $2,000 dissaved; in income groups around $5,000 the median rate of saving was about 6 per cent of income; and in income groups around $10,000, about 10 per cent.

STATISTICS ON INDIVIDUALS' ASSETS

In 1962 about 15 per cent of the 59 million spending units in the United States had a net worth of over $25,000.[3] The total worth of this small minority represented at least two-thirds of the net worth of all American families. This ratio of concentration is obtained when families are arranged according to their total wealth. When they are ordered by income, we find that the 10 per cent of families with the highest income have assets that represent about 40 per cent of all assets. The share of these families in total income is only about 30 per cent. Wealth is more highly concentrated than income. When the assets of wealthy people are scrutinized, we find further evidence of concentration: The few very rich have a disproportionately large share of all wealth. In a study which, to be sure, was carried out in one metropolitan area alone, it was found that among families with an income between $20,000 and $50,000 a year, the middlemost family's net worth exceeded its income five times; among families with more than $50,000 income a year, the median net worth was eight times the median income (see Ref. 3).

There are three ways of accumulating assets: saving out of income, capital appreciation, and inheritance (or gifts). The third source of assets is probably the least important in terms of the number of people concerned. Among the very wealthy (income over $50,000), only 12 per cent said that their fortune was entirely or mostly inherited. Many others said that they had inherited a small part of it, but about half of these high-income people asserted that they had not received any inheritance. In the entire population, 19 per cent reported that they had inherited some assets (7 per cent of those under 35 years of age and 34 per cent of those 65 years of age or older). When asked to relate their inheritance to their current financial assets, only 4 per cent of all families said that most

[3] Included in net worth are checking and savings accounts, bonds, stock, homes owned, other real estate, unincorporated business and farm assets, and the value of automobiles. All forms of debt are deducted. Excluded are insurance policies, pensions, jewelry, clothing, house furnishings, trust funds, and currency. See Ref. 7.

of their current assets had been inherited and 5 per cent that some had been inherited and some accumulated through saving. (The other 10 per cent said they had inherited little and saved most of their assets.)

No information is available which would permit us to estimate the respective roles of saving out of income and accumulating assets through capital appreciation. The role of the latter must have been substantial in view of the known increase in stock and real estate prices in the 1950s and early 1960s. The important role of saving money over many years is demonstrated by data on the distribution of assets by age. When we ordered American families by the age of the head for the year 1962, we found a steady increase in net worth up to approximately 50 years of age. In the age brackets 25 to 34, most families had very little net worth; even homeowners carried large mortgage debt and their financial reserves were usually quite small. The middlemost family in the age group 35 to 44 had a net worth of $6,000; in the age groups 45 to 54 and 55 to 64, the middlemost family was worth approximately $10,000. Families in the age groups over 65 had on the average slightly lower assets than those 55 to 64 years of age. Similarly with liquid reserves (deposits, bonds, and stock): In 1962 the proportion of families having at least $2,500 in liquid reserves was 15 per cent among those with a head under 35, 24 per cent in the age group 35 to 44, 36 per cent in the age group 45 to 54 and 40 per cent among those over 55 years of age. For most people, it takes at least two decades of saving before they reach their peak assets. After retirement, most people use some of their reserves, but in most cases the rate of use is slow.

It appears then that among younger people accumulation of reserve funds is not common. They buy a variety of goods on the installment plan and appear as savers primarily when they repay their debt. Prior to the age of 35 or 40, the accumulation of consumer goods (one-family homes, automobiles, appliances, home furnishings) has preference over the accumulation of financial assets.

Statistics may supply evidence for a variety of statements, and the data on the relation of assets to age have been used to state that, on the average, families with heads under 65 are poorer than families with heads over 65 years of age. (Therefore, it has been argued, Medicare is based on false premises; the younger people with their smaller assets should not pay for the retired people's health needs.) It is, of course, correct that the average net worth of all families under 65 is lower than that of older families. Many young families with very small net worth are included in the first group, and they depress the average. But it is equally correct to point out that in the age group 45 to 64 the average assets are the highest and that the incomes of people under 65 are much higher than the incomes of those over 65. In addition, the low incomes of older people are permanently low, while those of younger people are often temporarily low. Finally, attention must be called to the distribution of net worth within different age groups. Up to 50 or 55 years of age, the distribution is fairly normal—there are many families in each age group with assets in the middle range, and fewer with larger or smaller assets. The distribution of assets of older families is different. Quite a number of them have assets above the national average, and this is particularly true of net worth, since older families are rarely in debt. These people have earned a fair income over a longer period of time than the younger families and thus accumulated larger reserve funds. On the other hand, an unusually large proportion of families over 65 years of age have practically no financial assets. Obviously, these people are in a much worse position than younger families without any assets because their earning power is much smaller.

One final aspect of the statistics of wealth must be presented. The composition of assets differs according to whether a family has sizable or small assets. Those with a few thousand dollars have, at the most, a small equity in their home, a car, and some bank deposits. Those with $25,000 or more have much of their assets in common stock, business ownership, or real estate, in addition to having a home, a car, and bank deposits. As we proceed upward on the income scale the amounts held in every one of the diverse savings outlets increase. But the increase is slow in homeownership and is very rapid in the ownership of securities, particularly common stock. The home of a person making $50,000 a year is worth, on the average, five times as much as the home of a person making $5,000 a year, while the value of the common stock held by the former is many times greater than that of the latter. Holdings of common stock are, as we shall show in the next chapter, the most highly concentrated of all major savings instruments. Because of the large amounts of securities and business investments held by upper-income people, the share of bank deposits in the total assets decreases as income rises.[4]

Diversification of family investments is a goal toward which people consciously strive once they have any investments. This stage is not reached, however, until a family has accumulated several thousand dollars in reserve funds. Interest in having common stock and, especially in small towns, in investing in real estate is stimulated by not wanting to have all one's eggs in one basket. But even in the portfolio of the average $10,000-income family, fixed-value assets played the major role in 1962. During and shortly after World War II government savings bonds (war bonds) were the favorite investment of the majority of savers; in later years it was savings accounts, including accounts with savings and loan associations.

INFLATION

In all the postwar years neither experience with inflation nor the expectation of further inflation detracted from people's will to save and hardly worsened the competitive position of fixed-value assets (bonds, bank deposits). For fifteen years the Survey Research Center asked the following question from representative samples of the population:

> Suppose a man has some money, over and above what he needs for his expenses. What do you think would be the wisest thing for him to do with it—put it in a savings account, buy government savings bonds with it, invest it in real estate, or buy common stock? Why do you make that choice?

At all times the majority expressed a preference for banks and bonds. This was even true of the upper-income groups—say, of families with incomes over $10,000 in the 1960s—although, as we shall see, not of the truly wealthy. The size of the minority opting for stocks and real estate varied somewhat according to whether inflation played a greater or smaller role at a given time. These variations indicate that there was a minority who changed their preference according to the presence or absence of inflationary fears. These people were interested in the possible advantages of variable

[4] This is true on the average. Some older high-income people, however, hold large bank deposits, probably because of estate-tax considerations.

value investments, but most of them still kept some of their savings
in bonds or in banks; hardly anybody considered transferring all their
savings from bonds and banks to stocks and real estate.

In discussing inflation in Chapter 14 we quoted one respondent
who explained why he kept his money in a savings account, although he was aware of the diminution of the purchasing power of
money. Implied in his story was the notion that there were no
alternative savings outlets in which the value of savings would be
assured or would even increase with inflation. The reasons for keeping some and often most of one's savings in savings accounts were
primarily: (1) stocks and real estate were considered speculative
and risky, a point about which more will be said in the next chapter,
(2) many people were aware of important advantages of bank
accounts, and (3) they believed in diversifying their savings.

Savings accounts with savings and loan associations, mutual
savings banks, and commercial banks are extolled as being secure,
liquid, and convenient. No signs of recollection of the bank failures
of the 1930s could be found in the 1950s. The highly desired savings
must be safe beyond question. People in all walks of life believe
that this goal is achieved only when the money is in United States
government savings bonds or in banks. For millions of people the
money in savings accounts is subjectively earmarked for a variety
of long-range purposes—for retirement, for the education of children, for paying for certain large purchases or a trip, etc. But even
in these cases people wish to have their savings readily available on
short notice. Studies carried out during the late 1950s indicated that
United States government savings bonds were not considered as
liquid as savings accounts with banks. Even though the bonds were
redeemable at any time, cashing them appeared less convenient
than withdrawing money from a bank and was undertaken only
with hesitation. Banks are generally considered the most convenient
place to keep savings. Yet in emphasizing the prevalence of the
desire for ready availability, we should not fail to mention some
people who consider savings accounts and savings bonds as having
the opposite advantage, namely, of keeping their money not so
readily available. These people feel that money in banks or bonds
has been "put away" where it is safe from being squandered.

Since a substantial share of the reserve funds held by the American middle class is in fixed-value investments, it has been argued
that the middle class has suffered great losses due to inflation and

would suffer further substantial losses if inflation were to continue. The classification of asset holdings according to surveys made in 1960 seems to bear out this contention: among holders of savings and reserve funds exceeding $5,000, only 17 per cent were found to have their savings invested overwhelmingly in stocks and real estate; twice as many families (35 per cent) had practically all their financial reserves in fixed-value investments. (The remaining 48 per cent had both kinds of investments; see Ref. 5.) But a very important asset is not considered in these calculations. This is home-ownership. The majority of people with "non-inflation-proof" reserve funds were found to own their homes, and their equity in the home represented a substantial proportion of their reserve funds. When it is also considered that repayment of mortgage debt becomes easier when inflation progresses, the conclusion emerges that homeownership offers substantial protection against possible losses on bank accounts and bonds. Thus the continuation of creeping inflation in the United States does not represent a major threat to the net worth of the broad American middle class.

INTEREST RATES

In our discussion of the perceived advantages of savings accounts we have made no reference to interest payments. The impact of higher and lower interest rates on people's saving performance is not easy to study. It would be impossible to get valid answers to such theoretically relevant but unrealistic questions as how saving would be affected if interest of, say, 10 per cent a year, or even 6 per cent, could be earned on convenient investments that were considered safe, or if interest on liquid savings were to be abolished. We were, however, able to learn something about the very realistic problem of the effect on saving of an increase in interest rates by one or two percentage points, because this is something with which the American people had some experience during the last decade.

Middle-class savers have some awarenes of prevailing interest rates. During and shortly after the war it was fairly generally known that war bonds "pay 3 per cent a year"—even though these were actually discount bonds, and the interest was much smaller if the bonds were not kept for ten years, a fact which was not well known. In the 1950s and the early 1960s, very many people were found to have correct notions about the interest rates they received on their savings accounts. Interest rates are considered fixed by outside forces. What makes them rise or fall most people do not know, but they do not think that they themselves have any influence in the matter. They say that 3 per cent or 4 per cent a year is what one can get, and that is the whole story. Any rate that is paid over an extended period and is quite uniform among different banks is seen as the right rate. On the whole, the American saver was satisfied with the interest received, whether it was 3 per cent or 4 per cent at any given time.

To increase one's income through the receipt of interest (or dividends) is not one of the major purposes of saving. As we have shown before, the great majority of Americans save because of the threat of emergencies, or for retirement and the needs of their children, but not for the sake of receiving interest. The receipt of interest represents a bonus. If the bonus is higher than before, it is appreciated, but higher rates do not induce people to save more. No support could be found for the contention that 4 per cent interest on savings accounts stimulates saving more than 3 per cent.

This conclusion does not rule out some short-range impact of a change in interest rates. When the news comes, as it did in 1957 and in 1961, that savings and loan associations or commercial banks have raised their interest payments, it does influence some people. In 1957, as we mentioned in the discussion of findings relevant to business-cycle trends (Chapter 10), many people considered the higher interest rates to be unfavorable for business. The end of the easy-money period, which was associated with good times, was viewed with concern. Whether some people responded to the news by increasing their savings for a short while, we do not know. What is known is that differential rates offered by different savings outlets had some influence in shifting money. The preference for savings accounts over government savings bonds, consistently increasing during the fifties, could be traced to some extent to an awareness of existing interest differentials. (But this was just one factor, supporting other considerations discussed in this chapter.) When certain institutions—for instance, savings and loan associations—announced an increase in interest rates over and above what other institutions paid, some people decided to take advantage of the new offer and transferred their savings. Calculating behavior does exist, but it is not the rule. Habits and inertia remain powerful, although occasionally they are overcome, and people adjust to new possibilities.

THE TOP ASSET HOLDERS

Practically always the saver is at the same time a worker—an employee, a salesman, or a small businessman—preoccupied with the task of earning income rather than of taking care of his savings. One great advantage seen in the preferred forms of saving is that one need not be concerned with them. Savings deposits and savings bonds can be forgotten; one cannot lose anything by not devoting attention to them. Thus, as a saver, the average American does not conform to the theorists' notion of an "economic man."

Yet something resembling an economic man was discovered in a study, based on special methods of sampling, in which a fair number of investors with $100,000 or even more than a million dollars in assets were questioned about their investment policies (see Ref. 3). The process of decision making by the large-asset holders was found to be qualitatively different from that of the average saver in several respects:

1. Top asset holders are inflation-conscious. Their investment policy is consciously directed toward the problem of hedging against inflation.

2. Top asset holders are interest-conscious. They review their investments frequently and sometimes shift them, often on very short notice, to take advantage of interest differentials amounting to not more than one-eighth or one-fourth of one percentage point. Government securities other than savings bonds—treasury bills and notes, tax exempt bonds, etc.—as well as mortgage loans and foreign investments, practically unknown to the average saver, are familiar to many top asset holders. Considerations of yield influence the purchase or sale of these securities.

3. Top asset holders are tax-conscious. They devote time and energy to finding investments that serve to minimize income and estate taxes.

4. Top asset holders are concerned with leaving an inheritance to their children. The middle-income saver is hardly cognizant of this motive to save. He thinks in terms of giving his children a good education and possibly assisting them in starting in their business or professional career. He believes that everyone must make his way on his own. The transfer of assets from one generation to the next is, in most cases, accidental rather than intentional. The wealthy, on the other hand, are concerned with establishing and preserving a

family fortune. They often set up trust funds in order to preserve wealth for their grandchildren. (Most of the "wealthy" interviewed were over sixty years old.)

5. Top asset holders devote much time to managing their investments. The task of management consists not only of extensive reading but also of discussing financial matters with other investors. They also have access to professional advisers and make use of them (and some, of course, entrust the management of their assets to professionals).

These findings are important, because holders of large assets, though relatively small in number, control a very substantial part of the nation's wealth, are much more active traders than other people, and exert a great influence on the outcome of monetary policy through their reactions to new measures and regulations. But in some important respects no difference was found between top asset holders and other savers. First, both groups were found to be greatly concerned with the security of their investments. Capital appreciation and high yields as goals of investment policy are surpassed, even among the wealthy, by concern with the safety of the investments. Usually only a small part of the wealth of top asset holders is available for risky or speculative ventures. Secondly, inertia and past habits play a large role in the decision making of holders of very large, as well as small, assets. When asked about their satisfaction or dissatisfaction with their portfolios, the majority of wealthy people interviewed complained that they had left too large a share of their investments in the same form for many years and that they had not switched their assets frequently enough. The prevailing composition of assets represents a powerful constraint to new decisions. People become accustomed to the given situation, and abstaining from action is the easiest of all decisions. These are human traits which the very rich share with the rest of the population.

INFLUENCE OF WEALTH ON SAVING

Financial wealth in the possession of private individuals has grown greatly during the twentieth century. In consequence, economists have turned their attention to the question of the impact of increased wealth on consumption and saving. World War II stimulated such discussions, since in many countries the war was financed, partly at least, by selling government bonds; this raised the amount of liquid wealth available to the people. Since, in principle, consumer expenditures may be paid either out of income or from liquid assets, it was a simple matter to change the traditional equation $C = fY$ by writing $C = f(Y, W)$: Instead of saying that consumption is a function of income, economists postulated that it was a function of income and wealth. It was for most economists a self-evident conclusion that wealth, like income, would be positively correlated with consumer expenditures: The greater the income or the wealth, the greater the consumer expenditures and the smaller the amounts saved.

Several arguments have been used to explain such an influence of total wealth or of liquid wealth on consumer expenditures. First, in an apparently obvious analogy to the principle of diminishing marginal utility, incentives to save were supposed to weaken with an increase in wealth: The richer the family, the smaller the need to add to its wealth. According to a priori considerations, the only two purposes for liquid assets in the possession of households are to be available for investment opportunities and to be used for expenditures. The share of liquid assets earmarked for the first purpose may vary greatly, but some assets would usually remain over and above the reserves held for investment opportunities, and they would stimulate spending. "Money burns holes in people's pockets," or substantial liquid assets make it difficult to resist the temptation to spend—thus have run the arguments in favor of the assumed relationship. Many economists thereupon postulated that, given unchanged income, the greater the liquid assets, the larger the proportion of income spent. This appeared to be so indisputable that sometimes even the need to obtain empirical verification was denied.

I pointed out some years ago that from a psychological point of view only one of the arguments mentioned above appears convincing (Ref. 1). Available liquid assets do represent enabling conditions for consumer expenditures; and the larger the liquid assets, the greater their possible contribution to spending. Even in this respect, it should be kept in mind that a large part of the so-called liquid assets represents what people consider to be permanent savings, and subjective liquidity is not the same as legal liquidity. The argument that increased wealth reduces the strength of motives to save must be contrasted with the principle of levels of aspiration, which says that the more we accomplish, the higher we raise our sights. Should the latter be the operative principle, the felt need for greater liquid assets may even increase with the accumulation of such assets.

Probably the most important consideration is the enduring nature of dispositions to save. Thriftiness as a personality trait, the lack of many dependents, and the habit of saving contribute substantially to the accumulation of financial assets, since inherited wealth is relatively uncommon. These factors change slowly and tend to remain influential over long periods. Most holders of large assets have been large savers in the past, and it should be assumed that they will continue to be large savers.

Only empirical tests can determine the outcome of the various and partly conflicting influences. As a preliminary step, consumers' alleged saturation with large asset accumulations was studied. After determining the approximate size of financial reserves, representative samples of savers were asked the following question: "How do you feel about the amount of money you now have saved up—is it far too little, fairly satisfactory, fully adequate, or what?" The results presented in Table 9 indicate that people who say that their reserve funds are fully adequate are quite rare except when the reserves exceed several thousand dollars. At the other extreme, most of those who have hardly any reserves are dissatisfied. But dissatisfaction with the size of reserve funds is not restricted to people with small assets. A fair proportion of people who hold sizable assets say that they are dissatisfied. The table also shows that the rate of dissatisfaction of high-income people does not differ much from the average. If asset-income ratios, rather than assets alone, are related to dissatisfaction, the differences are smaller than those shown in the table.

The data permit the following interpretation: Some people with sizable reserve funds consider them adequate and, presumably, are not strongly motivated to increase them. Yet with many other people a goal once set becomes inadequate when reached. Many young people appear greatly bothered by the absence of any reserve funds and say that having a few hundred dollars in the bank would make a great difference to them. When, in due time, they have accumulated these funds, the amount often seems entirely inadequate. Similarly also with larger funds. A person may think that all he needs is a few thousand dollars in reserve, but after having saved up this amount, he may set his needs higher and may then strive for additional reserve funds with equal or even greater intensity.

Table 9. Subjective Notions about Adequacy of Current Savings*
(*Proportion of Asset Holders in Different Groups*)

Savings	All asset holders	Asset holders with incomes over $10,000	Amount of Savings				
			Under $500	$500 –2,500	$2,500 –5,000	$5,000 –15,000	$15,000 and over
Fully adequate	18%	22%	9%	12%	15%	32%	46%
Fairly satisfactory	28	30	16	30	40	29	29
Not satisfactory	51	47	71	56	44	37	21
Don't know, not ascertained	3	1	4	2	1	2	4
Total	100%	100%	100%	100%	100%	100%	100%

* The question asked in 1962 was: "How do you feel about the amount of money you now have saved up—is it far too little, fairly satisfactory, fully adequate, or what?"

A study of the influence of asset holdings on subsequent savings performance likewise yielded the conclusion that it is necessary to distinguish between different kinds of people. Alternately, it is possible that the saving behavior of people differs under different circumstances. The results of a panel study, carried out in three waves in 1960, 1961, and 1962, are presented in Table 10.

Table 10. Relation of Initial Liquid Asset Holdings to Subsequent Rate of Discretionary Saving

Saving-income ratio, 1960–1961*	Liquid asset holdings in early 1960†			
	$1–499	$500– 1,999	$2,000– 4,999	$5,000 and over
20 per cent or more	14%	14%	21%	32%
Between —9 and +19 per cent	76	69	50	37
—10 per cent or less	10	17	29	31
Total	100%	100%	100%	100%
Number of cases	274	258	148	143

* The amount of discretionary saving—in this instance, changes in liquid assets, securities, and also in installment debt—was determined for the two years 1960 and 1961 and is expressed in per cent of average income in these two years. Repayment of mortgage debt, life insurance premiums, and social security or pension accumulations are excluded.

† Amounts in checking accounts, saving accounts, and United States government savings bonds.

The saving performance of panel members with some initial liquid-asset holdings during a twenty-four-month period was grouped in three categories. The first contains the large savers—those who added 20 per cent or more of their income to their savings. The other extreme category contains the large dissavers—those who dissaved at least 10 per cent of their income. The middle category contains the small savers and those who broke even, as well as the small dissavers.

Table 10 shows that the middle category predominates among those who had small assets to begin with, as well as among the majority of all people. Large dissaving—not only in the form of reduction of assets, but also in the form of borrowing—is fairly rare among families with less than $2,000 in liquid assets; large-scale saving is likewise uncommon among these families. In contrast, substantial proportions of holders of sizable liquid assets add large proportions of their income to their assets, while other substantial proportions of these same groups do the opposite. It appears, then, that larger liquid-asset holdings have a twofold effect on subsequent saving—they are associated with both high positive and high negative saving-income ratios.[5]

Further statistical analysis indicates that the differences between the saving performance of families with small and those with large initial assets are not a function of income. When, for instance, only the middle-income families are considered—eliminating from the study both the high- and the low-income groups—the differences between the saving performance of people with large and small initial assets become greater still.

We may conclude, then, that for some people at certain times the propositions presented by economic theorists are valid. Liquid reserves are accumulated in order to be used during one's lifetime, and when the time of use arrives, dissaving may be substantial. As important as this effect of sizable asset holdings is the opposite effect. The relatively high percentage of large savers among those holding sizable assets may be explained by the persistence of habits of saving and the principle of rising levels of aspiration.

From the point of view of the influence of wealth on the economy, the aggregate effects of sizable asset holdings are of interest. In

[5] Similar data have been presented by the author in Ref. 1, pp. 167ff., and Ref. 2, pp. 133ff. See also Katona, "On the So-called Wealth Effect," *Review of Economics and Statistics,* Vol. 43, pp. 59ff., 1961.

other words, it would be important to find out which of the two divergent influences, namely, to increase saving or to increase dissaving, is the stronger. Concerning the number of people behaving one way or the other, there do not seem to be large differences according to the data presented in Table 10. Regarding the amounts saved or dissaved, tentative results seem to indicate that in some past years the negative and in some more recent years the positive influence of assets on saving was somewhat the stronger, although in neither period does the influence appear to have been great in either direction.[6]

Of importance for the purpose of understanding saving behavior is the following question: What is it that determines whether in a given year large-asset holders either save or dissave substantial amounts? It appears that change in income is a factor of some relevance: Among large-asset holders with a decline in income, dissaving was more frequent, and among large-asset holders with an increase in income, saving was more frequent. In addition, of course, the desire to purchase durable goods or to make other large discretionary expenditures influences the behavior of large-asset holders. As yet we do not know enough to give definite answers regarding the outcome of the interplay among conflicting motivational forces. But the results of the studies undertaken up to now yield certain clear-cut conclusions that invalidate widely held notions. We know now that many people with substantial asset holdings continue to save large amounts year after year. Therefore, it is not generally true that in a wealthy society there is little willingness to save.

---

[6] The above conclusions are derived from the finding that in regression equations calculated by R. Kosobud from the 1960 to 1962 panel data, in which saving was the dependent variable, liquid asset holdings appeared with a positive sign and a small not significant parameter. Among upper-income people a positive influence, and among lower-income people a negative influence, of assets on amounts saved was found.

21

Common Stock

A very substantial share of America's material wealth is owned by corporations and therefore, indirectly, by stockholders. Over the last few decades this share has increased as the result of rapid corporate growth and an increasing tendency to incorporate family-controlled business firms. The stockholders' wealth has also grown, because stock prices have increased greatly. It should, however, be kept in mind that a sizable proportion of corporate stock is not in the possession of private individuals. Corporations, including financial institutions (insurance companies, etc.), own large amounts of stock in other corporations, and double counting must be avoided in determining national wealth. Considerable amounts of stock are also held by fiduciaries and estates (these might be attributed to individuals), as well as by welfare funds and foundations. We are not concerned, however, with the question of who owns American corporations—as is well known, ownership differs greatly from control, since most individual stockholders have no influence whatsoever on the corporations in which they own stock—nor will we discuss entrepreneurial investments in the form of ownership of shares in closely held corporations. The topic of this chapter is common stock as a part of household wealth.

In 1962 approximately 20 per cent of 55 million American family units owned stock (including shares of mutual funds). In the early 1950s, less than 10 per cent of 47 million family units owned stock. This is a most significant change, and we shall discuss the factors contributing to it in some detail. Yet such data alone do not tell the whole story. For, while it is true that there has been a very great increase in the number of stockholders, correct social and economic inferences may be drawn only in the light of the additional fact that the increase has been in the number of small stockholders.

Among the 20 per cent of stockholding families, at least one-fourth own stock worth less than $1,000. More than half own stock worth less than $5,000. Even the approximately 6 per cent who own stock worth $5,000 to $25,000 do not control a major share of national wealth. The 3 or 4 per cent of family units holding stock worth more than $25,000 own substantially more than 50 per cent of all stockholdings in individual possession; possibly the few families with more than $100,000 in stocks own as much as half of all stockholdings.

There are some stockholders in the middle-income group, but even among families with $10,000 to $15,000 income many fewer than one-half own stock, and only among families in the top-income brackets is ownership of sizable amounts of stock very common. In 1962, 6 per cent of the family units with over $15,000 income were found to own approximately 60 per cent of all privately held stock. In 1961 a special study indicated that about 4 out of 5 families with an income of more than $20,000 were stockholders. At the $20,000- to $50,000-income level the average (mean) value of stockholdings was found to be $70,000; at the over $50,000-income level the average value was found to be $400,000. It follows that the concentration of stockholdings increases sharply the further one proceeds up the scale of income.

There is no indication that the rate of concentration of stock-holdings declined during the postwar period, that is, during the time when the number of stockholders increased greatly. In the 1950s and early 1960s, wealthy people saved much more than the less wealthy. In addition, those with large stockholdings profited more from the increase in stock prices than those with small stock-holdings. Thus there was progress in spreading the ownership of American business in terms of the number of people involved, but not in terms of the value of stockholdings.[1]

[1] The available data on stock ownership are subject to some error. The figures quoted represent approximations which, however, suffice for the con-clusion drawn. Because of inadequate representation of the very rich in

In discussing experience with and attitudes toward common stock, the wealthy must be considered separately from other stockholders because of the great differences in the size of their stockholdings and the disparity in their attitudes. In the next section therefore, we shall disregard the large stockholders and the high-income families.

PUBLIC ATTITUDES TOWARD THE STOCK MARKET

Shortly after World War II most Americans thought that common stock was a risky and speculative investment. Very many people

---

sample surveys, rates of concentration derived from those surveys represent minimum estimates. The data quoted in the text are from the Surveys of Consumer Finances. See the monographs (Refs. 5, 7, and 8) and, for earlier data, G. Katona, J. B. Lansing, P. E. de Janosi, "Stock Ownership among American Families," *Michigan Business Review*, vol. 5, pp. 12–16, January, 1953; M. Kreinin, "Factors Associated with Stock Ownership," *Review of Economics and Statistics*, vol. 41, pp. 12–23, 1959; and the book by J. K. Butters, L. D. Thompson, and L. L. Bollinger, *Investment by Individuals*, Harvard University Press, Cambridge, Mass., 1953. Regarding stock ownership of high-income families, see Ref. 3.

The New York Stock Exchange has also collected data on the number of stockholders, defining stockholders, however, as individuals rather than family units. Husband and wife, if both own stock or if the stock is in the name of both, are both considered stockholders (the same is true of minor children). The method used by the Stock Exchange consists of determining the names and addresses of random samples among the 42 million stockholders on record and eliminating duplications. The Survey Research Center's finding that there were approximately 11 million shareowning family units is (after making suitable adjustments) in fairly good agreement with the finding of the New York Stock Exchange that there were 17 million individual shareowners in 1962.

The crucial question concerning the distribution of the *value* of stockholdings has not been studied by the New York Stock Exchange. New data on this question will become available from a study by Jean Crockett and Irwin Friend who analyzed the dividend income reported in individual income tax returns for 1960. (See American Statistical Association, *1963 Proceedings of Business and Economic Statistics Section*.) According to their preliminary report the 0.1 per cent of individuals reporting over $100,000 income owned 19.5 per cent of all individually owned stock, and the 1 per cent reporting over $25,000 income owned almost half of the stock. Crockett and Friend found that the rate of capital appreciation was similar among middle- and high-income people from 1957 to 1963. Obviously, however, the amounts of unrealized capital gains were highly concentrated among large stockholders.

recalled the stock market crash of 1929. This was true not only of older people but of many young ones as well who told about their fathers or uncles having lost money. A sizable proportion expressed such extreme opinions as, "You always buy at high prices and sell at low prices because you are at the mercy of insiders or manipulators." That you need expert advice, if not inside information, in order to make money in the stock market was a fairly common belief. Since the first and foremost requirement of most Americans for their savings is that they be safe, common stock was generally placed at the bottom of the list when people were asked for their preferences among bank deposits, government bonds, real estate, and stock.

Over a period of ten years a slow and gradual change in these stereotypes and attitudes could be observed, and it was possible to identify some major factors responsible for the change. The upward movement of the stock market and acquaintance with someone, or a few people, who had made good in the market and who were people like oneself, rather than insiders, contributed most to the change in opinions as well as in behavior. The opinions were not reversed, however. Even in 1960 hardly any respondent with less than $15,000 income argued that a person "like myself" should have most of his savings in common stock. But the notion that one should diversify one's financial reserves, and that a proper way of diversification was to invest a small share of one's reserves in stock, was widely accepted. Relatively few Americans appear to have acquired the belief that stocks are a sure thing, with which they cannot go wrong and are bound to get rich quick. But confidence in stocks, expressed, for instance, by saying that sizable losses are out of the question and that small losses are much less probable than capital gains, has become widespread. Because of the awareness of possible losses and the belief that money invested in stocks is not always readily available, since the time when it is needed might not be a good time to sell, many people who decided to buy stock used only a small part of their savings for this purpose.[2]

[2] The number of employee stockholders, who regularly buy small amounts of the stock of the corporations in which they work, also increased greatly during the postwar years. According to a study conducted by the New York Stock Exchange in 1960, 233 of the approximately 1,100 companies with shares listed on the Exchange had stock purchase plans in which 1½ million employees participated.

In two surveys conducted in the fall and winter of 1962, respondents who had bought stock that year were asked ". . . why did you think stocks would be a good investment?" It should be noted that the question was asked after the stock market decline—the market broke on May 28, 1962, and had not yet recovered greatly when the surveys were conducted—and most respondents had made their purchases before the break, presumably at higher prices than those that prevailed at the time of the interview. The distribution of answers received was the following:

Reasons for Buying Stock in 1962*	*Proportion of Buyers*
Prices low, capital gains expected	20%
Yield high or satisfactory	16
Hedge against inflation	5
Persuaded by friend or broker	10
Company stock; continuing arrangement to purchase	18
Speculation	3
No definite information obtained	28
	100%

* Some people mentioned two reasons for buying stock; only the replies given with emphasis are presented here.

The answers suggest fairly conservative attitudes on the part of purchasers of common stock. To be sure, speculation as the motive for stock purchases may be admitted less often than it prevails. The infrequent mention of inflation may be related to developments in 1962, but inflation was not found to be the major motive for stock purchases in any postwar years.

Most purchasers of common stock say that they sought and received information before they bought. The broker is mentioned as the most usual source of information (by over 40 per cent of buyers), but also frequent is the mention of friends (more than 20 per cent) indicating the great role of group influence. It appears that among middle-income people either most friends and colleagues own stock or none own stock. The answers received to the following two questions usually coincided: (1) "Would you say that some of your neighbors, friends, or colleagues own common stock?" and (2) "Do you own any common stock?"

The following questions were inserted in a nationwide survey conducted in August, 1962, that is, a few weeks after a major slide in stock prices:

1. Do you happen to know what the stock market has done during the last few months?

2. Tell me about it.

3. Why do you think this happened?

4. Nobody can know for sure, but what do you think stock prices will do during the next few months?

The decline in stock prices was fairly well known. Among all respondents 46 per cent, among stockholders 66 per cent, and among respondents with more than $10,000 income 68 per cent, reported that stock prices had declined. About one-third to one-half of these described the developments in such emotional terms as "collapse" or "crash," or said that the decline was substantial. These findings were not unexpected. It was reported before that following large movements in the stock market, a fair proportion of people gave a correct answer regarding market trends, while following a period in which stocks made no decisive movements in either direction, a much larger proportion professed to be uninformed (see Ref. 2, p. 146).

Of interest were the answers to question 3. Three different kinds of reasons for the stock decline were mentioned frequently:

Nineteen per cent of all people said that government action, or specifically the dispute about steel prices, was responsible for the stock decline.

Nineteen per cent referred to speculation or manipulation as an explanation of what had happened.

Twelve per cent said that stock prices had been too high before the drop.

(Some respondents who mentioned two of these reasons were tabulated twice.)

The first answer referred to what, at that time, was probably most often mentioned in the mass media; the third had been given publicly by spokesmen of the government at the time the survey was conducted. The frequency of the second explanation was surprising, because half a year earlier, in answer to questions about investment preferences, relatively few people had characterized common stock as speculative. Yet after the sharp, and for many people mysterious, drop in prices, the old notion that speculators and manipulators cause stock prices to advance or decline was suddenly revived.[3]

Since many people thought that the stock market had declined because of a one-time action by the government or because of manipulation, the influence of which might be transitory, the answers to question 4 may be understandable. Only two answers were given with any frequency: stock prices would go up, and stock prices would remain where they were. Practically nobody expected them to go down further. A rather substantial group said that stock prices would return to their previous high levels.[4] When, in September, 1962, I reported on these findings to a group of statisticians, the comment was made that the answer indicated the prevailing lack of information and lack of understanding of economic developments by the American public. Yet a few months later stock prices had regained their previous top levels.

The most relevant question addressed to stockholders read as follows: "Has the recent decline in the stock market made a difference to you financially, or not much difference, or what?" Only one out of ten stockholders said that the decline had made any difference. A few respondents were found, even in the small sample survey, who complained about having lost their savings or having been compelled to spend less as the result of stock market losses. But most stockholders, including most large stockholders, argued that the market decline did not really affect them because (1) they had long-range investments, or (2) they had suffered paper losses only, or (3) the difference was too small to matter.

When, in the fall of 1962, the economic attitudes expressed by stockholders were compared with those of people who did not own stock, only small differences were found. Most stockholders as well as most people informed about the stock market decline viewed business trends no differently from other people. They believed that what happened to the stock market was not closely related to what happened to the economy. Excluding the top asset holders, we find

[3] Data compiled by the New York Stock Exchange indicate that in 1962 individuals sold more stocks than they bought, and pension funds and institutions bought much more stock than they sold. One wonders whether the relatively small purchases by individuals are related to the change in attitudes revealed in the surveys.

[4] This opinion, elicited in the survey, about the future course of stock prices apparently did not induce very many people to buy stocks at that time, however.

that most Americans do not consider the stock market a barometer for business developments and, in fact, relegate the stock market to a relatively minor role in the economy. This is in line with their decisions about their own savings, for in most savers' portfolios, as reported above, investment in stocks does not play the principal role.[5]

THE LARGE STOCKHOLDERS

Many of the statements made thus far about stockholders do not hold true for top asset holders or high-income people. First, as a rule these people have the largest share of their wealth in stocks. According to the special study cited earlier (Ref. 3), publicly traded stock and business investment represent about 60 per cent of the assets of individuals with more than $25,000 income. Secondly, concern with inflation appears to be very widespread among top asset holders. In explaining their preference for stocks they uniformly referred to inflation. Finally and most importantly, top asset holders are frequent traders. Practically all of them buy or sell stock at least once a year and usually much more often. (Studies of all stockholders revealed that about half of them did not make any transactions during a twelve-month period, and among those who did, many bought company stock or shares of mutual funds, thus carrying out arrangements entered upon earlier.) Top asset holders employ professional help in order to take advantage of opportunities offered by the market. They are interested in buying stock for the sake of making a few points profit; their stock investments do not constitute funds that are meant to remain as they are until used.

This does not mean that top asset holders speculate on the market. They indignantly deny that they are speculators. There are exceptions, to be sure, as there are some middle-income people who

[5] Our analysis of the impact of the stock market decline in 1962 did not make use of psychoanalytic concepts. As an example of using such concepts we may refer to a speech by a psychoanalyst who related the 1962 stock slump to guilt feelings about money made too easily and about too great a prosperity. I concur in attributing significance to motivational factors of which the investors themselves are not clearly aware. But as of now I know of no psychoanalytic studies that have provided insights into the behavior of investors or that have advanced the understanding of fluctuations either in the stock market or in the business cycle.

purchase stock for the sake of short-term gains. Also some rich people were found to designate a small part of their assets to be used for speculative ventures. But on the whole today's American capitalism frowns on speculation. High-income people try to make use of economic opportunities. They act as the economic man is expected to act—which most people do not.

What makes stock market prices go up or down? Obviously this is a problem for psychological economics, because stock prices rise or fall as a result of similar decisions made at the same time by very many people about buying or selling stock. But this process of decision making has not yet been studied. There can be no doubt that the antecedents of decision making regarding the purchases or sales of stock could be studied. To be sure, the usual cross-section samples would not suffice for such an investigation. But it would be possible to draw samples of frequent traders or large investors and to enlist their cooperation. With the presently available techniques, studies of private investors would probably be more promising than studies of institutions and firms, since the operations of the latter, and especially their purchases and sales of stocks, are usually considered secret. As a starting point the investment policies of private investors might be studied to obtain data on their investment goals in relation to the composition of their assets. Then the factors inducing a review of investment portfolios and the precipitating conditions of transactions might be determined. Data on information received or sought, on personal contact and consultation, might also be of interest.[6] In addition to the behavior of individual buyers and sellers, the spread of news among groups of people and the mutual stimulation of group members also need to be analyzed. No doubt this is a large research project which would hardly produce significant insights in short order. Still, it is surprising that no large financial institution has as yet devoted even small funds to studies of this kind.

We conclude from our studies of stockholdings that the present distribution of wealth in corporate stock is far from equalitarian. By far the largest share of the value of stocks remains in the hands of a small minority of the public. Therefore, insofar as the influx of funds to the market by the growing number of small stock-

---

[6] The studies directed by the Securities and Exchange Commission in 1962–1963 did not extend to an analysis of the information given by brokers and investment counselors to their customers.

holders and especially by pension funds has contributed to raising stock prices, the major effect has been to make the rich richer. This is not to imply that the growth in the number of American families owning stock is meaningless. The ownership of some stock, however little, by millions of Americans may serve to stimulate more general public interest and deeper involvement in economic news and developments.

22

Installment Credit

The important role of installment credit in a mass consumption economy was mentioned early in this book. Consumer discretion is greatly enhanced by the possibility of making large purchases at a time when the consumer has but a small part of, rather than the entire, purchase price readily available. We also had repeated opportunity to call attention to fluctuations in the use of installment credit in connection with postwar business cycles (Part Three). The relation of recent recessions to installment buying is illustrated in Chart 7, which shows the movements of the major and most volatile element of installment credit, namely, automobile credit. Repayments of automobile debt were fairly steady from 1956 to 1962, while the extension of new credit fluctuated sharply. The shaded portions of the chart, representing the excess of repayments over extensions of automobile credit, indicate, not only the periods in which car sales were low, but also the duration and extent of the recessions in 1958 and 1961.

It appears that recessions coincide with periods in which extension of automobile credit is small, and prosperity coincides with periods in which extension of such credit is large. It does not seem, however, that installment credit dropped or advanced much earlier than business activity in general. Conclusions about fluctuations in installment credit causing the downturn or upturn in economic activity are not justified from findings that indicate coincidence. We shall return later in this chapter to the question of whether or not installment buying contributes to economic instability.

If incurrence of installment debt is discretionary, it must, according to the theory of psychological economics, depend not only on ability to buy but to a large extent also on willingness to buy. This has been confirmed by statistical calculations. We found that income and the Index of Consumer Sentiment, as determined by the Survey Research Center, jointly explain 77 per cent of the recent

CHART 7

Automotive Installment Credit Extensions and Repayments
(Seasonally adjusted)

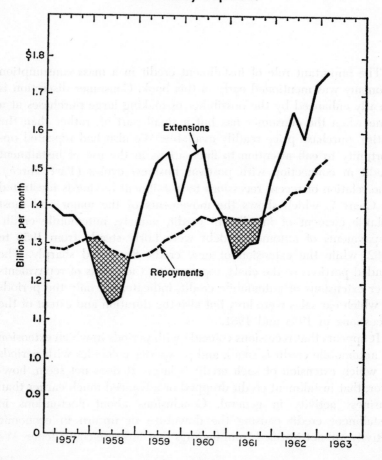

wide fluctuations in installment-credit extensions; the explanatory value of attitudes was found to be as large as that of income.[1]

A time lag was introduced into the calculations, which were based on measurements of attitudes and income as determined six to eight months before the extension of installment credit. Thus willingness to buy was found to have increased or decreased prior to the corresponding change in installment credit.

Some of the basic statistical data on installment credit are fairly well known. When World War II ended the American people were practically debt-free. During the first ten postwar years, both mortgage and installment credit increased sharply to an extent far exceeding the growth of income or GNP. During the years 1956 to 1962, however, the rise of installment credit was smaller than it would have been if it had corresponded to the increase in population and in income. Aggregate debt repayments stabilized in those years at approximately 13 per cent of disposable income. Close to one-half of all families owed installment debt at that time, while one-third had mortgage debt, and one-fourth short-term noninstallment debt. Altogether, excluding duplications, about two-thirds of all families had some kind of debt during the late 1950s and early 1960s.

Yet debt is far from being equally distributed among the American people. Whether a family buys on the installment plan depends primarily on its income and its age (or, more correctly, on the stage of its life cycle). Installment debt is a middle- and upper-middle-income phenomenon associated with younger people. The notion that the well-to-do pay cash while the poor buy on time is incorrect. Low-income people as well as high-income people buy on the installment plan less frequently than those in the $6,000 to $10,000-income groups. Older families use the installment plan less

---

[1] The following regression equation was calculated by Eva Mueller (Ref. 4) for the period 1952 to 1961:

$$E = 0.18Y_{-1} + 0.31A - 49 \qquad r^2 = .77$$

where E = extension of installment credit for cars and other consumer goods during the half year following survey; quarterly data at annual rates (Federal Reserve Board)

Y_{-1} = deflated disposable income during the half year preceding survey (Department of Commerce)

A = Index of Consumer Sentiment, Survey Research Center

r^2 = correlation coefficient, indicating the explanatory power of the equation frequently than younger families. Among younger families, those with children at home use installment credit most frequently. As Table 11 shows, in 1963 among families with children, the head of which was under forty-five years of age, 72 per cent owed installment debt and 42 per cent owed sizable installment debt. Among all American families the frequency of debt was much lower, namely, 50 and 27 per cent respectively.

Table II. Relation of Installment Debt to Income and Stage of Life Cycle, Early 1963

Spending unit income in 1962	Proportion of all units	Proportion owing installment debt in each group	Proportion owing installment debt of over $500 in each group
Under $3,000	26%	32%	9%
$3,000–5,000	20	53	28
$5,000–6,000	12	57	32
$6,000–7,500	13	62	37
$7,500–10,000	14	63	41
$10,000–15,000	10	53	35
$15,000 and over	5	30	23
All units	100%	50%	27%
Married with children, head under 45 years old	30%	72%	42%

NOTE: The table reads: In 1962, 26 per cent of all spending units had less than $3,000 income; early in 1963, in this income group 32 per cent owed installment debt and 9 per cent owed installment debt exceeding $500; etc.

In 1950 the use of installment credit was fairly rare among forty-five- or fifty-year-old people, who usually expressed unfavorable attitudes toward debt. By 1960 the cutting-off point between those who were in favor and those who were against installment buying rose to fifty-five or sixty years of age. Most users of installment credit were favorably disposed toward it; as we said earlier, the favorable attitudes were usually maintained when the users became older. Therefore between 1950 and 1960 the use of installment credit spread considerably among people forty-five to fifty-five years of age (see Ref. 6, Chapter 3). Younger age groups also increased their use of credit, but not to the same extent.

Over 60 per cent of new cars, but only 45 to 50 per cent of used cars, and not quite half of major appliances and furniture are purchased on the installment plan. The largest group of cars usually bought for cash is the inexpensive used cars. Credit buying of cars fluctuates to a greater extent than cash buying.

ATTITUDES TOWARD INSTALLMENT CREDIT

The Survey Research Center's inquiries about attitudes toward installment credit usually began with a simple question: "Do you think it is a good idea or a bad idea to buy things on the installment plan?" In the early 1950s about one-half of all people said "a good idea"; by 1960, about 60 per cent. The question served to introduce a more detailed study of consumer attitudes. We first inquired how people who were in favor of using installment credit explained their attitudes. Some people said that they, or their friends and neighbors, would have to go without various necessary and most useful articles if they could not buy on credit. Many other people emphasized positive aspects of credit buying. It appears justified, in their opinion, to pay for a car, a refrigerator, a washing machine, etc., while using those articles. The analogy with the accepted practice of buying a home with a mortgage is in the minds of many people.[2] Most people believe that automobiles and durable goods are expenditures that should be paid for out of income. It does not seem to be legitimate to use accumulated savings to pay for them. (Correspondingly, relatively few people mentioned buying a car as a reason for saving.) Installment credit is the method that makes it possible to pay for a car out of income. To be sure, the purchase is usually not paid out of one year's income, but out of the income of two or three years.

Yet many people are undecided when asked whether buying on the installment plan is a good idea, and even among those who approve, many do so conditionally. Two considerations are frequently noted: the size of the debt and the purpose of it. Some say that the credit is justified only if one does not borrow too much; one should know how far one can go and should never overburden oneself with debt. Others say that it depends on what one buys:

[2] Some homeowners in response to the survey question, "Do you own this house?" answer, "No, I am paying for it." An analogous notion may prevail in England regarding installment credit, as the British expression "hire purchase" suggests.

they approve of installment credit only for the sake of buying certain things and not other things.

In replying to specific questions, most Americans approved of the use of installment credit for the purchase of large necessary articles. In 1961, for instance, 84 per cent of a nationwide urban sample agreed that it was right to purchase an automobile on the installment plan. The proportion expressing the same opinion regarding large electrical appliances and furniture was only slightly smaller. But only 32 per cent approved of buying major clothing items and only 12 per cent of buying jewelry on time.

Opposition to installment buying is supported by three kinds of arguments. First there are people, representing about 10 per cent of the population in the early 1960s, who argue that debt is morally wrong. They believe that going into debt should be avoided under all circumstances. Then there is a similar proportion who think that installment buying makes for excessive spending. They say that people do themselves a disservice by "easy buying." The enjoyment of goods is paid for by future worries or even trouble. Thirdly, there are people who think that installment buying costs too much. In the early 1960s about one out of every six respondents raised the question of high costs when asked about the advantages and disadvantages of installment buying. We shall come back later to the problem of cost.

CHANGE IN THE RELATION BETWEEN BORROWING AND DISTRESS

Paramount among old stereotypes that linger on and impede the understanding of new developments is the notion that the consumer does nothing but consume. If, however, as we said in the first part of this book, investment consists both of business expenditures on plant and machinery and of consumer expenditures on durable goods, it can hardly be argued that borrowing for the sake of purchasing machinery is justified but borrowing for the sake of purchasing automobiles and appliances is unjustified. A second very old idea is the association of consumer credit with usury. In the distant past people borrowed when they were in distress, when illness, old age, bad harvests, or unemployment—all beyond their power to avert—made it necessary for them to get help from others. Because creditors frequently exploited the desperate situation of their debtors, personal credit was thought to require regulation while business credit did not.³ But today much of consumer credit, primarily mortgage and installment credit, is a sign of prosperity and a contribution to prosperity rather than being associated with distress of the borrower and with recession.⁴

The changed situation can be seen most clearly in the finding that consumers frequently buy on the installment plan, even though their liquid assets would permit them to pay cash for their purchases. In the late 1950s and early 1960s one-fourth to one-third of installment buyers had enough money in banks and bonds to pay cash. It is, of course, true that families having several thousand dollars in bank deposits hardly ever buy on the installment plan. But most others who would exhaust a large part of their liquid assets if they paid cash prefer not to touch them. It is not true that installment buying is resorted to only when it is unavoidable.

Additional information on this issue was obtained by asking survey respondents the following question (in 1959): "Speaking of buying a car on time, Mr. Smith has done so, although he has enough money in the bank to pay cash; why do you think he bought the car on time?" ("What kind of a man is he?" was a further probe added to this question.)

No fewer than two-thirds of all people could find a meaningful reason which explained to their satisfaction why Mr. Smith had bought his car on time, even though he had enough money in the bank to pay cash. The one most commonly given was that the money in the bank was earmarked for something else. Bank deposits should be kept for rainy days, many people said. Of interest are three further reasons attributed to Mr. Smith: one is that by buying on the installment plan one establishes credit; another, that by buying on credit rather than paying cash one gets better service, sometimes even a better price. Finally, a number of respondents said, in essence, that it is difficult to replace savings. In other words, after paying cash for, say, a car one is under no pressure to replenish

---

³ According to another notion of bygone days, poor people had only themselves to blame when in need of credit. They were called spendthrift and wasteful and thus were thought to deserve little consideration or accommodation.

⁴ This is true generally of dissaving also, the major forms of which are incurrence of debt and reduction of liquid assets. Nowadays the latter arises more often from unusual expenditures for which the savings were accumulated than from the need of paying for food or other necessities.

the depleted bank deposits. But after buying on the installment plan the monthly payments are made out of income, so after a couple of years one owns a car on which there is no debt and still has the money in the bank untouched. Questioning installment buyers with sizable liquid assets likewise indicated that such an awareness of one's own frailty is not uncommon.

Derogatory remarks about Mr. Smith, such as calling him a spendthrift or a foolish man, were made by only a small proportion of respondents. Many more people referred to him as a person who plans ahead or even as a cautious or intelligent person.

Consumer behavior in which there is clear evidence of advance financial calculations is not frequently encountered. The majority of American people today do not prepare detailed budgets for their expenditures. Some types of persons, of course, do so, and adversity or unusually constrained circumstances induce some others also to resort to budgeting. However, for most people installment buying and incurring other contractual obligations take the place of budgeting. Most people, when they buy a house for their own oc- cupancy, calculate the monthly mortgage payments they can afford to make. The same is true of large installment purchases, and most debtors know fairly exactly how much their installment payments are every month. Others, with several forms of debt, calculate all their contractual obligations—the mortgage payments of home- owners or the rent of tenants, plus taxes, social security payments, and life insurance premiums, as well as the monthly installment payments—and relate the total to their income. Many people intentionally set their contractual obligations fairly high. This is the way they make sure that they do not spend their income for unimportant things. The contractual obligations incurred for valuable purposes represent the first charge on income; most of what remains is needed for food and other necessities. In this way some people keep themselves from splurging and wasting money.

People with installment debt have been asked in many surveys whether it would be a hardship for them to make larger monthly payments or whether this would be easy. The proportion of those who said that it would be easy fluctuated between 20 and 30 per cent; it was relatively high among upper-income people and low among lower-income people. Of primary interest are people's ex- planations of their opinions. Those who said that it would be a hardship for them to make larger payments usually explained that their debt was up to their limit. The others asserted that they were not paying to their full capacity. Most people, in answering the question, revealed that they figured the relation of their installment payments to their income. This is in contrast to the opinion sometimes expressed that it is common practice, when no down payment is required, for people thoughtlessly to overburden themselves with debt.

OTHER FORMS OF CONSUMER CREDIT

The use of installment credit is of course not the only way of buying consumer goods without paying for them immediately. In 1960 close to 60 per cent of all American families and about 90 per cent of families with an annual income of over $10,000 had at least one charge account (frequently they had several). Charging purchases is not considered buying on credit. Buyers are reinforced in this notion by the absence of carrying or interest charges, even though many people are not very prompt in repaying their charge-account obligations.

Most people approve of having charge accounts; they express their approval by saying that charge accounts are very convenient and that they make it possible to purchase merchandise whenever it is needed or when good buys are available, even though the purchaser may be temporarily short of cash. Yet a substantial proportion of people are also aware of disadvantages. One may be induced to buy things not needed or more expensive than usual if one can charge the purchases; many people say that charge accounts make it hard to resist temptation.

Several new forms of consumer credit were introduced or became popular in the late 1950s. One was the use of credit cards, but little is known as yet about their influence on consumer behavior. Another is represented by credit arrangements introduced by department stores and other large stores, for which, in contrast to the charge accounts, interest is charged. The various forms of department-store credit requiring interest payments are viewed with some ambivalence by consumers. According to a survey conducted in 1961, broad groups of the population acknowledged the need for such credit and said that stores offering revolving credit provided a necessary service to their customers. A substantial proportion of people argued that without such credit, purchases of large clothing items, home furnishings, and the like, would often have to be postponed, or that the customer could not make use of clearance sales and special opportunities to purchase goods advantageously. Other people saw the same drawbacks in interest-bearing as in charge-account credit: One was tempted to buy more goods and more expensive goods than otherwise. Often the same people voiced both favorable and unfavorable opinions. Worries about how to pay the bills as well as concern about the expenses involved in using store credit were mentioned by many people.

It appears, then, that the notion of paying while using is widely accepted but is fully approved only if one buys goods of enduring value which are thought to be necessary. Many people advocate caution in using credit. Such attitudes must be viewed as beneficial to the economy as well as to the consumer credit industry. Both profit from slow and gradual growth; neither would gain from rapid and excessive increases.

During the first few postwar years, unusually large consumer expenditures were restricted to the purchase of cars and durable household goods. With increasing affluence consumers began to spend large sums of money on a great variety of goods and services. We shall speak later in this book of expenses for additions and improvements to houses, repairs, sports equipment, vacation travel, and education. The point we make here is simply that the purposes for which consumer credit was used were much more varied in the early 1960s than ten years earlier.

The increase in borrowing cash, rather than buying on credit, is probably related to the ever-expanding kinds of goods and services which consumers desire and for which they wish to delay payments. In addition, of course, personal loans are incurred for emergencies. Most of the loans granted by consumer-finance companies (small-loan companies) are for a few hundred dollars. Blue-collar workers are the most common borrowers; the following are some of the reasons they give in their applications for loans: to consolidate overdue bills, to pay for hospital and medical expenses, to repair homes or cars, to travel, to assist relatives. The stated reasons may not always be the real reasons; borrowing for purposes that are not admitted does occur but does not seem to be the rule.

ON THE COST OF CREDIT

Installment credit is expensive. This is not because the lenders are inefficient or noncompetitive, nor because they seek excessive profits, but primarily because of the high cost of operation. Investigation of debtors who borrow relatively small amounts and the collection of monthly payments create high operating expenses. On the other hand, reserves for losses can be kept fairly small in view of the low default rates. On the whole—although, of course, not in every individual instance—American consumers have proved to be conscientious debtors.

Most American consumers are not well informed about how much installment credit costs. This was shown in a nationwide survey conducted by the Survey Research Center in 1959, in which the following question was asked: "Do you happen to know how much interest or carrying charges one has to pay to buy a car on time? Suppose you need a thousand dollars which you would repay monthly over two years, about how much do you think the interest or carrying charges would be each year?"[5] About two out of every five respondents were unable to give a numerical estimate in replying to the question. Many said simply that they did not know. Among the respondents who gave answers in terms of dollar amounts or percentages, very many cited unrealistically low rates. Altogether, the interest per year was estimated

At 6% or less	by 23% of all people
At 7 to 15%	by 25% of all people
At 16% or more	by 13% of all people
No estimate	by 39% of all people
	100%

Since 10 per cent per annum was then about the lowest rate at which car buyers could finance their purchases in banks, and most installment credit cost considerably more, it is clear that either no knowledge at all or incorrect knowledge was much more common than correct knowledge.

On practically every item of knowledge or information we studied, we found that high-income people, people with college education, and people with personal experience in the particular item were better informed than other people. But this finding was not sustained concerning the cost of installment credit. We found that 30 per cent of people with more than $10,000 income, 31 per cent of people with a college education, and 31 per cent of people who made

---

[5] Intentionally the question was not made precise. No attempt was made, for instance, to find out whether the answers related to the amount originally borrowed or the unpaid balance. We tried to formulate a question that would be understandable to broad groups of people.

monthly payments of over $100 placed the cost of installment credit at 6 per cent or under.

The relatively great frequency with which costs of 4 or 5 and especially 6 per cent were mentioned may be interpreted as a carry-over from other information. Especially better-educated people dislike to confess to an interviewer that they do not know the answer to a simple question. As was noted earlier, the rate of interest paid on United States government savings bonds and on savings accounts is fairly well known. Most people also know that the cost of borrowing is higher than the interest on savings. On the basis of these pieces of information, some people appear to have surmised an answer to the question about the cost of installment buying. They mentioned some percentages with which they were familiar and which seemed appropriate to them. Actually, their answers represented uninformed guesses.

If consumers are uninformed about the cost of installment credit even though they buy on the installment plan, it is probable that cost is not the crucial consideration for them. This conclusion is justified because in many other respects people are very well informed about everything connected with purchasing an automobile. Regarding installment credit, most people are interested in something other than interest or carrying charges, namely, the size of the monthly payments.

It does not follow that many consumers are careless because they concern themselves with the size of monthly payments rather than with the cost of borrowing. How large a monthly payment they can afford to make represents the major factor that influences the decision to buy or not to buy. When in 1955 lenders lengthened credit terms considerably, many people could afford to buy a car who previously had not been able to. Cars did not get cheaper—interest paid over a longer period may even have made the purchase more expensive—but a car could be paid for out of three years' rather than two years' income.

This does not mean that people are not interested at all in the size of carrying charges. The great increase in the number of people who borrow from commercial banks rather than from sales finance companies (in the latter case the arrangements are usually made with the car dealer) may be traced directly to the knowledge that banks charge lower interest rates. Some people, however, prefer to transact their entire business at one place or believe that financing the car through the car dealer will result in advantages in service or even in a better trade-in price. It may be concluded from the inquiries into people's concern with and awareness of the cost of financing that the use of installment credit is quite insensitive to fluctuations in the interest rate. A change in the carrying charge by one or two percentage points per year would hardly influence the rate of purchase of consumer durable goods.

When in 1960 Senator Douglas introduced what has usually been called the "Truth in Lending Bill," which would require the lender to inform the borrower about the true rate of interest (in per cent of the unpaid balance per annum), the opposition centered primarily around the difficulty of calculating such an interest rate. No doubt disclosure of truth and prohibition of deception represent worthwhile objectives. In addition, enactment of the bill might result in increased price competition and might drive some lenders out of the market who charge unusually high rates. But it is doubtful that the bill would serve, as intended, "to assist in the promotion of economic stabilization." In the past the reduction of interest rates in times of recessions or their increase in times of prosperity has been about 0.5 or 1 per cent (if it occurred at all); since this is a very small change in comparision with the cost of installment credit, the impact of publicity about such a change could hardly be substantial.[6]

THE FUNCTION OF INSTALLMENT CREDIT

The most relevant aspect of the debate in connection with the bill requiring disclosure of interest rates concerns the economic function of installment credit. The preamble to the bill as submitted in 1960 and 1961, speaks of "the excessive use of installment credit" and of the dangers of such use for borrowers as well as for the

[6] In 1960 I went on record in opposition to an immediate enactment of the bill. (See *Hearings before Subcommittee of U.S. Senate Committee on Banking and Currency*, March 23, 1960, pp. 18ff. and 803ff.) At that time I was concerned about an impending recession—which did set in toward the end of the year—and feared that the bill would have deflationary effects over the short run. Some people upon learning that installment credit costs were, say, 16 per cent per annum, rather than 6 per cent as they had thought, might be shocked and postpone their purchases. Because of the possibility of such an "announcement effect," the time at which new information on interest rates is given to consumers is of importance.

entire economy. These views may be contrasted with the findings reported in this chapter on the fairly conservative attitudes most American consumers display toward installment credit. No doubt misuse of credit does occur, either in the form of borrowing too much or of borrowing for frivolous purposes, but the great majority of consumers were shown to view credit in a fairly restrained manner. The notion of its excessive use is also contradicted by the fact that over the period 1956 to 1962, aggregate installment debt did not increase in relation to income. The relation of debt repayments to disposable incomes stood at approximately 13 per cent over a period of seven years; this stability suggests that in those years insufficient use of credit by consumers may have even hampered economic growth.

In 1962 and 1963 credit extensions increased greatly; the 13 per cent ratio, to which many economic analysts had become accustomed and therefore considered normal, was exceeded. Should this development be greeted as a sign of economic upturn, or should it be viewed as a danger signal indicating excessive use of credit? Data are available that help clarify this question. Let me first make the point that an increase in aggregate debt may be due (1) to debtors having borrowed larger amounts than earlier, (2) to an increase in the number of borrowers, or (3) to both factors. When the ratio of aggregate debt to aggregate income increases, it is not necessarily true that the quality of borrowing has deteriorated; it may simply mean that there are more borrowers.

Table 12 indicates that the major new development, at least until early 1963, was indeed an increase in the number of borrowers (corresponding to an increase in the number of automobile buyers). From 1962 to 1963 the proportion of spending units owing installment debt rose from 46 to 50 per cent, even though the number of spending units also continued to grow. Yet the proportion of individual units with a relatively high debt-income ratio (more than 20 per cent) did not increase; indeed, in the mid-1950s this proportion was higher than in 1962 or 1963. In terms of income, new debtors were quite similar to the earlier debtors. Table 11, presented earlier, showing the percentage of spending units in various income groups who had installment debt at the beginning of 1963, differs only very slightly from a similar table prepared in 1960 or 1961. In all these years the great majority of debtors used less than 20 per cent of their income to repay their debts.

Table 12. Ratio of Annual Installment Debt
Payments to Disposable Income
(*In Per Cent of All Spending Units*)

	1954	1957	1959	1960	1961	1962	1963
Make installment debt payments with payment-income ratio: *							
Under 10 per cent	15	15	17	18	18	16	17
10–19 per cent	14	16	17	17	18	17	19
20 per cent and over	13	15	13	12	10	12	12
Not ascertained	1	2	1	1	1	1	2
Total	43	48	48	48	47	46	50
Make no installment debt payments	57	52	52	52	53	54	50
Total	100	100	100	100	100	100	100

* In surveys conducted in January–February of each year, respondents were asked about the size of their monthly payments and about their income during the preceding calendar year. The debt payment-income ratio was obtained by dividing the monthly payments by one-twelfth of the disposable income of the same respondents.

Who are the people with unusually high debt-income ratios? Detailed studies indicate that mostly they are young people and people with optimistic income expectations. For some of them, the income in the preceding year, to which their debt had been related, was unusually low. Some figured their newly incurred debt in relation to expected income increases. In all these respects there was no change from 1961 to 1963.[7]

It does not follow, however, that the increase in the aggregate debt-income ratio in 1963, or further increases in future years, is necessarily devoid of danger. The greater the debt and the greater the contractual obligations in general, the less the economy can afford income declines or even the frustration of optimistic income expectations. The process of figuring how much debt one can afford in relation to current income or to an increased income that the debtors expect to receive in a year or so may become precarious

[7] See Refs. 7 and 8. That debtors did not feel overburdened with debt in 1963 was also indicated by direct questioning. In 1963 the distribution of consumers' answers as to whether it would be hard or easy for them to increase their payments on debts was substantially the same as a year earlier or three years earlier.

should incomes fall or fail to rise. Should incomes decline, install-ment credit would contribute to the instability of the economy. But credit itself does not cause declines in income; it should therefore be considered as a factor that potentially reinforces recessions rather than a factor that initiates them. By the same token, of course, substantial credit extensions may reinforce booms.

One final argument that has been used against credit purchases maintains that carrying charges represent waste. Obviously, by paying cash, consumers would save the expense of the carrying charges. It does not follow, however, that abolishing or restricting installment credit would result in more money being available for the purchase of goods. The accelerating influence of credit buying must be taken into consideration. In a society in which incomes rise with age, installment buying plays a particularly important role. We have pointed out before that over the past fifty years there has been a shift in the working population from farmers and unskilled workers to white-collar and professional people and that, with the change in the distribution of occupations and with in-creased educational levels, the peak income is now earned at a later age in life (Chapter 12).

Without understanding these basic changes that have taken place in our society, it is not possible to comprehend the role that con-sumer credit plays in the present-day American economy. Were it not for the institution of consumer credit, our young people would have to be satisfied with a lower standard of living. Arriving at a mature age, they might find that they had accustomed themselves to a simple way of life and might have no use for the things they could then afford. It has been said in the past that young people should save for their old age. The new situation is that people, in effect, borrow while they are young, when they benefit most from things bought on credit, and delay the accumulation of financial reserves until later in life.

Saving money in advance of its use is not necessarily preferable to buying goods first and saving through repaying the debt after-ward. Today in America, a home, a car, appliances, and house furnishings are usually acquired before financial reserves are accum-ulated. For many people borrowing and saving are not at opposite ends of the pole but activities of different stages of the life cycle. The practice of installment buying does not detract from the desire to save.

Installment credit has made it possible for millions of American families to acquire what they consider necessities at a fast rate, in anticipation of future earnings. Today Americans marry young and have children shortly after marriage. They believe that children should be brought up in a home they own, located in a nice neighborhood, and equipped with a refrigerator, a washing machine, and many other appliances. The question is no longer whether young couples should have children *or* durable goods; thanks to installment credit, they have both.

There is nothing normal about a 13 or 14 per cent debt-income ratio. An increase in that ratio is probable in the not too distant future and would benefit the American economy. During the second half of the 1960s the growth of the economy will be retarded unless the amount of installment credit outstanding increases. In those years the war-baby-boom generation will reach the stage of marriage and household formation. Desires to buy homes on mortgage credit and durable goods on installment credit will then become more widespread. Both ability to buy and willingness to buy will depend primarily on the employment situation and employment prospects. But the availability of consumer credit and the use made of credit opportunities will represent important factors influencing the rate of economic growth.

A rapid increase in the use of installment credit is partly a consequence of a mass consumption economy and partly a factor promoting its growth. In this respect fifty years of American developments have been replicated in Western Europe in a much shorter period of time. In most Western European countries installment credit doubled in the course of a few years in the late 1950s and early 1960s. In those years the economic boom in the Common Market countries, which began with large investments by business firms and governments, changed into a consumer-goods boom. What happened with cars in America in the 1920s and with automatic washers and television sets after World War II has all been happening at the same time in Europe, and in Japan as well. Very broad groups of the population, including millions of blue-collar workers, have become aware of the pleasures of vacation trips and camping.

Europe on the move and Europe in search of consumer goods which may be bought on credit—these new developments have become important economic stimuli. In Europe, as in America, the expansion of installment credit has contributed to increasing prosperity. As a consequence of the eagerness of European workers to purchase more durable goods and to raise their standard of living, their demands for higher incomes likewise rose sharply. It is precisely such developments, leading to the emergence of mass consumption societies, that we hope may one day result in the economic welfare—and ultimately even in the political welfare—of more and more nations of the world.

PART SIX

Spending

23

Automobiles

There is little necessity to justify studying automobiles as a major item of discretionary spending in the United States. The automobile is not only one of the most important possessions of the American family but also one of the major factors in the economy. It provides a livelihood to one American out of every seven. As a result, the great fluctuations that occur in the demand for cars tend to cause alternating periods of prosperity and recession. The number of cars bought in the first half of 1958, for example, was almost 25 per cent lower than in the first half of 1957—which itself was far from a good year—and changes by as much as 20 per cent from one year to the next occurred in later years as well.

On the average, about one out of every four families purchases a car each year. Almost two-thirds of these buy used cars and slightly more than one-third, new cars. The average price of a new car—about $3,000 in the early 1960s—far exceeds the average price of a used car—about $800. Comparisons, however, should be made on the basis of amounts of money spent rather than of prices, since more than 80 per cent of new-car buyers, but only 50 per cent of used-car buyers, trade in a car or sell a car when they buy a newer one. The net outlay, that is, the amount buyers have to pay or finance, averages about $2,000 for new cars and $650 for used cars.

Buyers of new cars differ from buyers of used cars by age and income. In general, the higher the income, the higher the proportion of new-car buyers; but up to the group with a $10,000 annual family income the number of used-car buyers exceeds the number of new-car buyers in every income group. Young people usually buy used cars. The proportion of income spent on car purchases does not vary much with income. The net outlays of different income groups, expressed in per cent of income, are fairly constant except that among those with high income the proportion is somewhat smaller, and among those with low income somewhat higher, than average.

Two-thirds of the American labor force commute to work by private automobile. The proportion of car owners using their cars to get to work is higher still. One out of every five family units does not own a car. This proportion has declined rather slowly during the last ten years. Nonowners are common in the low-income groups, among older people, and among inhabitants of our largest cities, especially those who live in the central districts of those cities. Ownership of two or more cars by one family rose rapidly in the 1950s and jumped sharply in 1962–1963. In 1963 close to 25 per cent of all families owned more than one car. In addition to high income, suburban living and a working wife are factors associated with multiple car ownership.

FLUCTUATIONS IN AUTOMOBILE DEMAND

The study of automobile demand can best be approached by asking: What makes for more and what makes for fewer car purchases? Since changes in ability to buy—income, assets, debts—are slow and gradual, while the demand for cars often exhibits sharp and sudden variations, the importance of psychological factors is clearly indicated. Some of these, amply discussed in previous chapters, are not specific to the auto market. Optimistic views of personal financial prospects and of the general business outlook contribute to an increase in the willingness to embark on discretionary purchases. Buying new cars is, of course, discretionary in most instances. Relatively few new cars are bought by those people who need transportation either because they have no car or because their car is in bad condition. Usually the new car replaces an older one which is technically still in good condition, and sometimes it represents changing from a one-car to a two-car family. In either instance the purchase can easily be postponed until times seem more suitable. It follows that pessimistic personal and business expectations make for a smaller, and optimistic and confident views for a larger, demand for new cars.

A second set of factors is represented by characteristics of the car supply. Prices exert an influence in the sense that car buying is adversely affected when consumers believe that prices have gone up substantially. This was indicated in surveys by the relatively large number of people who, after prices had risen, said "This is a bad time to buy, because prices are high." Conversely, car buying is stimulated when most people think that car prices have remained about the same for some time. Many people are quite sophisticated about automobile prices. They are aware of fluctuations in trade-in prices as well as in discounts, which are often more important than changes in the list prices of new cars.

Reactions to new models and especially to the assortment of cars offered represent further important considerations that are influential in determining the demand for cars. It has not yet been possible to make reliable measurements of the extent of this influence. The fact of its existence and importance will nevertheless emerge clearly when we discuss the data collected in connection with the changes in automobile demand from 1955 to 1963.

When automobile purchases over a time span of five or ten years are studied, rather than the fluctuations from one year to the next, the influence of certain enduring considerations becomes apparent. The demand for automobiles tends to grow because of the increase in the population, the increase in the number of cars on the road, and the resultant increase in the number of cars scrapped. Also, car demand may be expected to be stimulated by an increase in real incomes. Therefore the car market can be pictured by a fairly steady-rising trend line, superimposed on which are the variations caused by changes in willingness to buy. These changes influence the number of cars bought over a time span of several years as well as from one year to the next. Even fluctuations in scrappage rates depend as much on people's willingness to upgrade their cars as on the number of old cars on the road.

1955 was the best automobile year in the postwar period; the automobile boom of that year sparked the economic upturn and led to several years of prosperity. There was an improvement in general optimism and confidence in the course of 1954, and the models introduced in the fall of that year were greeted most favorably. In addition, there was a unique influence at that time that may hardly ever be repeated: Installment credit maturities were lengthened substantially. While in 1953 it was difficult to finance a new car for more than twenty-four months, by 1955 financing over thirty-six months became quite common. Lengthening of the financing period results in a reduction of the amount of monthly payments. Since the ability to make monthly payments out of income represents a crucial consideration in car buying, many people were in a position to buy cars in 1955 who could not have done so earlier.

Turnover rates were unusually high in 1955: People turned in their cars for new cars after having used them for a much shorter period than usual. In this sense car sales in 1955 impinged on the demand of the next few years. Nevertheless, the auto boom of 1955 was not followed by a slump. In 1956 and 1957 sales remained fairly high, although not as high as in 1955. Thus there is no justification for assuming that one good auto year necessarily saturates the market. The good economic climate coupled with frequent income increases served to stimulate auto buying, even though complaints about rising car prices and dissatisfaction with the models offered were expressed occasionally as early as 1956 and frequently in 1957. The industry's rule of thumb—if you have a good thing you should give the buyer more of the same—backfired. People did not react favorably to increased length and width and to more chrome and fins, even though those features had had great appeal at the time of their introduction. "All cars look alike" was a common response in 1957, and some people commented that they had nothing to choose from.

In the recession year 1958, auto sales fell more sharply than most other major economic indicators, and an increased share of the cars bought consisted of small foreign imports. During the subsequent economic recovery, compact cars were introduced. They were greeted with enthusiasm: most people made some favorable comment about one feature or another, and few were critical. From 1959 to 1962 close to one-third of all the people interviewed argued that a compact car would be a better buy for them than a regular-size car. Attitudes are, however, advance indicators of purchases, and it frequently takes some time before new attitudes are reflected in demand. Many people with favorable attitudes toward compact cars decided not to buy one until they were tested over a period of time and their worth proved.

The introduction of compact cars had a great and beneficial

influence on the entire automobile market, including regular-size cars. Year after year, before their introduction, the majority of people expressed the opinion that cars cost more than the year before. Beginning with 1960, the opinion "Car prices haven't changed much" became predominant. Cheaper cars were available; if a buyer paid more than a year earlier, it was by choice rather than necessity. The number of different makes and models on the market increased greatly; one had much to choose from, and many people found one or another new feature of the cars offered most attractive.

While the improvement in attitudes toward cars was evident in 1960, the upswing in demand was delayed by the recession of 1960–1961. But when people became aware of improved economic conditions, there was a sudden change. Expressed intentions to buy cars soared as early as May, 1961, and remained unusually high during 1962 and 1963 (see Chart 8). The 1962 car models, introduced in the fall of 1961, sold very well, and the 1963 models still better, further contradicting the notion that the new-car market is quickly saturated. In these years automobile demand was stronger than the demand for most other products and served as the major factor that prevented the economy from slipping into stagnation or recession.

The high level of car sales in 1963 was again stimulated by satisfaction with the assortment of cars offered and their prices and was given a further boost by a completely new factor in the economy: In 1962 or 1963 the first large group of World War II babies reached their sixteenth year, that is, the age at which most Americans start to drive. This factor will remain influential for several years, but made the greatest change when it first appeared.

An increase in the number of drivers' licenses issued is, of course, not identical with an increase in car ownership. But the prices of used cars were unusually firm in those years, indicating an upward trend in the number of people buying their first car. Higher prices for used cars, and thus higher trade-in values, amount to a reduction in the cost of new cars. The increase in two-car families was also related to the presence of an increased number of drivers in many families.

While there were fluctuations in consumer sentiment, and in general economic trends as well, expressed intentions to buy new cars remained fairly stable and consistently high from May, 1961,

CHART 8

Intentions to Buy a New Car During Next 12 Months*

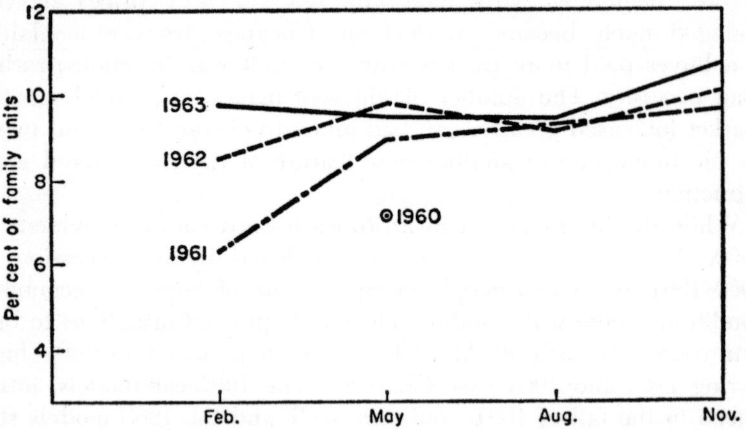

* Survey Research Center data. Family units that reported they would or probably would buy, plus one-half of those who said they might buy, during the next twelve months. Respondents who were uncertain whether they would buy a new or a used car were apportioned equally between the two categories. The data are not adjusted for seasonal variations or for population increases.

to November, 1963 (see Chart 8). Intentions to buy cars are worth citing, even though, as explained in Chapter 9, they reflect a relatively late intercept in the process of decision making. In addition, buying intentions are subject to some seasonal variations. Probably they are relatively high shortly after the introduction of new models. Therefore year-to-year changes are more relevant than changes from one quarter to the next. Moreover, intentions, when presented as a percentage of families, fail to reflect the impact of population growth (the number of families increases by approximately 2 per cent a year). In order to go beyond determining changes in the proportion of advance planners and to consider the marginal buyers as well, measures of consumer sentiment—toward personal finances, the business outlook, and market conditions—take on great importance.

It took eight years before the record car sales of 1955 were equaled: both in 1955 and 1963 approximately 7½ million new cars were sold in the United States. (Car production in 1963 was still not as high as in 1955, because in 1963 car imports were much higher and exports somewhat lower than in 1955.) In 1963 consumers kept the economy moving forward. In the words of the President's Council of Economic Advisers, "Much of the strength in 1963 centered in residential construction and automobile buying."[1] This was the case even though neither residential construction nor automobile buying was booming in 1963. From 1955 to 1963 population rose by 15 per cent and real per capita disposable income rose by 13 per cent, while automobile buying increased hardly at all. Thus sales of 7½ million automobiles could be considered remarkably high in 1955 but not in 1963. In view of the continuing increase in population, in incomes, and in the number of cars on the road, sales of only 7½ million cars in the late 1960s would indicate that consumers willingness to buy new cars was fairly restricted.

The experience with fairly steady car sales in 1962–1963 offers no assurance that there will not be substantial fluctuations in the future. There is always the possibility of consumers' willingness to buy being unfavorably affected by reactions to prices and the assortment of cars offered or by considerations not related to the car market. Furthermore, the very fact of high automobile sales causes some people to defer buying, since high sales are thought to worsen the buyer's bargaining position. Then, too, the increase in multiple-car owners, though apparently assured over the long run, is usually interrupted by plateaus.

ATTITUDES TOWARD THE AUTOMOBILE

During the lean auto years, from the fall of 1957 till the fall of 1961, many writers argued that the American people's attitudes toward the automobile had changed. In earlier years the car had been recognized, not only as a highly valued possession, but also as the family's most visible status symbol. It was then argued that Americans bought new and fancy cars to keep up with the Joneses and to support their children's struggle for status within their peer groups. In addition, the kind of car selected was believed to reflect the buyer's hidden personality traits. All this supposedly changed radically, and between 1958 and 1961 some critics spoke of the end of the auto era.

Probably the generalizations were exaggerated in both periods.

[1] See *Economic Report of the President,* January, 1964, p. 48.

Survey findings are available indicating that there were some changes in attitudes toward the car between the first postwar years and the early 1960s. Yet the changes were far from radical. The car remained very important for most Americans, but for many it was no longer an end in itself but a means to an end. The variety of the good things of life which Americans aspired to possess was much larger in the early 1960s than in the late 1940s. The automobile became just one among several greatly desired objects, yet one which was necessary in order to accomplish other desired goals.

As we noted in Chapter 8, there is much justification for speaking of a proliferation of wants as a result of increased affluence. When, shortly after World War II, survey respondents were asked about things they would like to have or would like to spend money on if they had the funds, relatively few things were mentioned. A new car, a one-family house, and a few major appliances were the only articles that received frequent mention. In the early 1960s, however, when respondents were asked about things they would like to have or do, but could not with their present income, the list of things mentioned by sizable proportions of people was quite lengthy. In addition to the valued possessions of ten or twelve years earlier, a summer cottage, a motorboat, numerous hobby and sporting goods, power tools, and additions or repairs to the home were each mentioned by a sizable proportion of respondents. Very substantial was the increase in the frequency with which travel was mentioned—vacation trips as well as trips to visit distant parts of the United States and foreign countries. Educational needs both for children and adults were likewise often referred to in discussing unsatisfied wants.

It is sometimes said that "people have run out of things they can't do without." As a result of having bought a great variety of goods over many years, American consumers are thought to be well stocked up, and their wants are thought to have become less insistent. Yet when the Survey Research Center asked a question intended to elicit a mention of unfulfilled wants and desires, the proportion of the population *not* mentioning any wants was the same in the 1960s as in the 1950s. The question, addressed to respondents after they were asked about their buying plans, read: "Now about your wishes, are there any special expenditures you would really *like* to make, or anything you would like to spend money on?" The negative answer, indicating no special desires, only fluctuated over the years between 28 and 31 per cent. More important still are differences in the frequency of negative answers among income groups and age groups.

Proportion not wanting to make any special expenditures (1962):

Income groups:	Under $3,000	$3,000 –4,999	$5,000 –7,499	$7,500 –9,999	$10,000 and over
	43%	33%	24%	23%	25%
Age groups:	19–34	35–44	45–54	55–64	65 and over
	16%	24%	29%	43%	53%

Only among older people or those with lower income, do we find a substantial proportion with no wants. The population groups which make the largest discretionary purchases also have the largest number of unfulfilled desires.

In 1963 we experimented with a somewhat different formulation of the question. Following inquiries about past transactions, respondents were asked: "Are there things you feel you would like to have or do, but can't do with your present income?" (If "Yes": "What kinds of things are these?") Again a variety of answers were received, with durable goods, travel, leisure-time expenditures, and additions to or repairs of houses receiving most frequent mention. Only 27 per cent of a representative sample of consumers answered in the negative. Primarily older people and, not surprisingly in view of the stress on income in the new question, respondents with more than $15,000 income constituted this group.

It appears then that a decade or two of a continuously high rate of buying on the part of very many Americans did not make for saturation. Moreover, even our desires are reality tested; most poor people dream of fewer expensive things than wealthier people. Obviously, after purchasing a new car or a second car, our car needs are saturated for a while; but other needs and wants, previously less noticed, may become salient. We raise our sights when we feel that we are making progress. Newer articles or articles used by relatively few people and not belonging in the "standard package" are desired primarily by people who are well provided with the standard goods.

We may also derive certain conclusions about automobile demand from the finding that a greatly increased number of people are interested in owning a summer cottage or a boat, in hunting or fishing, and in traveling. To satisfy these desires, an automobile is indispensable. The car is needed in order to reach one's summer home or boat, and it is the most frequently used as well as the preferred method of travel. We shall speak of the paramount importance of the automobile for family excursions and travel in Chapter 25 and may say here only that long-distance family travel makes people want large and powerful new cars. At the same time the spread of suburban living and the absence of public transportation in most outlying districts increase the need for a car for other purposes. Cars have become necessities for commuting to work, for taking children to school, for shopping, and for visiting, in addition to the widespread discretionary use of the car during leisure time.

No doubt the place of the car in American life has changed somewhat. The generation which grew up without a car has almost disappeared. A necessary article is taken for granted and may lose some of its glamour. Especially families having two cars may view their second car from a strictly utilitarian standpoint. But these changes have not reduced people's felt need for a car and even for two or three cars in the family. Only in a few central districts of very large cities—Manhattan is a prime example—are there people who profess not to need a car.

These long-lasting considerations that indicate continuing needs and desires for cars do not assure the prevalence of favorable attitudes for cars at all times. It will not be easy for the industry to bring its products in line with consumer wants, because divergent and even inconsistent tendencies can be observed in consumer tastes. To the extent that the automobile has become a necessary means to an end rather than an end in itself and to the extent that it must compete with other desired goods, the public may be expected to become increasingly price conscious. Therefore, smaller and cheaper cars, that can be parked more easily and consume less gas, are desired. (Since gas is an ever-recurring expense, its cost seems to be subjectively more important than would be warranted by rational considerations.) At the same time, and often on the part of the same people, high value is placed on such expensive features as automatic transmission, power steering, bucket seats, and various new accessories. Although most consumers are fairly well informed about everything connected with cars, they do not give clear direction to the industry.

The automobile is no longer cherished without criticism, and people do not necessarily approve of whatever the manufacturers do. Criticism can be easily evoked. For instance, in a 1960 survey respondents were asked about the annual model changes in a question formulated as follows: "How do you feel about the practice of changing the appearance of new cars every year?" About 40 per cent answered in unfavorable terms as against 30 per cent who thought that the changes were necessary or useful. (The remaining 30 per cent mentioned both sides of the argument or said, "It doesn't matter.") The higher the income, the more frequent was the notion that changing the appearance of cars every year served no useful purpose and was wasteful. At the same time, however, many people said that they wanted one or another of the features available in the new cars, and this response was given both by some who were in favor and some who were against annual changes. Substantial differences in the success of different car models and types indicate that consumers make up their own minds. Advertising and merchandising efforts may contribute to the success but do not insure it. Whether the great expense of the annual model changes pays off or the auto industry would be better off if it made changes less often and used the savings to reduce car prices —this is a question to which no reliable answer can be given.

Overwhelmingly, the American people expressed satisfaction with the performance of their cars in the early sixties. They thought that the cars were "better" than those produced some years earlier. People also approved of the various major accessories and thought that the repair shops to which they took their cars frequently did a good or fair job.[2] To some extent perhaps these judgments reflect the ease with which survey respondents express satisfaction. But a comparison with attitudes toward major household appliances is illuminating and reveals some unique features of the automobile on the American scene.

HOUSEHOLD APPLIANCES

In 1961 the Survey Research Center asked the following question in nationwide surveys: "We are interested in the quality of house-

---

[2] About one-half of all car owners said that during the preceding year they had had repairs on their car other than upkeep or small adjustments. The middlemost estimate of the annual repair costs per car owner exceeded $100.

hold goods—appliances, house furnishings, and the like. Do you think their quality has improved during the last few years, or remained as it was, or did it get worse?" In reply 37 per cent of families said that the quality had improved, 21 per cent said that the quality had remained the same, 29 per cent said that the quality had deteriorated, and 13 per cent were uncertain or did not know.

The answers were rather uniform in the various income and age groups; if anything, high-income people and people with many appliances were somewhat more critical than others. Almost as many people believed that the quality of major household appliances had deteriorated as believed that it had improved. Only one out of every three families felt there had been quality improvement—even though new models are presumably introduced because they are thought to meet consumer needs better than the older models. Many people said that newer appliances performed better than those produced a few years earlier, but many others complained about the lack of durability of merchandise produced at the time of the study.

Studies were also made about the frequency of service calls in connection with major household appliances. The questions were: "How about repairs on household appliances, TV set, plumbing and heating equipment—did you have someone come to your house to fix any of these during the last twelve months or so?" (If "Yes") "How many service calls were there during the last twelve months?" The data show that service calls and repairs are frequent and expensive. About 45 per cent of all families said that in 1961 they had had no service calls; 15 per cent recalled one; another 15 per cent, two; 14 per cent, three or four; and 10 per cent, five or more service calls. Among families with more than $10,000 annual income, who own a larger number of appliances than lower-income people, only 25 per cent said they had had no service calls and 30 per cent remembered four or more. Among those who had had service calls, the middle-most annual expense had been approximately $30 per family.

Dissatisfaction with the cost of repairs on appliances, plumbing, and heating equipment was expressed quite frequently: about one-third of those who had had service calls complained about the charges made. The dissatisfaction may be attributed to the fact that in most instances consumers have no basis for comparison. In the case of auto repairs it is usually possible to drive to several

repair shops to obtain cost estimates, but when one calls a serviceman to the house, one must pay whatever the charges are. On the
other hand, most people said that they were satisfied with the work
done.

Regarding major household appliances, there is no support for
notions about pronounced dissatisfaction with the kind of goods
offered, but there is no evidence either of heightened interest in
new products or new models that would stimulate consumers to
upgrade their possessions. In this respect, in the early 1960s the
automobile industry was in a more favorable situation. In another
area of consumer attitudes, however, the appliance industry was
at least as well regarded as the automobile industry. Satisfaction
with appliance prices was pronounced, and the majority of people
who had an opinion on the subject said that appliance prices had
not gone up in the last few years and were reasonable. Nevertheless,
in the early 1960s there was an upsurge in car demand and no
similar movement in appliance demand. It appears, therefore, that
willingness to buy is greatly dependent on satisfaction with the
assortment of goods offered and the attractiveness of new models
and products.

There exist many further differences between the situation of the
automobile industry and the industries producing other major durable goods. Furniture and major household appliances are bought
by a larger proportion of people—40 per cent of all families buy
at least one of these items every year—than automobiles; the
amounts spent are lower (on the average $400 a year per family,
since many people buy more than one article in a year). Trade-in
is much less important in appliances than in car purchases. In the
case of major appliances the frequency of buying does not increase
with income, as it does in the case of automobiles. On the other
hand, both types of goods are bought more frequently by the
younger than the older age groups, and credit buying is very
important for both.

To some extent automobiles and major appliances are competitive
goods: relatively few families buy both kinds of goods in the same
year. It makes sense, therefore, to consider the purchases of all
major durable goods together. In most of the years since 1955, about
one-half of all families made such a purchase. On the average, the
net outlay on these goods amounted to 12 to 13 per cent of income
in the early 1960s. The proportion was higher among low-income

people and among younger people, and lower among upper-income and older people.

During the last few years the development of the automobile industry has been much less favorable in America than in some foreign countries. In the six Common Market countries 4.6 million motor vehicles (cars, trucks, buses) were produced in 1962 as against 800,000 in 1950. In this same period the share of these countries in the world's automobile production rose from 7.5 to 26 per cent. On the other hand, American car production was only slightly larger in the good year 1962 than in the good year 1950. Three European countries—Germany, France, and the United Kingdom—each exported more cars in the 1960s than the United States.

The enormous strides in the motorization of Western Europe are reflected in these figures, but they do not give a correct picture of the success of the American automobile manufacturers. As is well known, American firms are represented abroad through subsidiaries and thus profit from the growth of automobile demand in the Common Market as well as in the rest of the world. Instead of exporting cars, the United States exports know-how, capital and, to some extent, automobile parts. Car imports to the United States, in which the foreign subsidiaries of the American manufacturers participate to a small extent only, rose greatly in the late 1950s. The increase was arrested with the introduction of compact cars. The American industry strengthened its control of the domestic market in the 1960s.

The sizable increase in the number of young families which will occur during the second half of the 1960s will give rise to increased automobile demand. But whether those years will be unusually good or only mediocre automobile years will depend on the four major considerations discussed above, namely, on people's personal financial situation and prospects, on their general economic outlook, on their perceptions of car prices, and on the attractiveness of the assortment of goods offered. The rate of increase in the number of two-car owners will likewise be of major significance and, in view of prevailing desires, will depend primarily on income trends. Future automobile demand will, of course, also be influenced by the congestion of streets and highways and the availability of parking facilities, on the one hand, and the rate of deterioration in public transportation, on the other.

24

Housing

Certain short-term population movements may be predicted with great confidence. Because of the war-baby boom, in 1970 the number of people between twenty and twenty-five years of age will be approximately 50 per cent higher than in 1960. Some consequences of the population trend are likewise predictable. The number of high school students showed a sudden and sharp increase in the early 1960s, and the number of those applying for a college education will surely go up a few years later. At the age of sixteen or seventeen, the young people get their drivers' licenses. Soon thereafter the rate of purchase of inexpensive used cars increases, because many new drivers desire to own a car and some are in a position to buy one. A great increase in the number of marriages, when the war-baby generation reaches eighteen or nineteen years of age, can also be predicted with confidence (and is projected by the Census Bureau). The birth rate will increase somewhat later, although the extent and speed of its increase depend somewhat on economic considerations. But the rate of marriages is not the same as that of household formation. Net household formation depends on the disappearance of households which, in turn, depends on the economic situation of the aged and is not easy to predict. In addition, the newly married may postpone the establishment of their own households. Furthermore, the first home is usually rented rather than bought. It became clear during the postwar period that it was not possible to predict residential construction from data on marriages and household formation (see Table 13).

Table 13. Marriages, Household Formation, and Housing Starts

Period	Marriages*	Net household formation*	Private nonfarm housing starts†
1947–1949	1.8	1.6	.9
1950–1954	1.6	.9	1.1
1955–1959	1.5	.9	1.2
1960–1962	1.6	1.0	‡
1963–1965§	1.8	1.1	?
1966–1968§	2.0	?	?
1969–1970§	2.2	?	?

* Average number per year in millions.
† Average number per year in million dwelling units.
‡ Different series available only, not comparable to earlier data.
§ Projected.
SOURCE: I am indebted for the form of this presentation to Robinson Newcomb; see his article in *Dynamic Aspects of Consumer Behavior*, Report of the Foundation for Research in Human Behavior, Ann Arbor, Mich., 1963.

In the first few years after World War II, marriage rates were unusually high and in many cases two families that had been living together separated; therefore, new households were formed at an unprecedented rate.[1] The number of marriages declined slowly but household formation declined rapidly after 1949. Yet this decline was not accompanied by a slackening of residential construction, and home building activity even increased in 1955–1956 without any demographic factors contributing to its growth.

REASONS FOR BUYING A HOUSE

Two considerations which economic analysts traditionally relate to housing trends help to explain what happened in the postwar years. One of these is easy money. Mortgage credit was amply available at fairly low rates until 1957 and, compared to prewar rates, could not be judged expensive even in the following years. More important still were income developments. With rising income, the American people could afford better houses and made great strides in acquiring them during the postwar period. About

[1] On the widespread resistance to living with relatives, see J. N. Morgan, M. H. David, W. J. Cohen, and H. E. Brazer, *Income and Welfare in the United States*, McGraw-Hill Book Company, New York, 1962.

one-third of all dwelling units were classified as substandard by the 1950 Census, less than one-fifth by the 1960 Census. The high rate of disappearance of housing units—about 800,000 units disappeared each year in the fifties—is related to rising incomes and the demand for better housing.

The generalization that replacement demand is important only for articles that are used up or wear out quickly and unimportant for houses and office and factory buildings that have a very long average life is not supported by any evidence. The boom in the erection of new skyscraper office buildings in Manhattan in place of structures that could have been used for many more decades or the abandonment of numerous factory buildings in the center of practically every American city illustrates the true principles of obsolescence. The availability of more advantageous products—air-conditioned office buildings, factories located in outlying areas, etc.—represents a major factor that shortens useful life. The same applies to automobiles and some other durable consumer goods. Similarly, the useful life of one-family houses cannot be calculated without taking new developments into account.

In the 1950s a sample of homeowners, who had moved into newly built houses shortly before being interviewed, was asked by the Survey Research Center about their previous residences and their reasons for moving and buying a new home. Only about 10 per cent of these people were found to have bought their houses simply in order to have a place in which to live. Formation of new households and separation of multiple ones thus accounted for a very small proportion of residential building. The typical pattern is to start married life in a rented rather than an owner-occupied house. About 20 to 25 per cent said they had bought their house because they had moved to a distant community. Many in this group were former homeowners who had been transferred to another part of the country. In this case, buying was not a discretionary decision. But for about two-thirds of those who had bought newly built houses and for the majority of those who had bought older one-family houses, the reason for moving was that the buyer wanted a more suitable home.

In many instances renters had bought one-family houses because they considered them more suitable than rented apartments. (We shall discuss the powerful motives to become a homeowner later in this chapter.) In some other cases, the more suitable home was smaller than the one previously owned; children had grown up and moved away. Many more had bought larger houses, usually because of an increase in the number of children in the family. But considerations relating to the respective sizes of the old and the new home were not the most frequent motivational forces. Most buyers spoke of having wanted a "better house," or a house in a "better location." Increased income often represents the condition for such decisions. The house in which one has lived for a few years no longer appears satisfactory in view of the improved financial situation. Concern with the neighborhood is a frequent determinant of home buying because some neighborhoods deteriorate, because living in certain areas adds to one's status, and above all because there is a widespread desire for fresh air, trees, and parks, as well as leisure-time and sport facilities, that can only be found in suburbs or outlying districts.

The rate of home buying then depends on the extent of "upgrading" that appears possible and desirable. Deprivations and dissatisfactions which push a family away from its old home are less powerful motivational factors than attractions which pull it toward something new. Changes in housing accomodations are influenced less by what one must have than by what one would like to have. The importance attributed to the psychological climate is not negated by the fact that rising income trends represent enabling conditions. The availability and the cost of mortgage funds likewise remain important, because home buying is a well-considered and even a calculated decision on the part of most buyers. Changes in interest rates, found to be ineffective in changing the rate of installment buying, did cause short-term fluctuations in home buying, indicating that in the latter case monetary policy may have an influence on consumer behavior.

POTENTIAL RESIDENTIAL MOBILITY

We turn now to a study of the longer-range housing plans of the American people. In former times many people bought a house with the idea of spending the rest of their lives in that house and possibly of passing the house on to one of their children. Nowadays the prevalent pattern is to change housing several times during the life cycle and, in this way, to adjust one's living quarters to changing needs and preferences. Survey respondents were repeatedly asked whether they expected to stay in their house (or apartment) for the rest of their lives or expected to move sometime in the future. Table 14 shows that in 1961 to 1963 only 35 per cent of families planned to stay in their house or apartment for the rest of their lives, while 58 per cent had at least some tentative plan to move. Among those who expected to move, more than half thought they would move in the next five years. Data obtained in earlier years were quite similar.

Table 14. Expectations about Changing Residence, 1961 to 1963*

	All families	Homeowners	Renters
Expect to move:			
Within five years	34%	23%	58%
Later	10	12	6
Uncertain when	14	13	14
Total	58%	48%	78%
Expect to stay for rest of life	35	47	15
Uncertain about plans	7	5	7
Total	100%	100%	100%

* The questions were: "Do you think you will stay in this house (apartment) for the rest of your life or do you expect to move sometime in the future?" and (If "expect to move") "Do you expect to move fairly soon, or within the next five years, or later?"

These data reflect the very great mobility of the American people. Each year in the late 1950s and early 1960s one out of every five families moved. Many families have changed their place of residence every two or three years. Yet the majority of movers stay in the same community or county. Residential mobility therefore is largely independent of job mobility. When the people themselves are asked why they think of moving, their explanations are quite similar to the reasons given for past moves or past house purchases. Some of those who think of moving speak of inadequacies of their present home or its location, and many more of their desire to have a larger, better, or better-located home. Among renters, preference for homeownership is a frequent response. Less than 10 per cent of all families, and therefore less than 20 per cent of the potential movers, say that their job will or might require them to move.

The potentially mobile families are predominantly young people. They are also people who have been in their present home for a short time only. Among families who have been in their present house or apartment less than six years, fewer than 30 per cent intend to remain there the rest of their lives, and nearly 40 per cent plan to change within five years.

Satisfaction with the house where one lives and its location does not detract from potential mobility. It is not uncommon for a strong desire to improve one's place of residence to exist side by side with a feeling of satisfaction with the place where one lives. Dissatisfied people often feel unable to change their situation, while satisfied people see the possibility of improving it or of arriving at still greater satisfactions.

To study their location preferences, respondents were asked, "If you could do as you please, would you like to live closer to the center of the city (town), or further out in the country, or just where you are, or what? Why is that?" About 60 per cent of all respondents replied in 1963 that they would stay where they were, 30 per cent said that they would like to be farther out in the country, and fewer than 10 per cent expressed a preference for living closer to the center of the city. As expected, the first choice (staying where they were) was least frequent among central city residents and the second choice (farther out) most frequent among them. But the differences between the answers given by city and by suburban residents were small. Only 8 per cent of people living in the suburbs spoke of wanting to live closer to the center of the city, and 29 per cent expressed the desire to move farther out. The younger the family, the more frequent was the desire to live farther out in the country. When people were asked about the reasons for their preferences, it became apparent that the urbanization of suburban areas—shopping centers, factories, fewer open spaces— continually reinforces the desire to get away from the urban environment. Dissatisfaction with noise, traffic congestion, and commercialization reinforces the desire to be close to the outdoors.

The potentially mobile people are predominantly optimistic about their financial prospects, while many of those who expect to stay in their home or apartment for the rest of their lives expect stable rather than rising incomes. Optimism about economic conditions and confidence that in a few years the family will be better off financially are associated with plans to move. Clearly, the realization of moving and house-buying plans will depend on the fulfillment of optimistic expectations. Trends in the housing market not only shape economic conditions, but also depend on them and on people's perception of economic prospects.

THE MEANING OF HOMEOWNERSHIP

America is a nation of homeowners. This was true before World War II, but the strides made toward widespread homeownership since the war have been spectacular. In 1946 about 50 per cent of 38 million nonfarm families lived in houses they owned; in 1962 about 60 per cent of 52 million families. The number of homeowners thus rose from 19 to over 31 million.[2] Homeownership has spread to younger age groups. While in 1950 the ownership rate did not reach the national average until people attained the age of forty or forty-five years, in 1962 only among those under thirty or thirty-five did one find below-average homeownership rates. Homeownership is also relatively infrequent among nonwhites and among those who live in the center of large metropolitan areas. The very large number of newly built owner-occupied one-family houses in the outlying areas of American cities and towns testify to the home-ownership trend of the last decade and also represent visual evidence of the great reduction in substandard housing that has taken place since World War II.

The rate of homeownership does rise with income, but the increase is rather limited. In 1962, even among those with only $2,000 to $5,000 annual income, 45 per cent owned their homes. Homeowners as a group, however, have higher incomes and also spend more on housing than renters. Looking only at monthly mortgage payments, which represent just one of the expenses of homeownership—to be sure, for those with mortgage debt the largest one—we find that the middlemost mortgage payment is larger than the middlemost rent (about $90 a month as against $65 a month). Of course, economists rightly point out that a large part of the monthly mortgage payment serves to repay the debt and therefore constitutes an amount saved. From the point of view of the homeowner, however, monthly mortgage payments, like rent payments, are expenses for which provision must be made from monthly income. Almost all newly built homes are purchased with the help of mortgage debt. (Purchases of old houses more often represent an

[2] The statistical data presented in this chapter, other than demographic data, are from the Surveys of Consumer Finances. See also E. T. Paxton, *What People Want When They Buy a House,* U.S. Dept. of Commerce, 1955, and *Psychological Research on Consumer Behavior,* Foundation for Research on Human Behavior, Ann Arbor, Mich., 1962.

exchange of one mortgage-free house for another.) But the repayment of the mortgage debt proceeds at a fairly fast rate. In 1962 slightly more than one-third of those who owned homes owned them debt-free.

The median mortgage debt, for those who had a mortgage, was $7,500 in 1962. It rises from about $3,000 among low-income families to over $12,000 among families with an income of over $15,000. The value of the owner-occupied houses, about which survey data are fairly reliable, exceeds the debt by a substantial margin in each income group. The middlemost home was worth somewhat more than $12,000 in 1962. With a family income level of under $3,000, the house was worth about $8,000; and with an income level between $10,000 and $15,000, it was worth about $17,000. The average value of houses in which families with over $15,000 income lived was much higher still. Nevertheless, owner-occupied houses represent the type of asset which rises least sharply with income. In the case of all other consumer assets, for instance bank deposits and especially securities, the difference between the average holdings of the high- and the low-income families is much larger.

Among low- and middle-income families who own their homes, the house typically represents a very large share of their total wealth. Beyond an income level of $7,500, this share begins to decline and drops sharply at a $20,000 income level. Among the wealthy, discussed in Chapter 20, the home represents a fairly insignificant part of their wealth.

As we mentioned in Chapter 3, the value of all owner-occupied one-family houses was estimated at close to 400 billion dollars in 1962. Even though homeowners' net equity is less than two-thirds of that amount, a very substantial part of consumer wealth is in homes owned. This investment has proved inflation-proof. Since World War II the value of buildings has probably risen to a similar extent as the general price level, while the value of land has increased to a much larger extent. Then, too, the consumers' equity advanced disproportionately, since mortgage debt was repaid with dollars of lesser value. The lower and middle-income families profited from this development much more than from the upward movement of the stock market.

Surveys of attitudes toward homeownership, conducted in the early 1950s, revealed major motivational forces which have remained operative ever since. Many people felt that being settled meant owning the houses in which they lived. The beliefs that children should be brought up in homes belonging to the family and should play in the family's own yard, rather than on the street, and that a substantial citizen is a homeowner were shared not only by professional and managerial people but by many wage earners as well. Financial advantages of homeownership were also frequently cited. Finally, in the 1950s the widespread desire for suburban and outlying locations could be satisfied only through homeownership.

In the early 1960s new apartment houses were built in very large numbers. While in the middle 1950s the number of apartment units built represented less than 10 per cent of residential construction, in 1962 the proportion jumped to over 25 per cent. In fact, the entire increase in residential construction in the early 1960s consisted of increased building of apartment houses.

There is no evidence that the American people's attitudes toward homeownership have changed in any way. The answers renters gave about their moving plans and desires in 1962 reflected the wish to become homeowners as frequently as in earlier years. The new development consisted of the building industry catering to a new type of customer. Most new apartment units are intended for one- or two-person households. The number of these has increased and will continue to increase, especially among older people and also among the very young.

Some rather conspicuous luxury apartments in central locations of large cities represent just one aspect of the new building trend. New apartment houses have been erected in large numbers in suburbs and small towns as well. Thus in the early 1960s it became possible to be an apartment dweller and nevertheless share in the greatly coveted pleasures of suburban living. Some new apartment houses furnish a swimming pool and other recreational facilities, without burdening the inhabitants with the tasks of upkeep, lawn mowing, or gardening. Whether or not the new kind of supply will alter people's attitudes toward homeownership remains to be seen. Very probably future studies will confirm that in this respect, too, social learning is slow and gradual.

ADDITIONS TO AND REPAIRS OF HOMES

About 5 per cent of American families purchased a house every year in the early 1960s. Many more than one-half of the buyers bought old houses. The cash expense connected with house buying was relatively small. New mortgage money was borrowed to the extent of more than 20 billion dollars a year, and much of the remaining purchase price was covered by the sale of old houses. Thus bank deposits and securities were not greatly reduced for the sake of buying houses. The large items of expense out of income in the housing field consisted of (1) mortgage and real estate tax payments by homeowners and rent payments by renters and (2) the cost of upkeep and repairs as well as of additions to homes owned.

Expenditures for additions and repairs increased greatly with the increase in homeownership. Each year during the late 1950s and early 1960s about 40 per cent of nonfarm families reported having made some such expenditures. The estimated money outlays were about $500 on the average, and therefore the total amounts spent exceeded 10 billion dollars a year. Since some of the repair work consisted of many small projects and in other cases the owner participated in the work and purchased materials himself, the survey estimates of total expenditures are somewhat unreliable. Yet home improvement costs derived from aggregate statistics are likewise subject to great errors. The one assured conclusion is that the total amounts spent on additions and repairs are very substantial, both in the aggregate and from the point of view of individual family budgets.

Renters' expenditures on alterations are included in the above figures, but few of them make such outlays, and those who do spend insignificant amounts compared to what homeowners spend. About one-half of all homeowners spend money on repairs and additions year after year, indicating that many people carry out some major upkeep or modernization job every year and still more people every second or third year.

The proportion of homeowners making such expenditures increases slowly with income—to two-thirds among homeowners with over $15,000 income—while the amounts spent increase rapidly. In 1961 the discretionary-income group, with an annual income of between $6,000 and $15,000, spent about two-thirds of the total amount spent on additions and repairs. Many of the middle- and upper-income homeowners' expenditures serve the purposes of making additions and modernizing and are therefore discretionary, rather than necessary for preventing the deterioration of the house. A study of the age of the houses on which the owners spend money leads to this same conclusion.

Among the owners of the oldest houses, which their owners had bought before World War II, only 38 per cent spent money on additions and repairs in 1962, and the median amount spent was about $250. The frequency of expenditures as well as the amounts spent increased among more recent home buyers. Among owners of houses bought in 1959, 1960, and 1961, about 56 per cent spent some money on additions and repairs in 1962, and the median amount spent was over $400. Expenditures of over $1,000 per homeowner occur commonly only among relatively recent buyers. Time of purchase is of course not identical with the age of the house, but the two sets of data are related. (Among houses bought more than ten years ago by their current inhabitants, there cannot be any which were built during the last ten years, etc.) Large expenditures on the improvement of houses often represent a form of upgrading and therefore an alternative to buying a new house. In the absence of major technological innovations in housing, home improvements are very frequent. In addition, of course, appliances and furniture are often bought shortly after the purchase of a house. One major discretionary decision, in this instance, buying a house, leads to a chain of further major outlays that are discretionary in the sense that they may easily be postponed if circumstances make postponement advisable. The expenditures connected with the purchase of a house rarely cease with the transfer of the deed, and this is true even with newly built houses. Improvements and additions are made over several years following the purchase.

25

Leisure-time Activities

The emergence of new wants following the gratification of other wants represents a major feature of a mass consumption society. In discussing attitudes toward automobiles, we have already shown that a variety of new wants emerge when levels of aspiration are raised following the satisfaction of more basic or more standard wants. People who have a home, car, and some major household appliances become interested in other durable goods and, above all, in leisure-time activities.

LEISURE AND RECREATION

Expenditures connected with recreation and travel, as well as with education and cultural aspirations, have increased greatly since the end of World War II. This trend may be traced to the growing affluence of broad population groups, coupled with an increase in leisure time. In addition, people's tastes, inclinations, and interests have also changed in a manner that permits a prediction of future trends. Leisure-time activities, and expenditures for goods and services connected with them, will continue to grow. The many people who have engaged in these activities in the early 1960s have found great satisfaction in them and desire to continue and, if possible, devote still more time and money to them.

In bygone and almost forgotten times, leisure may have been a time for contemplation and meditation. Today, even the association of leisure with rest is rare, and relaxation has become identified

274

with an active life. Therefore leisure no longer consists of doing nothing and cannot be defined as the time when we do no work. It is rather *work* that must be defined specifically as consisting of duties imposed upon us, in order to distinguish it from *leisure*. But even though the distinction between leisure-time activities and work is conceptually unsatisfactory, and the same activity may be work for one person and leisure for another, we always seem to know whether we are engaged in either work or leisure. Sometimes, some of us like our work; leisure, most of us like most of the time and consider it one of the good things in life.

When representative samples are asked whether or not they have too much or too little leisure time, satisfaction is expressed by half the people, but more than one-third say that they do not have enough leisure time (see Table 15).

Table 15. Evaluation of Leisure Time

Amount of leisure time*	Men	Women
Too little	37%	36%
About right	48	51
Too much	7	6
Depends, don't know	8	7
Total	100%	100%

* The question asked by the Survey Research Center in 1960 was "Some people say that American men (women) nowadays have too much leisure time; others say that they have too little. Do you feel that you have just about the right amount of time for leisure activities, or too little, or too much?"

SOURCE: These data and the data on outdoor recreation are from Eva Mueller and Gerald Gurin, *Participation in Outdoor Recreation: Factors Affecting Demand Among American Adults*, ORRRC Study Report 20, Washington, 1962.

Those who say they have too much leisure are predominantly older people. "Too little" is the answer most frequently given by people under forty-five years of age who have more than $7,500 annual income. In all other population groups close to 30 per cent say that they do not have enough leisure.

What do people do in their leisure time? Mueller and Gurin tried to find out in surveys conducted in 1960. Prior to asking questions, they had to define leisure time. Survey respondents were told that leisure time was "the time you have after work, both indoors and outdoors, in the evenings, in your time off, and on weekends." A distinction was thus introduced between leisure-time activities after work or on weekends and activities during vacations. This same distinction will be followed in this chapter, and vacation and travel will be discussed separately.

In answering the question "How do you usually spend most of your leisure time?" members of a representative sample of adults mentioned a variety of activities spontaneously. Looking at TV, various active sports, reading, gardening and working in the yard, workshop and homemaking hobbies, visiting with friends and relatives—these were the activities listed by the greatest number of people in the order given. When later in the interview a printed card listing leisure-time activities was presented to the respondents and they were asked which of those they did "quite a lot," the same activities were mentioned frequently, as well as two more: pleasure driving and participating in clubs, organizations, and church work.

Participation in outdoor recreational activities is widespread. In replying to specific questions, nine out of ten American adults said they had engaged in one or more such activity in the course of the preceding year. "Automobile riding for sight-seeing and relaxation" received the greatest number of "ayes," close to 50 per cent of adults saying that it was a frequent activity. Even when pleasure driving was disregarded, 85 per cent of adults were found to have occasionally engaged in various forms of outdoor recreation, of which many were the more active sports—primarily swimming, picnicking, fishing, boating, and hunting. One-half of the adults named four or more such activities in which they had engaged during the preceding year, and the proportion who said they had done so "often" was as high as the proportion who had participated "a few times" during the preceding year.

Not so very long ago leisure may have involved very little expense. Today leisure is expensive. The cost of two activities that are fairly inexpensive, reading and looking at TV, is dwarfed by the large expenses involved in most other things we do in our leisure time. Statistical data on amounts spent are rare and often not reliable. This is so because leisure-time activities involve expenses both on goods and on services, and the allocation of certain expenditures is difficult. It has been estimated that the American people spend on recreation—including vacation and nonbusiness travel—as much as 60 billion dollars a year, which would make recreation our largest industry. But even if this total is based on definitions and allocations that are too inclusive, reliable estimates indicate surprisingly large expenses for various segments of the recreation business. To mention just one of the smaller segments: In 1960 Americans spent about

4 billion dollars on garden tools and supplies, nursery products, fertilizers for backyards, and the like. These expenses increased fourfold from 1950 to 1960. With the growth of suburban living the maintenance of yards has become a major expense, supporting an industry of considerable size. Expenditures for sports equipment are, of course, substantially larger. Sailboats and motor boats, swimming and hunting equipment, picnic and camping accessories, summer houses and cabins take up a fair share of family budgets and add up to a sizable sum in the aggregate. The cost of building and maintaining public and private facilities for outdoor recreation must, of course, be added. These facilities are used primarily by people who reach them in a few hours at the most by car, although they are also the goals of much of the vacation travel. Power tools and the like constitute expensive items for indoor recreation. While in nineteenth-century England a few exclusive firms catered to the hunting passion of a small upper class, in America recreation industries supply masses of consumers.

For millions of people, outdoor recreation represents a new way of life. It is cherished, not only for the fun it provides, but also because it is a social activity that can be shared with others, and because it is believed to contribute to good health. The broad middle-income group has been the leader in the trend toward a new life style characterized by informal living. When, in the survey cited above, respondents were asked about their desires regarding various leisure-time activities, many people—about two-thirds of the total—expressed the desire to engage in one or more additional outdoor recreational activity. This finding was, of course, not unexpected. The study also revealed that lack of time was the major factor preventing greater participation in such activities. Lack of money emerged as an important but secondary factor. With the prevailing trend toward a reduction of working hours, an extension of outdoor recreation thus seems to be assured.

VACATION TRIPS AND TRAVEL

Travel by American middle-class families increased greatly in the 1950s and 1960s. It may well be that the experience of taking automobile trips and finding them pleasurable was the major factor which evoked the inclination to take more trips and determined the taste for informality in travel.

In a survey conducted in 1960, the heads of 53 per cent of all family units said that they were entitled to a vacation with pay of a week or more. If the self-employed as well as those not in the labor force are excluded, since the question about vacation with pay does not apply to them, we find: 76 per cent of employed family heads were and 24 per cent were not entitled to vacation with pay. These proportions had doubtless changed considerably from those of a few decades earlier. The change reflects the increased number of white-collar workers as well as the spread of vacation privileges among blue-collar workers.

The great majority of people spend at least a part of their vacations traveling. The survey question asked about "overnight vacation trips, other than weekend trips." Among all families 43 per cent said they had made a vacation trip (12 per cent had taken two or more such trips), while 13 per cent said they had spent their vacation at home, in 1960. The remaining 44 per cent said they had taken no vacation in a twelve-month period.[1] The frequency of vacation trips rises with income but is not much influenced by age. Vacation trips are made with similar frequency by all age groups between twenty-five and sixty-five years of age.

When respondents were asked what they would most enjoy doing in their free time ("if you could do as you please"), nine out of ten said they would travel. When they were queried about their ideas of "a really good vacation," people replied either in terms of activities (outdoor activities, driving, sight-seeing) or by naming geographic areas, often distant ones, they would like to visit. The actual location where their previous vacation had been spent, however, appears to have been determined frequently by the residence of friends or relatives who had been visited.

Attitudes toward travel were also studied by asking respondents to complete such incomplete sentences as "People who travel a lot are . . ." This sentence is completed most often by the words "fortunate," "wealthy," and "well informed." Those who stay at home are characterized as having no money, having small children, being old, or being in poor health. These and similar studies indicate that there is only a small minority who have no desire to travel. The taste for travel has been spurred by the recognition of its educational value.

---

[1] The 43 per cent making a vacation trip and the 13 per cent who spent their vacation at home, added together, exceed the 53 per cent who were reported to be entitled to a vacation with pay. This is because some self-employed people who had no paid vacations had made vacation trips.

In studies of travel in general—including nonvacation trips for personal as well as business reasons—when a trip was defined as one that took a person at least 100 miles away from his home, it was found that two-thirds of American adults had traveled in 1962. Table 16 indicates also the modes of travel and their changes

Table 16. Frequency of Trips (at least 100 miles away) during a Twelve-month Period by Different Modes of Travel

	By automobile	By airplane	By railroad	By bus	By any of these four
Per cent of adults traveling, 1955 ...	57	7	11	7	62
Per cent of adults traveling, 1962 ...	62	11	8	9	68
Among those traveling in 1962 for nonbusiness purposes:					
Making one trip	31	65	70	65	*
Making two trips	15	14	15	13	*
Making more than two trips	51	14	11	18	*
Number of trips not ascertained ...	3	7	4	4	*
Total	100%	100%	100%	100%	*

* Not available.

SOURCE: John B. Lansing, *The Travel Market, 1961–62*, published by the Survey Research Center.

since 1955, as well as the frequency of multiple trips by the different modes.

Approximately two-thirds of American adults made at least one trip 100 miles or more from home in 1962. The proportion of those who used the family car for travel is only slightly lower. It follows that most people who travel by air, rail, or bus also travel by car. Business trips constitute a sizable proportion of air travel but not of other modes of travel. Trips by car differ from trips by common carrier in several respects. Nonbusiness travelers by car frequently take more than two trips during a twelve-month period, while about two-thirds of those who use plane, train, or bus make one trip only. (By definition each trip includes the return as well.) On the average, car trips are much shorter than trips by common carrier. Travel by car usually includes at least two and often several members of the family; travel by plane is most common when only one family member travels.

The higher the income, the greater the proportion of adults who took one or more air trips and the smaller the proportion of adults who took one or more bus trips in 1962. Travel by rail did not differ much among income groups. Travel by car has become quite common at fairly low-income levels. Almost half of the families with incomes between $3,000 and $5,000 took car trips in 1962; among families with higher income levels, the proportion rose slowly to 67 per cent of those with an income of over $15,000.

In the population as a whole, more people react favorably to travel by car than to travel by plane, rail, or bus. When asked about the best way to travel, without regard to cost, 40 per cent mentioned the car and 28 per cent the airplane. Among frequent travelers and high-income people, the preference for plane travel exceeds the preference for auto travel.

The cost of vacation travel was studied among people who said they had spent more than $100 for their vacation trip in 1962 or 1963. These people—less than one-third of all families—estimated that they had spent, on the average, approximately $400 on vacation trips, which amounts to over 6 billion dollars in the aggregate. Only 12 per cent of all families had traveled distances of over 1,000 miles. The higher the income, the more frequent are trips that take people far away and the more money is spent on vacation trips. Total expense and the distance traveled vary greatly with income. Yet the incidence of vacation travel varies much less with income, and the extent of liking to travel varies hardly at all.

CULTURAL ACTIVITIES

Not all use of leisure time can be characterized as fun, entertainment, or sport. To an extent that has increased greatly during the postwar period, Americans use their free time for what may be called cultural activities. Various forms of adult education—reading serious books; going to lectures, the theater, concerts and museums —have become popular. The word *activities* is rightfully used in this context, because most people participate in cultural pastimes in places away from their homes and often in groups.

Reliable statistical data on time spent on these activities or on the amount of money spent are not available. It has been estimated, for instance, that enrollment in adult-education classes exceeds enrollment in elementary and high schools, but the term enrollment is not used in quite the same way in the two instances. The growth

of groups performing serious music and theater, as well as of painting and sculpturing groups, in all regions of the country, including
many middle-sized towns, has been well documented, as has the
increase in book publishing, in which area the sales curve of serious
paperback books is most impressive.

This expansion of people's horizons is probably related to the
spread in formal education as well as to affluence, so that the
greatly increasing education of American youth is relevant in our
context. In the early 1960s the proportion of young men and women
going to college was almost as high as the proportion of boys and
girls going to high school at the beginning of this century. This
trend continues at an accelerated pace. Recent studies indicate that
not less than 60 per cent of parents with children in elementary
and high schools expect their children to go to college. These expectations, although far too optimistic in view of the lack of facilities, reflect the high esteem for education in our society to which
we have pointed on several previous occasions and which is the
basis for adult educational activities. Willingness to postpone entry
into the labor force and to earn money in order to get a college
education, and even postgraduate training, must be explained in
terms both of material and of spiritual values. The young men in
college and in medical school, law school, or graduate school know
that they enhance their earning power through additional training.
However, nonmaterial motives must also be effective; they often
lead to financial sacrifices for the sake of more schooling.

Primarily because of the expense of going to college, the education of children has become a big item in the budget of many
families. It has been calculated that going to college costs, on the
average, $1,750 a year and that 60 per cent of that sum is paid by
the parents. In the aggregate, in the early 1960s Americans spent
more than 5 billion dollars a year on private education in addition
to the taxes they paid for public schooling.

Our own report on cultural leisure-time activities can be made
only on the basis of very preliminary and clearly insufficient survey
data collected in 1962. A representative sample was asked, "During
the last few months did you people spend any money on such
things as education, lectures, books, concerts, theater, and the like?"
Then a subjective judgment was obtained about the size of the
expenditures, if any, and finally, those who said they had spent some
money were asked whether they would like to spend more, and

those who said they had not were asked whether they would like to spend any on those things. The data obtained for the entire population (Table 17) may be summarized as follows:

35% said they had not spent any money and would not like to
18% said they had not spent any money and would like to
15% said they had spent some money and would not like to spend more
32% said they had spent some money and would like to spend more
———
100%

Spending money on cultural activities is relatively rare among low-income people but becomes increasingly frequent as one proceeds upward on the income scale.[2] The desire to spend more on cultural activities also correlates with income, but to a much smaller extent than actual spending. Table 17 indicates that recent past spending ranges from 22 per cent (low-income people) to 73 per cent (upper-income people), while the desire to spend more ranges from 33 to 59 per cent. Especially among middle-income people are there many who would like to increase their spending on cultural activities. The data presented on recent past spending may be viewed as encouraging or discouraging according to the reader's notions and expectations, while the data on desires point toward a probable increase in the cultural trend.

It may also be mentioned that the desire to spend more referred on the part of 24 per cent of the families to education and books, on the part of 12 per cent to theater and concerts, and on the part of 10 per cent to both. Wanting to spend more on theater and concerts was expressed primarily by upper-income families, while wanting to spend more on education and books was not related to income. Studies of adult education indicate, however, that its beneficiaries are primarily those with substantial formal education.

Some experts disparage the increased exposure to and participation of the American people in the arts, maintaining that it has led to a popularization of lowbrow tastes rather than to creative performance. Not much is known of the relation between exposure and participation on the one hand and expertise and creative performance on the other. In two different fields, the sciences and sports, it seems to be true that participation by many often leads to peak performance by a few. It is not the province of this book to assert

[2] Mueller and Gurin (*op. cit.*, p. 35) also showed that "going to plays, concerts, lectures and museums" is highly correlated with income and education.

Table 17. Past and Desired Expenditures on Education, Books,
Theater, and the Like*

	All families	Family income			
		Under $3,000	$3,000 –4,999	$5,000 –7,499	$7,500 –9,999 and over

Spent during last few months						
Quite a lot	19%	7%	15%	18%	28%	36%
Small amount, very little	28	15	19	36	39	37
Did not spend	53	78	66	46	33	27
Total	100%	100%	100%	100%	100%	100%
Would like to spend						
More than at present	50	33	44	61	58	59
Not more than at present	50	67	56	39	42	41
Total	100%	100%	100%	100%	100%	100%

* The questions were: "During the last few months, did you people spend any money on such things as education, lectures, books, concerts, theater, and the like?" (If "Yes") "Was it very little, quite a bit, or what?" "Would you people like to spend money (more money) on such things?"

that in the arts either the same or a different relationship prevails. Let it be said simply that the growing sales of recordings of good music, as well as of original paintings to many consumers who never had any art objects, or at best poor reproductions, in their homes may be noted as a sign of spreading desires and levels of aspiration; they can hardly be viewed as standing in the way of great creative performance.

SERVICE EXPENDITURES

The increase in the proportion of consumer expenditures that is spent on services and the decrease in the proportion that is spent on goods between the late 1940s and early 1960s have frequently been noted by economists; these developments have usually been attributed to the lessened importance of production as compared to distribution in an affluent society. It is worth mentioning that the recent gain in the share of service expenditures is to some extent a statistical artifact and has little to do with the growth of leisure-time activities or even with the rising importance of discretionary expenditures. The following are the three major factors responsible for the statistical data which indicate that in the postwar period expenditures on services increased to a larger extent than expenditures on goods:

1. The amount of imputed rent rose sharply. The Commerce Department calculates what income homeowners forego by having part of their funds invested in their homes (or what homeowners save by not paying interest to themselves), and adds that amount both to national income and to service expenditures. Increased homeownership—which represents better housing—and the repayment of mortgage debt caused a great increase in these imputed expenditures.

2. The amount of interest paid on mortgage and installment debt likewise grew greatly from the late forties, when debt was very small, to the early sixties. The increased rate of homeownership and of purchases of durable goods contributed to this growth as did the rise in interest rates.

3. Prices of services increased, on the whole, to a greater extent than prices of goods. Therefore the share of service expenditures compared to expenditures on goods increased less in real terms than in current dollars.

In addition, such service expenditures as automobile insurance and the cost of repairs to homes and to durable goods rose substantially during the postwar years. In none of these instances did the consumers *decide,* as a result of changed inclinations or affluence, to shift their expenditures from goods to services. Such decisions may have occurred to a small extent regarding one further service expenditure that increased substantially, namely, medical expenses. (Preventive medicine, check-ups, etc., may be considered instances of discretionary decisions.) Yet on the whole there are only three areas of growing service expenditures in which the increase may be attributed to a change in the inclinations of consumers. The increase in these areas, although substantial, plays a minor role in the increase of total service expenditures. These areas are education, leisure-time activities, and personal care. Discretionary decisions were made in the subjective priority given to these areas, and they related to both goods and services. Collectively, consumers decided to devote a larger share of their money to buying books as well as to paying fees for lectures; to buying boats, sport and photographic equipment, and garden tools as well as to spending on travel and on tickets for sporting events and theaters; to buying cosmetics as well as to paying for hairdressers' services.

Leisure-time activities appear to stimulate expenditures on goods at least as much as on services. The distinction between goods and services is not of major importance in assessing the changes brought about by the emergence of a mass consumption society. The growth of the discretionary dollar represents the foremost change. With regard to the use of the discretionary dollar, the growing importance attributed to leisure-time activities represents a relevant factor. Whether we engage in these activities, how much time we devote to them, how much money we spend on them, and how we divide the money spent—these are discretionary decisions which influence our personal well-being and the total economy as well.

26

Marketing Research

The major conclusion that emerges from the discussion of the last three chapters is that changes in consumers' motives and attitudes exert a strong influence on their major discretionary expenditures. We shall refrain from citing further illustrations of this principle and from discussing consumer expenditures in areas other than housing, durable goods, and leisure-time activities. Rather we shall conclude our study of consumer spending by emphasizing the importance of research on consumer needs and wants. Since it is through marketing research that producers and merchandisers seek to inform themselves about consumer spending and the factors influencing it, it seems appropriate to explore here the functions as well as the limitations of that kind of research.

Survey research in which data are collected on consumers' economic transactions, their demographic characteristics, and their psychological propensities may be classified as follows:

1. Research concerned with the purchase of specific brands
2. Research concerned with the kinds of goods and services purchased (e.g., automobiles, travel, common stock)
3. Research concerned with changes in consumers' total spending and therefore with the analysis and prediction of economic trends

The work carried out by the Survey Research Center falls overwhelmingly into categories 2 and 3.[1] The objectives of marketing

---

[1] As the reader has by now doubtless become aware, however, the studies of the Survey Research Center are concerned primarily with discretionary consumer expenditures (and with discretionary savings as well), rather than with nondiscretionary expenditures on food, clothing, etc.

and advertising research, on the other hand, fall primarily into category 1. Yet it would not be justified to assume that there is a sharp dividing line between the two kinds of consumer research.

Obviously, marketing research cannot concern itself with the sales of a particular firm or brand without giving some thought to the overall picture of total expenditures in the given field, if not in the economy as a whole. Conversely, many findings of research of types 2 and 3 have direct implications for type 1, especially in terms of consumer psychology. There remain, nonetheless, significant differences between the traditional forms of marketing research and the more general consumer research.

THE FUNCTIONS OF MARKETING RESEARCH

A theoretical model of market research might be constructed in a number of different ways. One extreme model, for example, might relate to the introduction of a new product into the market. The new product, P_1, has been developed, and the aim of market research is to find out how the desired image of that product may best be transmitted to as many consumers as possible.

$$P_1 \longrightarrow C_n$$

where P stands for product, C for consumers, and n for needs. According to this model the initiative is taken by the merchandiser (producer, seller, advertiser), and the consumer is viewed as a passive recipient of information, who is to be convinced and persuaded to buy the product.

According to a rather different kind of model, the purchase situation resembles a problem-solving situation as usually described by psychologists. The consumers have a problem or an unsatisfied need and search for the best solution; after investigating and discarding several solutions, one solution is found satisfactory and product P_1 is bought.

$$C_n \longrightarrow \begin{pmatrix} P_1 \\ P_2 \\ P_3 \end{pmatrix} \longrightarrow P_1$$

In this model the consumer is an active agent, and the supplier is passive. For instance, having moved to a different city, a person searches for a house and, after comparing several houses on the market, decides to purchase one with no help or advice from the marketer (the real estate agent in this case).

Obviously, both models are faulty. They may correctly describe limiting conditions but cannot serve as general models of the usual purchasing situation. The basic shortcomings of both are that they neglect all interaction between consumers and merchandisers and leave out important variables. According to the first model the merchandiser tries to influence the consumer's mind, which is blank; consumers are puppets to be influenced. In the second, the merchandisers' activities are neglected. In both models insufficient attention is given to consumers' habits, past experiences, and satisfactions with products.

A valid model must unite some features of both of those suggested. Merchandising efforts must relate to consumer habits, experiences, and satisfactions, as well as to consumer needs and the active steps taken by consumers to solve their needs. If one wishes to persuade and convince others, it is necessary first to determine the characteristics, the opinions, and the feelings of those to be convinced. Marketing research must be, and usually is, greatly concerned with the study of consumer practices, motives, and needs. Such study is useful for all marketing and advertising research, whether it be concerned with the type of goods to be sold or with a particular brand.

Marketing research is often thought of as directing its activities exclusively toward the consumers, and ultimately its goal is indeed to facilitate the task of selling the products to the consumers. In many instances, however, this purpose may best be accomplished if the research findings are first directed toward the producer or distributor. Having determined the business policies and strategies or the type of product most pleasing or most acceptable to the consumer, it is the function of market researchers to persuade business management to adapt its policies and merchandise to satisfy existing or incipient needs. Influencing the firm to adjust its strategies to the inclinations and wants of consumers is usually easier than influencing masses of consumers to change their dispositions. Changes in consumer tastes and wants should be determined in order to bring the product and the way it is marketed in line with consumer likes and dislikes. When this is achieved, the products and the manner in which they are marketed and advertised may help to reinforce incipient tendencies in consumer wants.

GENUINE DECISION MAKING

Awareness of two major aspects of human behavior must govern the activities of the market researcher. People, in their role as consumers, as well as in all other roles, are both creatures of habit and sensible human beings. Even though impulsive behavior that appears to defy analysis does occasionally occur, habitual behavior and genuine decision making are the two most common determinants of purchasing behavior. There is no contradiction in a person's reacting, in one situation, almost automatically as a matter of routine or habit and, in another situation, acting on the basis of a real attempt to understand the requirements of the situation. Neither a scholar nor a businessman nor a consumer can or should consider every one of the multitude of actions he undertakes as a problem which requires deliberation, weighing of alternatives, and solving. In most instances people act as they have acted before in similar circumstances. Whether it is a question of a motorist deciding which route to take in driving home, or of a businessman deciding how much raw material to buy, or of a housewife deciding what to serve for dinner or which brand to buy, habit is usually the decisive factor. Market research is, of course, fully aware of the role of habitual behavior, as has been indicated by the valuable studies it has produced on brand loyalty and store loyalty.

Deviating from the habitual course of action represents one of the major instances of genuine decision making. The circumstances under which careful consideration and choosing among alternatives take place, or which are likely to elicit such behavior, are not fully known. On the basis of fragmentary evidence it is possible to present the following, possibly incomplete, list of expenditures and conditions which cause consumers to reflect and make what we have called genuine decisions before making a purchase.[2]

1. Expenditures which are subjectively thought to be major and which are fairly rare. Many of these expenditures are large (e.g., a house or, in many but not all cases, a car, etc.), but some may be small and yet of great importance to the buyer (as, for instance, a dress or a present for a specific occasion).

2. Unsatisfactory past experience, especially disappointment of expectations.

[2] Cf. George Katona and Eva Mueller, "A Study of Purchase Decisions," in L. H. Clark (ed.), *Consumer Behavior* I, New York University Press, New York, 1954.

3. Some (by no means all) purchases of new products or the first purchase of a product.

4. Awareness of a difference between one's customary behavior and that of the group to which one belongs or an important reference group.

5. Impact of strong new stimuli or precipitating circumstances; these stimuli may consist of general news (threat of war, inflation, etc.) or of news regarding specific products, which may be transmitted by advertisers.

6. Certain personality characteristics, often associated with education.

It follows that genuine decision making is not restricted to a few transactions which involve large amounts of money. It is also probable that with increasing education levels the frequency of genuine decision making is growing in our society.

When genuine decisions are made, consumers are not marionettes that can be manipulated. The main reason for this is that consumers' problem solving is commonly guided by a desire to understand. As has been said before, understanding usually does not mean having a scientifically valid and proven explanation but rather simply having an answer to the question of why. The buyer is often satisfied, for example, that he knows why he has chosen one or the other make of car, even though his knowledge is incomplete, and his explanation might not stand up in a conference of experts.

In many respects today's young housewife, who on the average has much more education than her counterpart of fifty or even twenty years ago, has become an expert shopper who tries to do well at her task of buying for the family. For this purpose she needs information and is often not satisfied to get it from her mother or neighbor, that is, to copy what was done in the past or what her peers are doing now. Advertisements have become an important source of information on products but not information which is accepted uncritically. Information about merchandise is sought in order to understand the characteristics of different products, as it is sought on economic developments in order to understand why certain things happen in the marketplace.

LIMITATIONS OF MARKETING RESEARCH

In an appraisal of the mass consumption society we are greatly concerned with the limitations of marketing research. Understandably enough, little has been said, and indeed little is known, about those areas in which it cannot perform all the functions assigned to it. It seems clear, however, that there are two basic limitations inherent in market research. The first relates to the study of the whys and wherefores of purchasing behavior. Even if the art of asking the question of why were developed much better than it actually is, the facts that consumer motives are learned and are constantly changing and that there are a multiplicity of prevailing motivational forces make it hardly possible for market researchers to give definite and reliable answers to many questions that business management rightfully asks. Secondly, consumers on the whole lack sufficient imagination to enable researchers to depend on them in guiding business to genuine innovations.

The limitations of the direct question of why are of a rather elementary nature and have long been understood. Most survey respondents when asked, even shortly after they have purchased a car, "Why did you buy a car?" reply by saying, in one way or another, "I needed it." It is, of course, possible to go beyond this uninformative reply by formulating the question more precisely. For instance, by asking "Why did you buy the car at that time?" or by studying the reasons for buying one make of car rather than another, useful information can occasionally be obtained. The argument of the so-called motivational researchers—answers to direct questions of why are rationalizations and therefore useless, while indirect psychological tests tap the true unconscious motives—is only partially correct. Even rationalizations are of importance, and knowledge about what are the salient and easily recognizable motivational forces is useful in interpreting the more elusive notions brought to light by such indirect methods as picture-, story-, or sentence-completion tests. Yet this controversy, rampant some years ago, has been more or less resolved by now. Market research must produce statistically reliable data, based on samples of sufficient size, on conscious as well as on elusive motivational forces. A further technique that has been found to produce very important information about motives is correlation analysis. A great contribution to answering the question of why is made by establishing functional relations among various factors. For instance, by finding that traveling by plane is highly correlated with income and certain occupations, as well as certain attitudes, or that installment buying is undertaken most commonly by middle-income younger families who have optimistic expectations, theory as well as practice may be advanced much further than either by direct questions or by psychological tests.

In spite of progress along these lines, there remain some inherent shortcomings of research on consumer motivation. The fact that in practically all instances human behavior is multiply motivated need not bother us much provided the conflicts between different motives are resolved. To be sure, there is a tendency toward congruence, and in certain areas dissonance is not tolerated. Yet in a multitude of practical situations our wants and desires are far from congruent, and often we are not even aware of wanting one thing and at the same time wanting its opposite as well. Furthermore, the temporary resolution of a conflict through action—e.g., buying something which satisfies certain vectors but not others—does not guarantee similar future resolutions. Changes in motives, through learning from experience, often precede action but not necessarily. Therefore product planning based on motivational studies, though helpful, does not insure success.

Let us proceed from theoretical principles to practical application. To cite an instance of ambivalence in consumer desires: The automobile industry found in the early 1960s that people, often the same individuals, surely the same groups of people, wanted both speed and economy. Long and low cars with top performance (quick starting and plenty of power, as well as reliability in performance) were desired at the same time as economy in price, in gas consumption, and even in the size of the car. To mention another example: Saving labor has long been acknowledged as one of the major ways of appealing to the busy housewife. Precooked or frozen food and appliances that make work easier capitalize on this motivational force. At the same time, the housewife does not want to be replaced and even desires to exercise her skills. The attitude of wanting "to get it done and be finished with it" prevails side-by-side with pride in workmanship. Without being aware of conflicting desires, people abstain from resolving conflicts. Generally, satisfaction with products purchased in the past or, say, with the kind of TV program viewed in the past, prevails side-by-side with desires for something new or better. Copying a successful competitor or relying on the continued success of one's popular merchandise is not necessarily good business policy.

All this, of course, does not mean that research on consumer preferences is useless. The consumers' advice is worth listening to, even though they do not always speak with a clear voice. One lesson to be learned is that business should not place too great a reliance on conformity among its customers. The uniformity of the American market has sometimes been exaggerated, and when it is recognized that the market is segmented, the dividing lines are frequently neither simple nor easily recognizable.

Often the kinds of people who buy different things differ and must be approached differently. This is an area in which more general consumer research may part company from specific market or advertising research. Especially regarding preferences for brands and makes, group differences and individual differences prevail both in people's reasoning and their feelings. It is the function of marketing research to find out what conscious or unconscious motivational and emotional factors make different kinds of people responsive to the products of different manufacturers.

Turning to product planning, it must be recognized that the advice market research may give can frequently be expressed in negative terms only. What not to do can often be determined much more definitely than what to do. Often it is fairly easy to find out what bothers or irritates people, while creative suggestions for product planning are hard to obtain, even regarding changes in familiar products. Such suggestions are practically unobtainable regarding new products. Because consumers as a whole are not well endowed with imagination and fantasy, consumer research cannot guide the process of technical innovation.

We have already mentioned this second limitation of market research in Chapter 7. There we referred to automobiles and room air conditioners as important new consumer goods which were not created because consumers desired or demanded them. More generally, we have had repeated occasion to point to conservative traits of consumers: As a rule their aspirations exceed the levels of their accomplishments only to a small extent. People feel a desire for only a somewhat better standard of living and only a few more consumer goods than they have, because even their wishes and dreams are reality-bound. Survey questions about desired innovations in home construction, in kitchens, or in transportation yielded answers indicating that the respondents had thought only of slight improvements in existing products rather than of something radically new. To quote a joke frequently told among market researchers, studies conducted at the time of the invention of the automobile would doubtless have revealed that the prevalent consumer desire was for a longer-lasting horseshoe. And yet radical innovations in consumer goods do occur, and some of them fail, while others are accepted as necessities and result in changing our lives. Market research can be of little help to the inventor but may be of great use in the second stage, when the question concerns the acceptance of the invention. When new products have been developed and business is confronted with the choice of concentrating production on one or another line, or of producing and selling several competing lines, that is when it is often possible and useful to ascertain the probable reactions of consumers.

It may suffice in this connection to call attention to the success of the compact car. At a time when the only cars manufactured by American industry were larger than ever and when the rising demand for small foreign cars was frequently described as coming from a special sophisticated group of the population that would necessarily remain small, survey research was able to indicate that the needs of a large proportion of consumers were not satisfied with the large cars. We may recall the findings cited in Chapter 23, according to which cars have become means to other cherished ends (leisure-time activities and travel) rather than being either status symbols or solely utilitarian means of transportation, as well as the findings concerning differences in the needs of two-car and single-car owners. These changes in motivational patterns and the incongruent desires for a car that was powerful—for psychological reasons as well as for travel—and at the same time economical spoke for a solution different from producing in America the equivalent of the small European car. At the same time consumer research showed clearly that the compact car, though successful, would not displace what has come to be known as the regular-size car.

ADVERTISING[3]

If consumers' behavior were irrational or if it never changed, because of the enduring power of habits, market and advertising research would be of limited use. The most important single fact that makes market research important in spite of its limitations is that the consumer is sensible. He is a discriminating person capable

[3] This subject, briefly discussed in Chap. 7, calls for a few additional comments in connection with market research.

of learning and wants to understand what is good for him and why. Putting something over on the consumer or attracting him with false claims might work only for a short time, if it works at all, and with only a few people. Advertising has been described as the process of bringing the consumer from a state of unawareness to that of preferring, liking, and buying a certain product. Its messages might profitably be guided by such clues to prospective changes in consumer tastes and desires as transpire from consumer research. Although the guidelines which such research can presently provide are admittedly far from unequivocal, they may yet be very helpful.

Much has been written but little is really known about consumers' reactions to advertising. Let us cite a few examples of how consumer research might nonetheless serve in guiding advertising policy. In the course of inquiries about people's attitudes toward business and toward big business we were able, for instance, to arrive at certain indications of the potential value of institutional advertising. Most people believe that business, and especially large firms or old firms, are honest, trustworthy, and eager to serve. It is thought that large firms are good places in which to work and that their products are worth buying. Which are the firms that qualify? Obviously those which are known, and advertising makes the names of firms and brands known. Some of these names become old acquaintances through advertising, and it pays to keep up this sense of familiarity—even though the attempt to make the buyer differentiate between the products of different companies is not generally successful.

It has been shown in this book that the consumer learns slowly and does not change his opinions and preferences quickly. He must be wooed constantly and, being very patient, tolerates much wooing. Possibly the advertising industry has gone too far in this respect, especially in television commercials. Many sophisticated people seem to think so, and their number is increasing. And yet there is little evidence that the broad masses are irritated by advertising or have become hostile. Only rarely does one find either an active like or dislike of advertising. More often people seem to be weary of it, and very often they are simply indifferent. Millions of people have become adept at discounting advertising claims or have even developed an ability to disregard advertisements—for example, to close not only their eyes but also their ears while waiting for the resumption of their favorite TV program.

Since, then, thousands of advertising messages become ineffective, must the industry multiply the number of messages it sends out? If a little bit helps, more of it helps more has been a credo that has too often backfired. The problem of too much advertising plagues us today and threatens us to a much larger extent in the future. The economy is growing and with it the number of advertised products and the funds available for advertising. But the amount of time the individual has to read or hear messages remains unchanged. Should our periodicals become still thicker and the TV commercials longer and more frequent? Even if, following an argument presented in Chapter 7, all advertising consisted of useful and interesting information on products and product uses rather than of unreasoned appeals, these prospects are most disconcerting.

First of all, advertising must adapt itself to the rising educational level of the American people. This one factor of change alone would indicate that advertising might do well to lean less heavily on persuasion and testimonials and more on technical information and explanations of the purposes best served by the products it desires to sell. But only further extensive research could point out in detail the changes in advertising ultimately required by the necessity of appealing to the educated and sensible consumer. The only conclusive statement that can be made on the basis of present knowledge is that if there are no changes, advertising and American salesmanship will surely suffer. Advertising is no different from any other field of business. It, too, must keep itself attuned to changes in consumer preferences and attitudes and change its methods accordingly. Here are wide and largely unexplored areas for future research.

PART SEVEN

Toward New Economic Insights

27

Consumers and Businessmen

In attempting to summarize the lessons learned from the exploration of the mass consumption society, let us look at that society first in terms of the well-known economic principle of the consumers' sovereignty. This principle asserts that production is the means and consumption the end—that production is oriented toward meeting the wants of the consumers. According to a more recent version, the change in consumer wants and tastes is the autonomous variable in the economic process to which market performance is responsive. Neither of these formulations helps much in explaining our present economy. Viewed as postulates they have not stimulated productive theorizing.[1] Viewed as realistic descriptions of what happens in the marketplace, they are, and always have been, at least partially incorrect. In the first instance, any discussion of consumers' sovereignty should not exclude from consideration the interaction that takes place between producers and consumers. Secondly, it should lay great weight on the consumers' power to influence the economic growth of the nation. The first point will be the subject of this chapter but will be preceded by a brief résumé of the general principles we have learned from our studies of consumer behavior.

[1] The principle of consumers' sovereignty has often been linked with the postulate that whatever consumers want is optimal for them. Maximization of utilities becomes, however, an unproductive tautology if one assumes that whatever consumers want serves to maximize utility.

SUMMARY OF THEORY

In the introductory part of this book we referred to two theses that hinder full understanding of the consumers' role in the economy. These are (1) that consumption is a function of income and (2) that consumers receive their income from the other sectors of the economy which alone are capable of generating income. These postulates have been subjected to some criticism in the postwar years, primarily, however, in the form of asking what financial variables in addition to income, especially current income, determine consumption. Some critics have proposed that wealth should be added to income as an explanatory variable. Others have advocated that income should be redefined to mean relative rather than absolute income level, that is, the income position of one consumer in relation to others or lifetime, or permanent, rather than annual income. The proposed variations of the original proposition fall short of a real understanding of how the situation has changed since the United States has become a mass consumption society. The thesis of this book, based on the insights gained in our surveys, represents a more radical departure from earlier visions of the position of the consumer.

The first new insight gained was not in the realm of the psychological. It consisted rather of the recognition that in our present American society consumer investment is an economic factor to be considered side by side with government and business investment. It was found that the rate of fluctuations of tangible investment expenditures by consumers, as well as the economic impact of those investments, was different from that of other consumer expenditures. Consumer borrowing for the sake of investment outlays appeared in a new light, and the distinction between spending and saving as the major choice of consumers had to be reconsidered.

The second insight required the introduction into the economic picture of the concept of the consumers' willingness to buy. This concept has become a scientific one by our having found it possible to measure changes in willingness to buy and to correlate them with changes in expenditures. Discretionary consumer demand was found to be a function both of ability and of willingness to buy. It was further found that the latter, represented by motives, attitudes, and expectations, may change independently of changes in income, but current income remains the most important determinant of ability to buy. Under certain conditions, however, consumers step up their discretionary expenditures, or reduce them, to an extent not explained by any change in income or even contrary to the direction of income change. The explanation then lies in changes that have taken place in the consumers' motives and attitudes.

Thirdly, we found reason to doubt the value of the traditional equation relating to income and consumption which considers the latter to be the dependent variable ($C = fY$). The causal chain does not necessarily start with income and end with consumption. Income itself may be dependent on consumption or, more correctly, on consumer needs and wants. The consumer is frequently in a position to do something about his income, and the major factor that determines his action is represented by his perceived needs. The consumer will consider his income as given and take no initiative toward changing it when he feels satiated or when he perceives an advance as hopeless. When there appears to be no chance for improvement, usually because previous efforts have failed, aspirations are curtailed. Levels of aspiration decline with failure and rise with accomplishment. Upwardly mobile families exert efforts to make more money and thereby to satisfy some of their ever growing wants. As we have seen, some of the ways in which income has been raised when consumption made it desirable consisted of the wife's returning to work or the head of the family's taking on a second job.

It is not sufficient to treat willingness to buy as a variable explaining consumers' expenditures. The variables on which willingness to buy, in turn, depends, must also be understood. Survey research proved capable of yielding information on why at a given time consumer optimism and confidence had either strengthened or weakened. It could be determined which of the various economic and noneconomic news had been relevant for masses of consumers and what kind of affective connotations had been attached to different kinds of news. As for changes in willingness to buy as they developed over periods of several years or decades, it was found that they could best be understood in terms of the principles of social cognition. It became evident that the masses of consumers are capable of acquiring new beliefs but that, barring revolutionary developments, the process is slow and gradual. Consumers do try to understand what is going on, and news that appears to them ununderstandable fails to impress or influence them. Some progress has thus been made toward understanding the origin of changes in attitudes, both in the short run and in the long run, but much remains to be done in these respects.

The theory of psychological economics which emerges from such findings recognizes that there are certain conditions influencing economic action which do and others which do not change over the short run. Sociocultural norms and group goals as well as the given personality structure of the population represent fairly stable enabling conditions from one year to the next. The given distribution of income, assets, and debts, and the business and credit structure, as well as the basic facts of domestic and international politics, are relatively stable.

Those conditions which change over the short run are represented by changes in the environment. They constitute economic stimuli among which information received is the most important. Information may stimulate change in actions and sometimes also in attitudes and opinions. The attitudes of very many consumers tend to change in the same way at the same time, thanks to the similarity of the stimuli as well as of the consumers' cognitive processes. Although action may occur without a prior change in attitudes, the latter precedes action often enough so that the predictive value of a study of attitudes proved to be fairly high.

BUSINESS BEHAVIOR

We return to the discussion of consumers' sovereignty. There was a time when impersonal market forces were thought to allocate resources according to consumer wants. Later, when it was recognized that, in many instances, a small number of producers made the decisions about the kind and quantity of goods to be manufactured, it was argued that the consumers determined the decisions of the producers. In the post-World War II period, it became popular to voice the reverse proposition, namely, that it was the producers who made the consumers want their products—and this became the battle cry of the social critics' attacks against merchandising and advertising (see Chapter 7). In fact, of course, neither extreme position is accurate; there is rather an interaction between producers and consumers. The influence of consumers on producers depends primarily on how the latter perceive trends in consumer demand. Producers collect a great variety of market reports, for instance on the sale of different kinds of products, on discounts and rebates, and, in those diminishing instances in which prices are not administered, on changes in prices (e.g., used car prices). They interpret these data, sometimes viewing them as indications of significant and enduring trends; the data are then given great weight in determining the kind of goods manufactured as well as the rate of output. At other times the market data are disregarded as reflecting transitory aberrations. On still other occasions the verdict of the market is far from clear and leaves room for different interpretations by different producers. Finally, in certain instances—among which, as we said earlier, the marketing of new products is particularly important—it is often not possible to obtain meaningful market reports upon which the producer could base an estimate of the relevant wants of the consumers.

The crucial question, then, is: What are the considerations that influence producers in their evaluation of reports on consumer demand? To a large extent these considerations are the same as those that influence consumers in evaluating information they receive: opinions about the general economic outlook that form the frame within which specific reports are understood and the decision makers' norms, habits, and attitudes, as well as the influence of their group. Group belonging exerts a much stronger influence on businessmen than on consumers. News, rumors, and opinions about the actions or reactions of other businessmen and especially of competitors are of particular importance in the business community. There is a further consideration which plays a great role with producers and not with consumers: The producers' own wishes, the way they perceive their own interests, tend to color their reaction to market reports. If a producer is committed to a certain action, he may tend to place little importance on news that is adverse to it. He may then rely on his own power to alter conditions, for example, by stepping up his merchandising efforts and devoting more money to advertising.

A comparative study of consumer behavior and business behavior may shed significant light on the mass consumption society. Some economists, who proclaim the existence of consumers' sovereignty, deplore it, because, in their opinion, it results in a preponderance of lowbrow tastes (see Chapter 25). Catering to the tastes of the educated, the informed, or the expert is advocated by these admirers of the elite. The masses are viewed, not only as lacking in taste, but also as being an unruly rabble on which order must be imposed from the outside. Studies of mob psychology, descriptions of what happens under conditions of panic or revolutionary fervor, have been generalized and the conclusion drawn that the masses are inclined toward excessive behavior. Consumers' power over cyclical trends is then viewed as tending to exaggerate booms as well as depressions. The economy is thought to be kept on an even keel when directed by the decisions of the informed, or at least by the few rather than by the many.

Such views are sharply contradicted when the findings obtained in interviews with businessmen and with consumers are reviewed. Uniformity of attitudes and action prevails to a much greater extent in well-knit groups than among unorganized masses of consumers. A variety of powerful features were found to be inherent in consumer thinking which counteract excesses and exert a stabilizing influence on the economy. In social cognition, in the development of expectations, as well as in the spread of opinions, norms, and patterns of behavior, self-reinforcing tendencies leading to excessive behavior were found to be the exception rather than the rule. This conservative nature of consumer thinking must be compared with the characteristics of business behavior and especially of business investment.

In popular writings substantial profits or the prospect of such profits are often called the one condition which stimulates business investment. It is said that new ventures must look very promising in order to attract investors' funds. Contrariwise, when profit margins are low or government regulations and controls prevail, investors are believed to be unwilling to risk money on new ventures. Such notions, though they seem unassailable at first sight, are far from sufficient to describe the factors that cause increased or reduced business investment in today's economy. It must be kept in mind that the bulk of expenditures on business plant and machinery are made by large, established corporations rather than by individual investors, and the corporations are usually well provided with money in bad times as well as in good. The two major sources of investment outlays are funds set aside for depreciation and profits not paid out to shareholders. Depreciation funds accrue quite independently of profit trends (except under circumstances close to bankruptcy which we may disregard), and the proportion of retained earnings can be changed according to investment needs.

Internal financing is usually preferred to credit, which represents a secondary source of funds. Under these circumstances it is, not the availability of credit, but the willingness of corporate management to step up or reduce capital expenditures which is the main determinant of fluctuations in business investment. This willingness depends on a variety of factors; profits and profit expectations are but one of the variables that influence investment decisions.

We shall do no more than mention some of the major factors relevant for the investment decisions of business firms.[2] Some of the capital outlays of established firms for plant and machinery are habitual. They represent an almost automatic use of depreciation reserves for the replacement of assets after a fixed number of years. Disregarding habitual outlays, two considerations loom large. First, there are capacity considerations. When sales approach the available productive capacity, expansion is called for to counteract the threat of losing customers. An upward trend in sales, in conjunction with an upward trend in profits, represents the ideal condition for willingness to invest. But an increase in sales may stimulate investment even without an increase in profits. Secondly, business investment is dependent on technological innovations. The use which competitors make, or are believed to be about to make, of technological innovations represents a crucial consideration influencing business decisions. What other producers and sellers in the same line of business do usually affects a businessman's decision.

It follows that capital expenditures are raised or lowered by very many business firms at the same time. The pressure of sales approaching capacity is rather uniform, as is the pressure to change products or production methods. It follows further that what consumers do has great impact on the investment decisions of business: Sales increases occur when consumers step up their purchases, and the fear that capacity will be overtaxed prevails when consumers are expected to increase their demand. We may add that notions about the profitability of investments are likewise commonly shared

[2] See G. Katona, Ref. 1 Chap. 9; J. Meyer and E. Kuh, *The Investment Decision,* Harvard University Press, Cambridge, Mass., 1957; and especially Robert Eisner's papers in *American Economic Review,* vol. 53, Supplement, 1963, and in *Conference on the Economic Outlook,* University of Michigan, 1963. Regarding attitudinal data from surveys with business managers, see G. Katona and others, *Business Looks at Banks,* University of Michigan Press, Ann Arbor, Mich., 1957; and E. Mueller and others, *Location Decisions and Industrial Mobility in Michigan,* Survey Research Center, 1961.

by members of the same industry. Would-be builders of electric generators or of apartment houses cannot but be reinforced in their opinion that their investment will be profitable when they know that their ideas and calculations are widely shared. It is not asserted here that there are no perceptive business leaders who, at the appropriate time, may embark on new investments contrary to the general pattern;[3] what is argued is that it is businessmen who, to a greater extent than consumers, tend to react as a group to whatever trend is perceived and thus to exaggerate the trend.

No discussion of businessmen's economic activity, any more than of consumers' activity, would be complete without a reference to motivation. A theory postulating a single business motive—usually profit maximization—is not necessarily incorrect but is unproductive. If whatever business does is assumed to serve to maximize profits, information is lost. The very fact of postulating never-changing business motives, or uniform motives among all business firms, stands as a roadblock in the path of making motivational studies which might contribute to an explanation of business behavior.

The motivational patterns prevailing in the American business community today have been described by several of its students (including Katona in Ref. 1) as a mixture of pecuniary motives and public relations motives. The former are represented mainly by the desire for larger sales, especially for a larger share of whatever market one may be in, as well as for satisfactory or slowly rising profits. Profit motives were found to be especially strong in bad times when a reduction in profits or even losses threatened. Among nonpecuniary motives, those which tend to improve public relations have gained in significance since the end of World War II, especially among larger firms and in good times. To serve not only the stockholders but also the employees, the customers, the community, and the entire economy are often proclaimed as goals of business enterprises. The feeling of achievement and the acquisition of prestige are often evaluated in terms of other people's appreciation rather than in pecuniary terms. Needless to say, business decisions motivated by concern with public relations may indirectly serve egotistic and pecuniary purposes. Yet the emphasis placed on

[3] In a previous study it was shown that unfavorable prospects do energize a few business managers to undertake large business investments. See Katona and Morgan, "The Quantitative Study of Factors Determining Business Decisions," *Quarterly Journal of Economics*, vol. 66, 1962.

the general welfare results in a motivational pattern, sometimes referred to as the social conscience of business, which is greatly different from the pattern according to which it is considered legitimate business policy to charge whatever the market can bear. Present-day business motives tend to result in policies intended to assure a slow growth in sales and stable prices, rather than high short-run profits.

Most business executives see business nowadays as being something other than speculation. The resultant tendency is to consider it safe to proceed in the same way as other firms and risky or speculative to initiate new or different procedures. Studies of motivational patterns, then, yield similar conclusions as studies of investment behavior. Countercyclical policies are given lip service, but the prevailing motivational patterns favor running with the tide and thus increasing capital expenditures in good times and decreasing them in bad times when everybody else does the same.[4] We arrive again at the conclusion that business investment tends to accentuate cyclical fluctuations—booms as well as recessions.

It must be said that since World War II long-range planning by business firms has tended to make investment outlays less mercurial than they used to be. Also, to the extent that changes in business investment depend on what consumers do, the former will lag behind changes in the pace initiated by consumers (as, for instance, in 1955 and 1963) and may even become countercyclical. Finally, the fact that there was no long recession during the postwar years may have influenced some business executives to spread their expenditures on plant and machinery more evenly. Therefore, the argument presented on the preceding pages may apply with lesser force today than, say, ten or twenty years ago, but is, in the author's opinion, still valid.

If business investment, which is uniform among many firms, were indeed the sole dynamic factor in the private economy, it would be easy to find justification for state interference with the economy. In fact, before World War II, particularly in Western

---

[4] This is true both of expenditures on plant and machinery and of changes in business inventories. Although no reference has been made to the latter, many of the considerations related to capital expenditures apply to inventory policy as well. During the postwar period changes in business inventories played a sizable role in bringing about either an upturn or a downturn in business activity.

Europe, the notion that excessive and intolerable fluctuations in the business cycle were caused by business investment represented the major reason for the trend toward government planning and state control. Government interference with business was thought to be necessary to stabilize the economy. In the postwar years in the United States countercyclical measures of an automatic nature contributed to greater economic stability. Large fiscal deficits in times of recessions and, to a lesser extent, surpluses in prosperous periods have not only been accepted as appropriate, but indeed resulted automatically from tax receipts being higher in good times than in bad and government expenditures, especially to the unemployed, being higher in bad times than in good. But automatic stabilizers may not always suffice, and there are those who advocate more extensive and more active government interference. The greater the countercyclical effect of consumer behavior, the less need be our reliance on government to rectify all economic maladjustments. It would be consistent with the American preference for voluntary and private action in maintaining our system if we give increasing thought to the reinforcement of the stabilizing role that may be played by consumers.

28

Economic Policy

In the social sciences there are no great barriers separating knowledge from its use. We have already mentioned a few areas in which business policy has been influenced, or should have been influenced, by businessmen's understanding of certain features of the mass consumption economy. Of still greater importance are the requirements which the mass consumption economy imposes on the government's economic policy.

Of the three major aspects of a mass consumption economy—affluence, consumer power, and the impact of psychological factors—the first has been given the greatest recognition in economic policy. When welfare economists, and many politicians as well, became aware of the affluence of the American society, they recognized that poverty was intolerable. In the 1950s the remedies advocated represented nothing more than a stepping up of such old palliative measures as making unemployment compensation and old-age insurance more comprehensive and more adequate. Less frequent was the recognition of such basic sources of poverty as lack of education and discrimination. In the early 1960s the high rate of unemployment among young people with inadequate schooling drew attention to the new situation in which only the skilled and the educated can make a good living. More and more experts advocated that the government increase its investment in human capital in order to spread the benefits of affluence and restrict the number of underprivileged.

RESPONSE TO TAX REDUCTION

Important as policies in support of education and against dis-crimination are, they are not germane to our topic. Some degree of recognition has recently been granted to the power of consumers in a mass consumption society, but until now the role this recogni-tion has played in influencing economic policy has been all too slight. The history of the major economic measures advocated by the Kennedy administration may serve as an illustration. In April, 1961, President Kennedy proposed to grant tax benefits to business firms which invested additional funds in new plants and equipment. His message stated that the program was required in order to stimulate the expansion and growth of the economy as well as to strengthen the government's anti-recession program. In the summer of 1962 Congress enacted a law which, by revising depreciation rates and granting tax credits, made it more advantageous for business to invest in plant and machinery. In the period immediately following, however, capital expenditures by business firms increased very little.

Obviously, this first tax proposal by President Kennedy and the law enacted by Congress stemmed from the old teaching that business investment represents the sole private means of generating economic expansion. The role of consumer investment in stimulating the economy was not then recognized. Little thought was given in government circles to the possibility of tax measures intended to increase certain expenditures by consumers.

Clearly, it would have been possible for government economists to argue at that time, and the question may come up in the future as well, that tax credits similar to those given to business firms undertaking investment expenditures should be given to buyers of houses, automobiles, and large appliances and to families making additions or repairs to their homes.[1]

As was shown earlier in this book, consumer investment expendi-tures are analogous in many respects to those of business, and both slowed down in the period 1957 to 1961. It could also have been argued that consumers would react to tax incentives faster than business firms. Business capital expenditures represent long-range

[1] I so proposed in a speech made in May, 1961, and which was reprinted under the title "Consumer Investment and Business Investment," in *Michigan Business Review*, vol. 13, pp. 17–22, 1961.

propositions and are subject to time-consuming efforts of coordination with ongoing investments. The mechanics of finding a site for a new factory, choosing plans for buildings, and selecting machinery require much time, as do the traditional methods of business decision making (committee meetings, consultation with outside experts). Since individual families may decide much faster, stimulation of consumer investment might fulfill the anti-recession function better than stimulation of business investment. Also, and this is relevant to the goal of accelerating economic growth, individual families may act under the influence of lesser incentives than managers of business firms (who commonly asserted in 1961 that the tax incentive was not large enough).

Skeptics may argue that tax advantages granted to consumers buying durable goods would serve only to advance purchases which would in any event be made at some time in the future. In other words, we would be borrowing from the future and merely postponing the day of reckoning. Naturally, this argument, if correct, would apply equally to the stimulation of business investment. But the argument has merit only if it is assumed that technological progress is nonexistent and that products offered for sale in future years will be no more desirable than those offered at the time of the tax incentive. (In addition, the argument disregards the effects of rising expenditures on income.)

Businessmen buy new machinery and consumers buy new durable goods when they believe that the new products are more appropriate for their purposes than the older ones. More appropriate may mean more efficient in operation, or more suitable in size, or even more pleasing to the eye. Attraction emanating from a new product creates incentives to buy and remains effective even if the products already owned are relatively new. A change in the composition of possessions would dampen future demand significantly only if in the years to come buyers were not attracted by the products offered or if their ability or willingness to buy were limited.

But there was little scholarly discussion of probable reactions to tax incentive plans in 1961 or 1962, even though the rate of economic growth remained slow. In the summer of 1962 President Kennedy put forth a new plan. He proposed an across-the-board, top-to-bottom cut in both corporate and personal income taxes. In August 1962 the President announced that the tax cut was not needed that fall. He waited until January, 1963, to submit to Congress his detailed proposals for placing several billion dollars in the hands of consumers and business firms. This was essentially the bill passed under President Johnson in late February, 1964.

Several aspects of the extensive debate concerning this first major cut in income taxes since their inception are highly relevent for a study of the mass consumption economy. The first thing to be said is that it recognized the strategic importance of the consumers. Those who favored its passage pointed out that an increase in the aggregate after-tax income of, say, 10 billion dollars would mean an increase in consumer expenditures of approximately 9.2 billion dollars (since in most postwar years consumers as a whole spent 92 per cent and saved 8 per cent of their income). Yet the immediate effect would represent only a part of the impact because higher consumption makes for higher incomes during the next period, which in turn results in still higher consumption. Such references to the *multiplier effect*, widely discussed by government economists,[2] did not appear to have convinced the traditionalists in economic thinking. They argued that the President's plan in which business and consumers shared the benefits of lower taxation was faulty; in order to stimulate the economy, business should receive all the benefits or at least the lion's share.

Most of the arguments followed the same pattern. An important business magazine maintained in 1962 that the main question was, "Will business invest fast enough to employ the nation's resources adequately?" One of the leading New York banks commented in its monthly letter early in 1963: "Many observers have found it surprising that the principal and most immediate stimulus of the Administration's tax program is directed at consumers." Another business magazine expressed itself even more pointedly: "Kennedy does not recognize the investment sector of the economy. . . . More consumer demand will not put idle plants and idle men to work." The fixed notion that business investment is the sole autonomous factor in the private economy appears to obscure fairly simple relationships: When consumer demand rises, idle men are put to work to produce more goods; when, because of rising demand, capacity output is approached, new plants are built. A sharp upturn in consumer demand in 1955 led to an investment boom in 1956.

---

[2] See Testimony by the Council of Economic Advisers at the *Hearings before the Joint Economic Committee* of the U.S. Congress, on the January 1963 Economic Report of the President, Part 1, 1963, pp. 1ff.

The tax cut was designed to include corporations as well as individual taxpayers at every level of income. In view of the very high marginal tax rates that had been imposed on high incomes during the war, it was understandable that they should be reduced, even though people with high incomes save a much larger proportion of their income than those with middle or low incomes, and therefore this part of the bill could curtail the multiplier effect. While equity required that taxes also be reduced for lower-income families, the share in the tax reduction received by people with sufficient income to permit discretionary expenditures is of the greatest importance to the economy. Equally important as how the tax savings are used is the impact of the tax cut on the psychology of consumers.

Few people today recall the early days of the New Deal. At that time pump priming by the government failed to stimulate the economy, apparently because the private sectors reduced their outlays when the government increased its own. The behavior of the private sectors was attributed to absence of confidence in the future —businessmen and consumers did not believe that government spending could bring forth an upturn in the economy. The problem of confidence or mistrust in the government's policy measures is equally crucial in discussing the impact of the tax cut.

We cited above the argument, presented by the President's Council of Economic Advisers, that about 92 per cent of the additional take-home pay would be spent and that the effects of growing consumer expenditures would multiply. One Senator asked what would happen if there were to be an increase in the rate of personal saving. If the rate "increases just 2 per cent you lose the whole effect of your tax cut," the Senator admonished the government economists (*op. cit.*, p. 64). They replied that such behavior by consumers would be possible, but there was no reason to expect it, and, obviously, a change in the other direction would be possible as well. Is that all that might be said? Is consumer psychology a mystery about which economists can only speculate, or could just such a question about possible consumer reactions to government action be subjected to scientific study and provide less equivocal guidelines for economic policy?

In Chapter 15, in discussing the American people's notions about government budgets and deficits, we cited some data on people's reactions to the tax proposal. We reported that in 1963 the majority were in favor of a tax cut, although the understanding of its economic implications was limited, and a sizable group had misgivings because of the government's need for money and also because of the ensuing deficit. Now let us look further into the study we made of people's probable reactions. What would people do with the money they would save through a reduction in income taxes? This important question was not easy to study. To be sure, the Survey Research Center did ask such a question in surveys conducted in 1962 and 1963. For some people the question was a simple one to answer. They were aware of priorities among their needs and wants and could easily state how they would use extra money. Most of these people answered in terms of specific spending plans—buying durable goods and travel were most frequently mentioned—as well as of repayment of debt. For other people the question was a puzzling one. It was an "iffy" question for those who did not believe that there would be a tax cut and therefore thought it not deserving of serious consideration. Many people with substantial income said that the amount would not be large enough to really matter or that they had no specific purposes in mind. "We will put it in the bank" was a common answer which, as we said in Chapter 18, frequently indicated only that the use of the money had not been decided upon. That this was so was clear from such further explanations as, "We'll bank it until we decide what we want."

It is sometimes more effective to determine people's attitudes or intentions by asking questions about what they think other people or most people will do, rather than what they themselves will do. This is particularly true when no decision has yet been made. Then, too, since saving is generally viewed as a virtue, some respondents might hesitate to report that they themselves did not plan to save.

In 1963 the Survey Research Center asked the following question in nationwide surveys: "Suppose income taxes are cut so that next year everyone will have more of his income left after taxes—what do you think most people will do with this money?"[3] Overwhelmingly respondents replied that people would spend the money on goods and services. About three-fourths of all respondents and a somewhat larger percentage of the high-income respondents were of this same opinion. Some respondents had no opinion, and only

[3] A similar question was also asked long before President Kennedy made his tax cut proposal, stimulated by my interest in tax reductions as a means of economic policy (see Ref. 2, pp. 244ff.). The answers received in 1961 were quite similar to those received in 1963.

relatively few thought that people would use the money to repay debts or would save it.

The notion that people in general are spending-minded rather than thrifty and virtuous appeared to influence these opinions. Spending by others is disapproved by many people, and yet it is also appreciated. Most people believe that the greater the purchasing power and the greater the rate of purchasing and spending, the better are economic conditions. Therefore the opinion that the tax cut would induce the American people to increase their spending was closely related to its corollary: As a result of the tax cut, economic conditions would improve. In addition, in the fall of 1963 surveys revealed that the tax cut, if enacted, would be viewed as a reason to expect a continuation of good times rather than the recurrence of a recession. It appears, then, that the bill was needed, even though economic conditions were good at the time of its passage. Surveys conducted several weeks before the tax reduction began to take effect revealed that the very anticipation of the tax cut had favorable effects on consumer attitudes and also on consumer demand.[4]

BROAD PRINCIPLES

The tax bill represents a single instance, albeit a very important one, which illustrates the necessity and the possibility of studying probable reactions to policy measures. The studies relating to taxes also revealed that practical problems of the day may stimulate basic research and that the results of such research may in turn be of practical use. Other examples could be cited as well. The consideration of such actions as anti-inflationary measures, changes in interest rates, and control of installment buying must always be based on the assumption that psychological factors are influential beyond the financial impact of the measures. People's perception of what is being done and their expectations about the outcome may radically change their reactions. Moreover, attitudes and expectations are themselves subject to change, and social learning may even be promoted through appropriate publicity.

[4] After the tax cut went into effect, the Survey Research Center embarked on a large-scale study of the impact of the tax cut on consumers' spending and saving behavior. The study was initiated by the President's Council of Economic Advisers and The Brookings Institution.

Rather than discussing findings pertaining to additional specific instances of economic policy, let us turn to some broad conclusions that may be drawn regarding the policy requirements of the mass consumption economy. Economic growth is not assured by the availability of natural resources or of capital. Even the prevalence of entrepreneurial dispositions does not suffice. Sociocultural norms and personality traits that are conducive to risk taking and profit making, much discussed in the past in connection with protestant ethics and the industrial revolution, are of importance. But something new has been added: In a mass consumption society consumer aspirations represent an additional important determinant of economic growth.

Prosperous times cannot endure if an increased rate of satisfaction of consumer wants results in feelings of saturation. Only if accomplishment continues to make levels of aspiration rise and consumers continue to set their sights higher after they have improved their standard of living, will mass consumption be sustained and will it stimulate further economic growth. People must be optimistic about their own and their country's economic prospects and must have confidence in their ability to improve their standard of living if they are to raise their sights rather than to feel satiated. Unless they can look forward to concrete rewards in the not-too-distant future, they will not work hard to improve their situation.

Rising incomes, then, are not simply a measure of economic growth but the motor that triggers hard work, the striving for advancement, and the desire for more of the good things of life. During the past decade some economists have advocated inflationary policies in order to produce rising incomes and economic growth. In their opinion the money illusion—a dollar is a dollar even if its purchasing power declines—would help to make creeping inflation beneficial rather than harmful. We found, however, that as of now people are quick to recognize price increases and cling to their deep-seated belief that inflation is bad. What is needed, then, is the confident expectation of rising incomes as well as of reasonably stable prices.[5]

These goals can be achieved because productivity is rising, as a

[5] Yet in the future some people might become habituated to small price increases so that possibly creeping inflation would not make for adverse attitudes and expectations, provided incomes were to increase to a larger extent than prices.

result both of technological progress and of mass consumption and its growth. We in America have achieved income increases far exceeding price increases for the past twenty years. This has not been an accident, but has demonstrated the possibilities inherent in a mass consumption society.

1963 was a good year, primarily as the result of rising consumer demand. Thanks to the tax cut, 1964 is well on its way to being better still. Yet enduring good times are not assured, and too slow a rate of growth may again threaten the American economy. Recognition of the consumers' role in today's economy by the government and the community of economists is still limited. Much remains to be done in this respect, and much more must be known than is known today about how to sustain high-level discretionary demand by consumers and how to transmit the benefits of such demand to technological progress and business investment.

As is well known, technological progress has adverse as well as favorable effects. Automation helps to produce better goods more efficiently, but it also leads to the displacement of workers. In the modern economy, there is less and less need for unskilled labor, while the compensation for special skills and knowledge is rising. Thus education becomes a key to rising incomes, and investment in human capital becomes a major requirement of economic policy.[6]

Widespread unemployment must be fought, not only for the sake of the unemployed and those threatened by unemployment, but also because it adversely affects even those who are not likely to lose their jobs. The confident expectation of an improvement in one's economic position and standard of living, which represents a necessary stimulus in a mass consumption society, is impaired by the presence of a large number of unemployed in one's community. People who have a lot and strive for more also have much to lose, are inclined to worry, and sometimes become insecure. We already mentioned this broad problem earlier in this book and cannot do more than refer to it again here. Widespread insecurity and anxiety constitute threats to our society. These threats extend, of course, not merely to the economic but to the personal, emotional, and social

[6] Such policies presuppose that motivations to improve their lot are not lacking among the poor. It should not be forgotten, however, that a large section of the poor—the aged, the disabled, the broken families—are not capable of becoming self-sufficient. (See the findings of Morgan, cited in Chap. 2.)

levels as well. The active man is preferable to the passive man, but constant striving and even achieving do not guarantee a happy life. Although it falls outside the province of this book, we want at least to acknowledge our awareness of the fact that government policy for the well-being of the people must go beyond the economic into the areas of physical and mental health, education, and social welfare. We repeat our strong belief, however, that all these other areas of concern can best be provided for if the economy is soundly based on a large, optimistic mass of consumers constantly seeking to improve their way of life.

29

Economics as a Behavioral Science

We have discussed the consequences of the mass consumption society for economic policy in the light of recent events and stressed the immediate impact of government measures on consumer attitudes. A much broader, and probably more enduring, perspective of the new economy emerges when we summarize some major features of psychological economics. In this chapter we shall show how economics as a behavioral science, which analyzes the factors that shape economic behavior, differs from nonbehavioral economics. There is always resistance to new approaches. This is particularly understandable here, first, because nonbehavioral economics has accomplished much in the past, and secondly, because behavioral economics starts from quite different premises.

RESISTANCE TO PSYCHOLOGICAL ECONOMICS

The origin of resistance to psychological economics on the part of some economic theorists may be summarized in three arguments. The arguments are presented here in rather extreme form in order to indicate the premises which are abandoned in psychological economics.

1. Economics should provide broad generalizations about economic processes which are valid at all times and under all conditions.

2. Information on the interrelation among economic data, such

as profits, sales, investments, and other "results of behavior," suffices for the understanding of economic processes.

3. Motives and expectations are fleeting, vague, and uncertain so that information about them does not contribute to objective, scientific analysis.

In view of what has been shown in this book, it is no longer necessary to discuss these arguments in detail. In contrast to the first argument, economics as a behavioral science asserts that economic principles should be derived from studies of human behavior in a given country at a given time rather than from generalized assertions about human nature. As to the second and third, behavioral economics acknowledges the importance of econometric studies that disregard psychological factors; it does not agree, however, that a study of the interrelations among economic data alone suffices for the understanding of economic processes or that motives and expectations are so vague and uncertain that a study of them cannot make a scientific contribution to economics. New economic insights can be obtained through behavioral research, because research techniques now make it possible to determine the influence of psychological factors on economic behavior. The statement of John Maynard Keynes that the factor of consumers' income expectations "is likely to average out for the country as a whole [and] is a matter about which there is, as a rule, too much uncertainty for it to exert much influence"[1] may perhaps be understood as a superficial conclusion drawn from experience in an earlier, very different, time. There is no a priori reason for the belief that the impact of income expectations, which typically do not average out, is more uncertain than the impact of past income changes, since the latter influence people with discretionary income according to their perceptions of and attitudes toward the changes. Whether the one or the other is more uncertain depends on circumstances.

Since science consists not in merely describing what is but rather in ordering facts through abstraction and generalization, it might seem that the complexity and variability of human behavior would rule out psychological economics as a science. In the first place, however, as we have said before, changes in attitudes among the

[1] J. M. Keynes, *The General Theory of Employment, Interest, and Money*, Harcourt, Brace & World, Inc., New York, 1936, p. 95. It should be noted that Keynes has made substantial use of an analysis of businessmen's expectations.

masses of consumers were found to be understandable and measurable. Secondly, research studies did yield generalizations. On the lowest level, they may be expressed thus: Under conditions a_1, b_1, and c_1 response X is probable, while under conditions a_2, b_2, and c_2 response Y is probable. Many empirically validated generalizations are of a conditional nature. But psychological economics goes further: It specifies the type of intervening variables between the stimuli and the responses that need to be studied. Motives, attitudes, and expectations represent some of the major factors on which the response depends; their changes are most relevant. Second-level generalizations consist, then, of principles concerning the relation between psychological factors and economic behavior.

No doubt the task of the economist would be much simpler if the consequences of, say, changing prices, interest rates, or taxes could be specified under all conditions and at all times. Unfortunately, such a statement as the following made by a leading economic theorist, Milton Friedman, regarding the study of the consumer is not valid in the behavioral sciences: "The necessity of introducing many variables is a sign of defeat and not of success; it means that the analyst has not found a truly fruitful way of interpreting and understanding his subject matter; for the essence of such a fruitful theory is that it is simple."[2]

The essence of a fruitful theory is its explanatory power. The theory must have "surplus value," that is, it must be applicable to sets of phenomena which were not considered when the theory was constructed. The theory must make use of abstraction so as to bring order among facts. While simplicity is a virtue, it would be well to keep in mind that the law of parsimony reads: *Entia non sunt multiplicanda praeter necessitatem.* Too many theorists remember only that concepts or variables should not be multiplied but forget the injunction *except when necessary.* The crucial question is whether or not the introduction of new variables is necessary for a better understanding of economic behavior (see Ref. 1, pp. 144ff).

The findings on diverse factors influencing the consumer, which are disparaged by Friedman, represent low-level generalizations. Psychological economics does not, however, end with them. Let us

[2] Milton Friedman, *A Theory of the Consumption Function,* National Bureau of Economic Research, Princeton University Press, Princeton, N.J., 1957, p. 231.

illustrate some of the insights gained through psychological economic research by citing some examples both of lower- and of higher-level generalizations.

EXAMPLES OF GENERALIZATIONS

We turn back first to our discussion of inflation (Chapter 14). As is generally acknowledged, inflation has certain precipitating circumstances of an economic nature. A sharp increase in government expenditures without a similar rise in revenues or even associated with a reduction in the supply of civilian goods, as occurs especially in times of war, or any credit expansion of an unusual type, represent typical stimuli. Concomitant are expectations of price increases, often associated with the experience of past price increases. The expectations may, under certain circumstances, induce businessmen and consumers to buy in advance and in excess of their needs, and the hoarding wave will then make for inflation beyond the influence of the economic financial forces. Under other extreme conditions, people's attitudes may counteract the inflationary forces, and then, in spite of an unusual increase in purchasing power, there may be no excess demand and no inflation.

In the years following the inflationary price increases that occurred during the first phase of the Korean War, American consumers were found to react to price increases by postponing some of their discretionary purchases, even though they expected inflation to continue. The conclusion that could be drawn from that finding, namely, that such attitudes as resentment of price increases which are believed to be unjustified restrict the influence of inflationary forces, represents a generalization that must be qualified. Changes in circumstances might result in different perceptions, in the expectation, for example, of sizable rather than slight price increases, and thus in different reactions. Again, there is no assurance that consumers will not in the future perceive a relation between price increases and income increases simply because, as we learned in our surveys, they have not thus far done so. To cite a further example, it would be possible one day for people to view inflation as a new way of life in which the traditional urge toward saving money in safe places (e.g., savings accounts) would no longer be felt and in which common stocks would be viewed as safe investments. Or, should good times continue with sizable income gains and fairly stable prices, the expectation of continuing slow inflation might one day no longer be viewed with alarm.

Does it follow that conditional generalizations about attitudes and reactions to inflation are of little value? It is true that no general rule can be set up which would postulate that creeping inflation will never be transformed into runaway inflation or that creeping inflation will always evoke the consumer reaction of reducing discretionary expenditures. In order to achieve understanding and make predictions, it will always be necessary to conduct empirical studies to determine whether, why, and in what direction people's attitudes and expectations have changed. Psychological economics does, however, provide higher-level generalizations that can serve as guidelines for those studies. We now know that economic-financial and psychological forces interact; that expectations of price increase may either accelerate or impede consumer purchases, according to the framework within which the expectations are held and which supplies their affective undertone; and finally, that social learning which may change the framework is usually slow and gradual. Thus we are in a position to make broad and unconditional generalizations about the origin of inflationary attitudes and expectations as well as about social learning, on the basis of which our conditional conclusions about the relation of inflation to spending and to saving may be revised whenever empirical studies indicate that revisions are warranted.

The important topic of consumer saving supplies us with further examples of the relationship between generalizations at different levels. Our studies indicated that large savings may serve either to stimulate or to restrict further saving. If that had been our only conclusion, criticism would be in order. When, however, the motivations to save were studied, we could arrive at the following formulation: Wealth (or large liquid reserves) exerts two kinds of influence on the process of saving—on the one hand, it may restrict saving to the extent that it represents an enabling condition for spending; on the other hand, it may stimulate saving if the achievement of certain savings goals results in raising levels of aspiration and thus creates desires for even greater savings—and finally, habits of saving may continue to prevail even among people with large savings (Chapter 20). Which of these motivational forces will be stronger depends on the circumstances that prevail at a given time, and therefore only conditional statements may be made about the aggregate effect of wealth on saving. Yet the conclusion that several contradictory motivational forces are operative among different people in the same situation is not conditional. This conclusion, in turn, permits the generalization that there will be a great diversity in the saving performance of wealthy people and, at the same time, provides the necessary guidelines for continuing studies of the relation between wealth and saving.

The influence of collective security arrangements on saving may be described, in a formal sense, in similar terms. Old-age insurance and private pension plans may serve either to reduce or to enhance the urge toward private saving. Once more let us point out that even this apparently useless finding is of value: It implies the fallacy of what many people consider to be mere common sense, namely, that social security and private pensions necessarily stifle individual saving (similarly, it is not true that wealth or inflation necessarily retard saving). In this case again psychological economics goes much further than discrediting old theories, since it specifies the motivational factors due to which favorable retirement prospects sometimes stimulate saving (Chapter 19).

Finally, a brief reference to psychological studies of the business cycle may be in order. It is quite true that we cannot make the following unconditional generalization: Change in optimism and confidence always exerts an autonomous influence on consumers' discretionary expenditures. For example, the conclusions derived from the observations made in 1954, when changes in attitudes that did not conform to changes in ability to buy were decisive, were not duplicated at all times; during the recovery from the 1958 recession, for instance, consumer attitudes followed rather than anticipated the changes originating in other sectors of the economy. Yet there is nothing conditional about our postulation of an interaction between economic-financial precipitating circumstances (changes in ability to buy) and psychological ones (changes in willingness to buy). We now know what kinds of environmental changes—income, production, domestic or international political affairs—influence willingness to buy, and we know something of the direction of their influence. Thus future studies on changes in consumer demand are provided with guidelines that will enable them to determine whether at a given time attitudes reinforce income trends or counteract them.

The generalization that heightened international tensions exert a negative influence on consumers' discretionary demand (Chapter 16) is a conditional one. It was established under conditions that prevailed between 1954 and 1961. It was then strongly confirmed when the solution of the Cuban crisis of October, 1962—that is, a substantial relaxation of tensions—resulted in uplifting consumer sentiment and adding greatly to consumers' willingness to buy. It remains conditional nonetheless, because what has happened before need not happen again. It is possible that in the future consumers would react differently to a new crisis or to progress in international negotiations (although social learning is slow). Therefore people's apprehension of new information must continually be studied; reliance on mechanical projections of past trends or on the analogy of past reactions is not permissible.

ON THE PROCESS OF ACCEPTANCE OF NEW APPROACHES

We have attempted to clarify the major features of psychological economics by pointing to reasons for resistance to its teachings. This discussion must be supplemented by an analysis of the process of the penetration and acceptance of psychological studies in economics. Historically, the failures of traditional methods of economic forecasting, especially shortly after the end of World War II, were of major importance. The desire to improve short-run predictions helped greatly in providing funds for research in economic psychology, and the interest in forecasting provided wide publicity for findings on consumers' expectations and plans. The growing use of the survey method in other areas was likewise most helpful. In sociological research and in studies of voting behavior, as well as in economic research, demographic data obtained from sample interview surveys became commonplace. When survey information on the kind of people—rich or poor, young or old, urban or rural—who bought new cars or owned common stock was widely accepted, the use of surveys for probing the question of why could hardly be denied. The search for motives has become legitimate both in market research and in economics proper.

Yet the acceptance of psychological economics began with its simplest and most mechanical approaches. The measurement of plans and intentions to buy became a tool in economic research much earlier than the consideration of consumers' cognitive and affective processes. The value of information that differed but little from traditional data was first to be recognized. Information on the number of people who bought automobiles in a given year and information on the number of people who planned to buy automobiles in the following year are akin in several respects, even though the first may be based on records of past transactions, while the second is compiled from opinions and guesses made by members of a sample in reply to questions by interviewers.

Closest to traditional economic data is information on intentions to buy in the near future. Many people, when asked whether they will buy a house, a car, or a major appliance in the next three months, answer with as much certitude as they do when asked whether they have bought such goods in the recent past. Either the decision making process already is far advanced—discussions among family members, shopping around, talks with sellers or agents have already taken place—or the negative answer is quite certain. Yet, as we pointed out in Chapter 9, survey information of this kind is the least useful of all data on intentions or expectations. However, any effort to determine purchase plans over a longer period of time must go beyond mechanical methods of prediction, because then the influence of people's attitudes becomes relevant.

There has been increasing recognition during the last few years of the value of this kind of research in what is sometimes called expectational economics. In the late 1950s when the Census Bureau as well as private market research organizations first began to study consumers' plans to buy, they emphasized that by querying about six-month, and sometimes even three-month plans, they stood on more solid ground than the Survey Research Center, which had begun much earlier with a study of twelve-month plans. In the early 1960s however, the Census Bureau in reporting on buying plans placed the primary emphasis on the predictive value of twelve-month plans.[3] More importantly, the experience of collecting data about buying intentions soon revealed to the Census Bureau

[3] The Census Bureau asks questions on buying plans over different periods of time, but on page 1 of its news releases presents only twelve-month data, in table form as well as in text, on intentions to buy new and used cars and houses. (For example, see the Census Bureau release P-65, No. 2, May, 1963.) The regression equations computed by the Census Bureau as representing the best fit between intentions and aggregate purchases are also based on twelve-month plans.

that predictions about consumer expenditures based on buying intentions had to be conditional, being subject to changes in market conditions, credit, and incomes. "Finally," says the Census Bureau in each of its news releases on buying intentions, "consumer attitudes toward spending or saving may also change independently of changes in objective economic factors."

Economics in general has made progress as a science during the last two decades through the collection of extensive quantitative data from which statistical relationships could be derived and used for the purpose of testing hypotheses. Psychological economics has proceeded along a similar path, as we emphasized at the outset when we pointed out that the crucial step in its progress was the newly discovered possibility of measuring changes in attitudes, motives, and expectations. Time series representing not only expressed intentions to buy durable goods but also changes in consumer sentiment, such as are supplied by the Survey Research Center's Index, are in line with prevailing scholarly trends; they are thus accepted by the profession much more readily than propositions that run against the stream of tradition.

The major function of behavioral studies in economics has not yet been generally recognized. The proposition here advanced says that the science of the interrelationship of economic processes must be supplemented by a study of the behavior of people from which those processes result. There are many people who do not appear to understand the twofold position of economics, parts of which are and parts of which are not behavioral. For instance, when the behavioral sciences subpanel of the President's Science Advisory Committee made a strong plea for large-scale behavioral research,[4] it failed to include an appeal for such research in the field of economics. The Committee report contrasts the great advances in the quantity and quality of available information about the economy with the prevailing lack of information about noneconomic aspects of behavior in American society. The authors say, "We know something of how people spend their money, but almost nothing of how they spend their time." It is, of course, correct to say that we know what proportions of national income are spent on food, clothing, durable goods, and services. But how much do we know about the reasons for the given, and constantly changing, distribution of ex-

[4] See *Science*, vol. 136, April 20, 1962.

penditures?[5] Only by answering the crucial question of why will our understanding of economic processes be enhanced and our ability to predict improved.

The behavioral sciences study the actions of man and groups of men by applying the scientific method—observation, measurement, testing—to man himself. Behavioral sciences exclude parts of the social sciences—the study of institutions and markets, for instance— and differ from physical or biological sciences. For human beings have images of the future which influence their behavior and which, since they are endowed with language, they can communicate to others. Access to such intervening variables as motives and expectations requires a unique methodology for psychological economics and represents a major contribution to the understanding of economic processes.

[5] I raised this question in my reply to the report of the subpanel in *Behavioral Science*, vol. 7, pp. 481ff., 1962. Needless to say, I am in full agreement with the report when it calls for studies of how people spend their time.

30

In Closing

Since the mass consumption society emerged first in the United States, and our empirical studies were restricted to the United States, we have made but fleeting reference to other countries. Yet what may be the most important overall comment on international aspects of mass consumption has already been made in connection with our reply to those who see little good in a consumer-oriented society (Chapter 8): Decent and rising standards of living for the common people represent the most realistic hope of the world for peace and freedom.

We live in one world. This is true, first, because conflict and war in any part of the globe affect all other parts and carry the threat of nuclear annihilation, and secondly, because quick communication between distant points has resulted, not in common economic realities, but in common economic aspirations. Enormous differences between the rich and the poor prevail, both within this country and to a far greater degree between this country and other countries; yet the strivings and desires of the poor are influenced by those of the rich and resemble them. Mass consumption, with its high living standards, has become an aspiration for all.

At the same time, we live in two worlds. There are two antagonists, the Western world and the Communist countries, and it is hardly possible for any country not to be involved in the conflict. The division in the economic area, the two worlds of the rich and the poor, is not the same as the political division. The standard of living of the masses in Soviet Russia is far lower than in the United

States and Western Europe but very much higher than in the less developed countries of Africa, Asia, and Latin America. Realistic prospects for a better life, in contrast to aspirations and dreams, differ enormously in the highly developed and underdeveloped countries, and the latter are far more populous.

The biggest and most conspicuous progress toward affluence has taken place in Western Europe. The economic miracle in the Common Market countries stemmed from the great energy expended, at low wages, on rebuilding industry and government facilities devastated during the war. During the late 1950s and early 1960s the traditional forms of investment were supplemented by consumer investment expenditures, the rapid increase of which greatly contributed to economic growth. In earlier times in Western Europe only a small upper class was affluent; the masses of people lived close to subsistence; and the middle class cherished the tradition of using and preserving the homes, furniture, and house furnishings inherited from parents and grandparents. The Americanization of the European economies has consisted of the quickly rising use of automobiles, refrigerators, washing machines, and central heating—all nonexistent before the war except among a few people—as well as the introduction and wide acceptance of mass distribution outlets.

We had occasion in an earlier chapter to comment on the rapid increase of consumer credit in Europe and must add just one point. As a consequence of rising standards of living and the heightened aspirations of European workers, their desires for an increased share in the national product have likewise risen sharply. In the early 1960s in the Common Market countries, the rate of wage increases exceeded the rate of increase in the GNP. The European workers' eagerness to purchase cars and other durable goods will no doubt continue and stimulate the struggle for higher incomes.[1]

[1] As an illustration of what has taken place in Europe we may mention a development in Sweden that puzzled many experts. In that country, neutral during World War II, no buildings were destroyed; the country has a relatively low birth rate; home building, being strongly supported by the social democratic government, was very substantial during the last decade and became well known from pictures of skyscraper apartment houses all around the beautiful lakes surrounding Stockholm. Nevertheless, Sweden has an enormous housing shortage. The explanation lies in the upgrading of tastes and wants. Families, which in earlier times were content with one- or two-room apartments, want bigger ones; young people are no longer willing to double up with their parents. Increasing prosperity creates wants the satisfaction of which makes for more prosperity.

For America, rising wages and rising living standards in Western Europe represent a favorable development. In the first instance, terms of trade may improve. Moreover, it is not the have-nots who buy industrial products. Trade flourishes among wealthy countries, and a highly developed economy is bound to profit from what other mass consumption economies produce and purchase. When middle-class standards prevail among the masses and the proletariat disappears, ambitions and aspirations do not dry up. They are channeled in new directions, away from goals of national glory and conquest toward such aims as improved private well-being as well as progress in the sciences and arts. Similar changes—or shall we say hopes—were mentioned earlier in connection with the Russian people's growing interest in consumer goods.

Basic tenets of psychological economics seem to bear some relationship even to the seemingly remote problem of the economic development of less fortunate countries. A leading student of this important problem, Robert L. Garner, concluded from his fourteen years of experience as vice-president of the World Bank and president of the International Finance Corporation that differences in geography, natural resources, and availability of capital do not explain why development has been rapid in some countries and slow in others: "I am, therefore, forced to the conclusion that economic development or lack of it is primarily due to differences in people—in their attitudes, customs, traditions and the consequent differences in their political, social and religious institutions."[2]

His conclusion has, of course, had no scientific validation. This could be provided only by measuring changes in motives, attitudes, and sociocultural norms and demonstrating that they do in fact correlate with the rate of economic development. Some progress has recently been made along these lines.[3] There are also indications that the acceptance of innovations in agriculture, manufacturing, and trade depends on people's attitudes. Very much must still be done in analyzing the sociocultural norms conducive to progress in underdeveloped countries, for instance, the absence of traditionalism and otherworldliness and the presence of what Riesman has called other-directedness and the presence of concern with achieve-

[2] Meeting of the Board of Governors, IFC, Sept. 21, 1961.
[3] See David C. McClelland, *The Achieving Society*, D. Van Nostrand Company, Inc., Princeton, N.J., 1961, and to some extent E. E. Hagen, *On the Theory of Social Change*, Dorsey Press, Homewood, Ill., 1962.

ment and standards of excellence, as well as of stress on hard work. Analysis of the psychology of entrepreneurs may point to the personality types needed for material progress in economically deprived countries. For, possibly, those countries must go through a phase of industrialization similar to that of Western Europe and the United States in the nineteenth century before consumers can promote economic growth. Possibly, however, there exist shortcuts toward mass consumption and improved standards of living so that the emphasis need not be placed on, say, steel mills but on the production of consumer goods and on consumer motivations to acquire them. Extensive studies are needed in this area. We can do no more here than to indicate the relevance of economic psychology to these broad problems.

We return to the main focus of our discussion, the mass consumption society in the United States in the 1960s. In the era of mass consumption the question What kind of a person is the consumer? becomes a crucial one. Great diversity prevails among American consumers, and yet it is possible to derive certain generalizations that are valid for the great majority. We may summarize some major findings of the studies reported in this book by listing the principal characteristics of the consumer of today, many of which denote sharp differences from the consumer of a few decades ago:

1. Fifty years ago the majority of consumers were unskilled or semiskilled workers and farmers with less than high-school education. Today the majority are made up of white-collar workers and their wives, both groups having gone at least to high school.

2. The majority of consumers reach their peak lifetime income in their late forties and fifties. After household formation there is a period of some twenty to thirty years of rising income. The experience of improvement in the standard of living, shared by most families during the last twenty years, contributes to the expectation that ways of living will improve still further for oneself and for one's children. This optimistic outlook spurs not only consumer expenditures but also the acquisition of reserve funds. The greater the contractual obligations and the larger the concrete rewards a person expects from saving (for instance, adequate provisions for retirement), the greater is the urge to save.

3. Work is no longer seen as an instrument for protection against deprivation. Nevertheless, consumers' wants have not become less

insistent. A variety of needs press for satisfaction, and under this pressure consumers strive to increase their income.

4. The American consumer is a sensible person and a discriminating buyer who seeks information and tries to understand what is going on. He is not irrational, even though he sometimes acts on impulse; when it matters, he ponders, weighs some alternatives, and tries to make an intelligent choice. This does not mean that he is an ideal "rational man." Old stereotypes and attitudes do persist even when no longer applicable, and habitual behavior—repeating previous actions almost automatically—is very common.

5. The consumer is not inclined toward excessive behavior. He is not a pawn moved about by marketers and advertisers at will, nor does he follow economic news mechanically. When times are good and everybody seems to be buying, cautious attitudes arise fairly soon; and when recession threatens or develops, long-range confidence does not vanish. Social learning is slow, and a sudden reversal of attitudes is a rare occurrence. The consumer thus contributes to stabilizing the economy.

It is a short step from findings of practical value to theory. Practical findings are enhanced and better understood when they are placed in a broad theoretical context. Yet, in considering the prospects of economic psychology in mass consumption societies, we must be aware of the admonition of John Maynard Keynes in his great book on economic theory: "The ideas of economists and political philosophers, both when they are right and when they are wrong, are more powerful than is commonly understood. Indeed, the world is ruled by little else."[4] This passage points to a major task of the next generation of social scientists. New and better theories about the economic behavior of the masses and especially about behavioral dynamics and social learning are the prerequisites to effective social and economic policies.

The development and acceptance of new ideas is, however, a slow process. As Keynes went on to say, "In the field of economics and political philosophy there are not many who are influenced by new theories after they are 25 or 30 years of age, so that ideas which civil servants and politicians and even educators apply to current events are not likely to be the newest." His thesis, then, is that

[4] J. M. Keynes, *The General Theory of Employment, Interest, and Money,* Harcourt, Brace & World, Inc., New York, 1936, pp. 383ff.

learning is slow among the opinion leaders. Social learning among the masses is slow as well. But both do occur. Though the penetration of new ideas is often opposed by vested interests, the power of these interests can ultimately be overcome.

Good theories bring order among the complex and varied facts of the real world and lead to an understanding of what is happening and to predictions of what will happen. The major theory of nineteenth-century economic philosophers presented an orderly picture but proved inapplicable to conditions of the mid-twentieth century. The postulation of rationality among consumers, consisting of the careful weighing of all alternatives and the selection of that outcome which maximizes utilities, is still pleasing to many who learned it twenty-five or thirty years ago, but the predictive value of this theory is quite limited under present conditions. The opposite extreme, sometimes implied but never developed into a comprehensive theory—the assumption of irrationality among consumers, who are thought to be triggered largely by unconscious impulses— may shed light on the behavior of one or the other individual, but it, too, fails to illuminate market processes. A full-fledged theory of the sensible and discriminating consumer and of the behavioral dynamics which govern the arousal of changed attitudes, expectations, and aspirations has not yet emerged. Empirical research on consumer behavior and its underlying forces has made progress, however, and reports on generalizations derived from this research represent the subject matter of this book. We are confident that a behavioral theory of social learning and social action will be developed in the not-too-distant future, because it is needed, and social needs do influence the growth of science.

Bibliography

I. PUBLICATIONS CITED IN TEXT BY NUMBER

1. Katona, George: *Psychological Analysis of Economic Behavior,* McGraw-Hill Book Company, New York, 1951.
2. Katona, George: *The Powerful Consumer,* McGraw-Hill Book Company, New York, 1960.
3. Katona, George, and J. B. Lansing: "The Wealth of the Wealthy," *Review of Economics and Statistics,* vol. 46, pp. 1–14, 1964.
4. Mueller, Eva: "Ten Years of Consumer Attitude Surveys: Their Forecasting Record," *Journal of the American Statistical Association,* vol. 58, pp. 899–917, 1963.
5. *1960 Survey of Consumer Finances.*
6. *1961 Survey of Consumer Finances.*
7. *1962 Survey of Consumer Finances.*
8. *1963 Survey of Consumer Finances.*
   Monographs 5, 6, 7, and 8 were published by the Survey Research Center of The University of Michigan during the year following that indicated in the title.

II. SUPPLEMENTARY BIBLIOGRAPHY

Bowman, M. J. (ed.): *Expectations, Uncertainty, and Business Behavior,* Social Science Research Council, New York, 1958.

Clark, L. H. (ed.): *Consumer Behavior, Vol. I,* New York University Press, New York, 1954.

————: *Consumer Behavior, Vol II,* New York University Press, New York, 1955.

————: *Consumer Behavior: Research on Consumer Reactions,* Harper & Row, Publishers, Incorporated, New York, 1958.

Foundation for Research on Human Behavior: *Psychological Research on Consumer Behavior,* Ann Arbor, Mich., 1962.

————: *Dynamic Aspects of Consumer Behavior,* Ann Arbor, Mich., 1963.

Friedman, Milton: *A Theory of the Consumption Function,* National Bureau of Economic Research, Princeton University Press, Princeton, N.J., 1957.

Galbraith, J. K.: *The Affluent Society,* Houghton Mifflin Company, Boston, 1958.

Katona, George: "Attitude Change: Instability of Response and Acquisition of Experience," *Psychological Monographs,* vol. 72, 1958.

————: "Consumer Investment and Business Investment," *Michigan Business Review,* vol. 13, pp. 17–22, 1961.

————: "The Relationship between Psychology and Economics," in S. Koch (ed.), *Psychology: A Study of a Science,* McGraw-Hill Book Company, New York, 1963, vol. 6, pp. 639–676.

———— and Eva Mueller: *Consumer Attitudes and Demand 1950–1952,* Survey Research Center, Ann Arbor, Mich., 1953.

———— and Eva Mueller: *Consumer Expectations 1953–1956,* Survey Research Center, Ann Arbor, Mich., 1956.

————, Stanley Steinkamp, and Albert Lauterbach: *Business Looks at Banks: A Study of Business Behavior,* University of Michigan Press, Ann Arbor, Mich., 1957.

Keynes, J. M.: *The General Theory of Employment, Interest, and Money,* Harcourt, Brace & World, Inc., New York, 1936.

Kuznets, Simon: *Capital in the American Economy: Its Formation and Financing,* National Bureau of Economic Research, Princeton University Press, Princeton, N.J., 1961.

Lampman, R. J.: *The Share of Top Wealth-Holders in National Wealth, 1922–1956,* National Bureau of Economic Research, Princeton University Press, Princeton, N.J., 1962.

Lansing, J. B., and others: *The Travel Market, 1958–1962,* Survey Research Center, Ann Arbor, Mich., 1963.

Morgan, J. N., M. H. David, W. J. Cohen, and H. E. Brazer: *Income and Welfare in the United States,* McGraw-Hill Book Company, New York, 1962.

Mueller, Eva: "Effects of Consumer Attitudes on Purchases," *American Economic Review,* vol. 47, pp. 946–965, 1957.

————: "Consumer Reactions to Inflation," *Quarterly Journal of Economics,* vol. 73, pp. 246–262, 1959.

————: "Consumer Attitudes: Their Influence and Forecasting Value," *The Quality and Economic Significance of Anticipations Data,* National Bureau of Economic Research, Princeton University Press, Princeton, N.J., pp. 149–175, 1960.

————: "Public Attitudes Toward Fiscal Programs," *Quarterly Journal of Economics,* vol. 77, pp. 210–235, 1963.

National Bureau of Economic Research: *The Quality and Economic Significance of Anticipations Data,* Princeton University Press, Princeton, N.J., 1960.

Toynbee, Arnold: *America and the World Revolution,* Oxford University Press, London, 1962.

III. ON SURVEY METHODS

The economic surveys conducted by the Survey Research Center of The University of Michigan, which supplied most of the findings cited in this book, have been described briefly in Ref. 1, Chapter 15, and Ref. 2, Appendix. The surveys conducted by the Survey Research Center are characterized by the use of carefully drawn representative samples of the noninstitutional population in the continental United States and of fixed-question–free-answer interviewing methods applied by well-trained interviewers.

The consumer survey program of the Center consists of:

1. The Survey of Consumer Finances, conducted annually with a sample of 2,000 or 3,000 respondents (heads of spending units). Main topics are distributions of income, financial assets, debts, and major transactions.

2. Periodic surveys of changes in consumer attitudes and inclinations to buy, conducted four times a year with a sample of 1,300 to 1,500 respondents (husband and wife are interviewed alternately). Main topics are consumer attitudes and expectations (as used in the Index of Consumer Sentiment), intentions to buy houses and durable goods, and reactions to major recent events.

3. Occasional surveys on topics of theoretical as well as practical interest. Among recent surveys those on poverty, on the influence of pension plans, and on travel and outdoor recreation were cited in this book. (In addition, the Center has conducted some surveys on entrepreneurial attitudes and behavior.)

Press releases are issued after the conclusion of surveys of general interest. In due time full reports, in the form of articles, monographs, and books, are published on all findings. The Survey Research Center does not engage in confidential research, even though its research funds are obtained through contracts with private business and government agencies in addition to foundation grants. The monographs 5 to 8 contain the findings of the Surveys of Consumer Finances and the periodic surveys since 1960 (earlier findings were published in the *Federal Reserve Bulletin*), as well as the questionnaires used and information on sample sizes and sampling errors.

As an indication of the extent of the sampling error, it may suffice to mention that the standard error for financial data (that are close to 50 per cent) is 1.3 per cent in surveys with 2,000 cases; for attitudinal data (close to 50 per cent), 1.65 per cent in surveys with

1,350 cases; the change in the Index of Consumer Sentiment has a standard error of 1.3 per cent.

Detailed information on the survey methods used can also be found in L. Festinger and D. Katz (eds.): *Research Methods in the Behavioral Sciences,* Holt, Rinehart and Winston, Inc., New York, 1953. (See especially the articles by George Katona and Angus Campbell on the sample survey, Leslie Kish on sampling, and C. F. Cannell and R. L. Kahn on interviewing.)

Regarding interviewing, see also R. L. Kahn and C. F. Cannell, *The Dynamics of Interviewing: Theory, Techniques, and Cases,* John Wiley & Sons, Inc., New York, 1957.

Regarding sampling, see also M. H. Hansen, W. N. Hurwitz, and W. J. Madow, *Sample Survey Methods and Theory,* John Wiley & Sons, Inc., New York, 1953; and Leslie Kish, *Fundamentals of Survey Sampling,* John Wiley & Sons, Inc., New York, (to be published).

Index

340   *Index*